Mastery and Escape

D1601717

Mastery and Escape

T. S. Eliot and the Dialectic of Modernism

Jewel Spears Brooker

UNIVERSITY OF MASSACHUSETTS PRESS

AMHERST

Copyright © 1994 by The University of Massachusetts Press
Printed in the United States of America
LC 93–45634
ISBN 1–55849–040–X
Designed by Susan Bishop
Set in Palatino type by Keystone Typesetting, Inc.
Printed and bound by Thompson-Shore, Inc.

Library of Congress Cataloging-in-Publication Data
Brooker, Jewel Spears, 1940–
  Mastery and escape : T. S. Eliot and the dialectic of modernism /
Jewel Spears Brooker.
    p.   cm.
  Includes bibliographical references and index.
  ISBN 1–55849–040–X (alk. paper)
    1. Eliot, T. S. (Thomas Stearns), 1888–1965—Criticism and
interpretation.   2. Modernism (Literature)   I. Title.
PS3509.L43Z64545   1994
821'.912—dc20   93–45634

British Library Cataloguing in Publication data are available.

Acknowledgment is made for permission to reprint from the following material under
copyright:
  "Gerontion" and excerpts from "The Love Song of J. Alfred Prufrock" and "The
Waste Land" in *Collected Poems 1909–1962*, by T. S. Eliot, copyright 1936 by Harcourt
Brace & Company, copyright © 1963, 1964 by T. S. Eliot, reprinted by permission of
Harcourt, Brace Jovanovich and Faber and Faber Ltd.
  Excerpts from "Tradition and the Individual Talent" and "A Dialogue on Dramatic
Poetry" from *Selected Essays*, by T. S. Eliot, copyright 1950 by Harcourt Brace & Com-
pany and renewed 1978 by Esme Valerie Eliot, reprinted by permission of Harcourt
Brace Jovanovich and Faber and Faber Ltd.
  Excerpts from "Burnt Norton" and "The Dry Salvages" in *Four Quartets*, copyright
1943 by T. S. Eliot and renewed 1971 by Esme Valerie Eliot, reprinted by permission of
Harcourt Brace Jovanovich.
  Excerpts from *Knowledge and Experience in the Philosophy of F. H. Bradley* by T. S. Eliot,
copyright © 1964 by T. S. Eliot. Reprinted by permission of Farrar, Straus & Giroux,
Inc.

For my beloved children

Emily Hope   Mark Spears   Kenneth Travis

Contents

CONTENTS

Acknowledgments

Carolyn Johnston, a dear colleague at Eckerd College, first suggested that these essays should be collected, and Bruce Wilcox, the director of the University of Massachusetts Press, embraced the project. I am grateful to both friends for their faith and encouragement.

One of Eliot's finest readers, Ronald Schuchard, studied the manuscript for me and, as on many previous occasions, provided insightful comments. Nathan Scott, a pioneer in modernist studies and one of the formative influences on my own scholarship, also read the manuscript and offered helpful suggestions. I am grateful to Professors Schuchard and Scott for their time and thoughtful comments. I am also grateful, in a general sense, to Eliot's widow and literary executrix, Valerie Eliot.

Part of the work on this book was completed while I was a visiting professor at Doshisha University in Kyoto, Japan. The first chapter, "Mastery and Escape," contains material from my 1992 T. S. Eliot Society lecture in Kyoto and from my 1993 lecture at Komazawa University in Tokyo. A version of the chapter on feminism and modernism was given as a lecture at Sophia University in Tokyo in 1993 and has been published in *The Rising Generation*, Japan's foremost literary monthly. My friends in Japan include many serious modernist scholars, and several have contributed in significant ways to my understanding of Western literature. My conversations about Eliot and modernism with Tatsuo Murata, Tetsuya Taguchi, and Hitoshi Sano were especially helpful for my work. I am grateful to them and also to Philip Williams, an outstanding American scholar who teaches in Japan. Professor Williams introduced me to the work of Japanese scholars and nominated me for the visiting professorship in

Kyoto. Professor Williams recently received an award from the emperor for his substantial contributions to American studies in Japan.

The following chapters first appeared as essays in the following publications: "Mastery and Escape," *South Atlantic Review* 59:2 (1994); "The Dispensations of Art," *Southern Review* 19:1(1983); "Old T. E. H." as "T. E. Hulme," in *British Poets: 1880–1914*, ed. Donald E. Stanford (Detroit: Gale Research Co., 1983); "Common Ground and Collaboration in T. S. Eliot," *Centennial Review* 25:3 (1981); "The Structure of Eliot's 'Gerontion,'" *ELH* 46:2 (1979); "The Case of the Missing Abstraction," *Massachusetts Review* 25:4 (1984); "Substitutes for Christianity in the Poetry of T. S. Eliot," *Southern Review* 21:4 (1985); "Keeping Time in Time" as "From *The Waste Land* to *Four Quartets*," in *Words in Time: New Essays on Eliot's* Four Quartets, ed. Edward Lobb (London: Athlone; Ann Arbor: University of Michigan Press, 1993); "The Education of T. S. Eliot," *Southern Review* 20:2 (1984); "T. S. Eliot and the Revolt Against Dualism," in *T. S. Eliot: Man and Poet*, ed. Laura Cowan (Orono, ME: National Poetry Foundation, 1990); "F. H. Bradley's Doctrine of Experience," *Modern Philology* 77:2 (1979); "Modernism and Belligerence" as "T. S. Eliot's Skepticism," *Southern Review* 27:3 (1991); "Tradition and Female Enmity," in *Making Feminist History: The Literary Scholarship of Sandra M. Gilbert and Susan Gubar*, ed. William E. Cain (New York: Garland, 1994); "'The Second Coming' and *The Waste Land*," *College Literature* 13:3 (1986); and "When Love Fails," in *Approaches to Teaching Eliot's Poetry and Plays* (New York: MLA, 1988).

Two of my students at Eckerd College were particularly helpful. Caroline Maun was my research assistant and Jerry Bartholomew helped with page proofs. Elizabeth Meyer also served as a research assistant. Their literary insights and computer skills were invaluable. Ellen Westbrook, who was my copy editor and indexer, also made important contributions. I especially appreciate her graciousness and professionalism. I am grateful to my children for years of spirited conversations on literature, philosophy, and theology, and to my husband, H. Ralph Brooker, for unending patience and helpfulness.

Finally, I would like to acknowledge the moral and financial support of Lloyd Chapin, academic dean of Eckerd College, and the financial support of the National Endowment for the Humanities, which in 1987 awarded me a Fellowship for College Teachers.

Abbreviations

A full note is used for the first reference to major works by T. S. Eliot. For subsequent references, the following abbreviations are used parenthetically in the text itself.

KE   *Knowledge and Experience in the Philosophy of F. H. Bradley*
OPP   *On Poetry and Poets*
SE   *Selected Essays*
SP   *Selected Prose*
SW   *The Sacred Wood*
TCTC *To Criticize the Critic*
UPUC *The Use of Poetry and the Use of Criticism*

Occasional abbreviations are used for in-text references to works by other writers. These abbreviations are explained in notes.

Mastery and Escape

Mastery and Escape

T. S. Eliot and the Dialectic of Modernism

And the end of all our exploring
Will be to arrive where we started
And know the place for the first time.
—"*Little Gidding*" V[1]

Modernism, a term used to describe the arts in Europe and America from the first decade of the century until the Second World War, is a capacious country. Its denizens include not only Virginia Woolf, but James Joyce, whose *Ulysses* Woolf considered pretentious and illbred; not only W. C. Williams, but T. S. Eliot, whose poetry Williams thought dangerous; not only the taciturn Picasso, but the flamboyant Dali. These figures may be said to inhabit the same country, but the divergence in ideology and absence of congeniality make it useful to imagine them as dwelling in different territories. Literary historians generally acknowledge as much and organize the cultural life of the first third of this century into at least two modernisms. The work of one group, consisting mostly of exiles (Pound, Joyce, Eliot), is characterized by internationalism, classicism, and intellectual complexity, all of which are conscientiously resisted by members of the second group (Williams, Robert Frost, Woolf). The modernism at reference in this collection of essays, most published in journals over the last decade, is the former. Sometimes called high modernism, its genealogy in philosophy and the sciences includes Marx, Darwin, Nietzsche, Freud, and Frazer; in literature, its forebears include first and foremost Homer and then Virgil and Dante. Its immediate ancestors include Flaubert, Henry James, Dostoevsky, and the French symbolist poets. My purpose is to clarify a defining

1. Except where noted all quotations from T. S. Eliot's poetry are taken from *The Collected Poems 1909–1962* (New York: Harcourt Brace Jovanovich, 1964).

1

feature of this modernism, namely, the tendency to move forward by spiraling back and refiguring the past. The main literary reference point will be T. S. Eliot, whose work is paradigmatic in regard to this characteristic.

The modernist motif of return is inseparable from the late nine-teenth-century focus on the Renaissance. Most modernists seemed obsessed with the idea that the retrieval of antiquity begun at the dawn of the modern era needs to be resumed and completed. Most insisted that going forward involves going back, that securing the future means redeeming the past. A parallel impulse is a process that Eliot, in his essay on Henry James, calls "mastery and escape." It is described in several of Eliot's literary essays and illustrated in his poetry. The genius of Henry James, according to Eliot, lies in "his mastery over, his baffling escape from, Ideas."[2] In another passage, in regard to the criticism of Samuel Johnson, Eliot remarked that it is only possible to escape Johnson after one has "mastered" him (*SP*, 67). In regard to Ezra Pound's vers libre, Eliot claims that Pound's escape from rigid forms had been made possible by his tireless mastery of them (*SP*, 150). Another version of the mastery and escape motif can be seen in "Tradition and the Individual Talent." "Escape from personality," Eliot claims, is possible only for the few who have personality; similarly, "escape from emotion" is possible only for the few who have strong emotions.[3] In all of these instances, mastery involves both knowledge of and control over. In this dialectic, as in much nineteenth-century dialectic, there is a dynamic interplay of conflicts. Escape, however, does not involve linear movement to an opposite or to synthesis. It is not escape *from* one's most recent position, but escape *to* a broader perspective; it is a transcendence (via a return) in which, as Eliot says of tradition, nothing is lost en route. As the concept culminates in *Four Quartets*, escape is a liberation effected by a return, after knowledge, to the place from which one started. In Eliot's case, the use of the "mastery and escape" motif is deliberate and informed by serious studies in philosophy, studies that pro-

2. T. S. Eliot, *Selected Prose of T. S. Eliot*, ed. Frank Kermode (New York: Harcourt Brace Jovanovich / Farrar, Straus and Giroux, 1975), 151. Subsequent references to this volume will be indicated in the text, abbreviated as *SP*.

3. T. S. Eliot, *Selected Essays*, new ed. (London: Faber and Faber, 1950), 10–11. Subsequent references to this volume will be indicated in the text, abbreviated as *SE*.

foundly shaped not only his developing critical mind, but his poetry.

Eliot is inseparably linked with international modernism. Not only did he contribute its major poem, *The Waste Land,* but in his early criticism, he proved to be its most articulate spokesperson. His mind and his art exemplify in rich particularity the tapestry of modernism. His understanding of history descends directly from thinkers such as Marx, Nietzsche, and Pater; and because it is a version of a perception broadly shared, it is highly instructive. Eliot's concept of tradition and the mind of Europe, again inherited from the late nineteenth century but modified to reflect his analysis of the early twentieth century, is indispensable in appreciating Yeats, Valéry, Joyce, and other contemporaries. Eliot's intellectual comprehensiveness—specifically, his rejection of synthesis and his insistence on a "both / and" logic of complementarity—illustrates a foundational pattern in modernist thinking. Finally, the movement of his mind—involving first surrender, then mastery, and finally transcendence —characterizes the mental dialectic of many of his brightest contemporaries. This pattern, a metamorphosis of Hegelian and Marxist dialectic, involves a play between opposites that moves forward by spiraling back (a return) and up (a transcendence). It goes beyond Hegel, however, in resisting linearity, eschewing mentalism, and evading synthesis. This dialectic, pervasive in most modernist work, appears with special clarity in Eliot, philosophically the best informed of the modernists.

The following discussion of the emergence of modernist dialectic will focus on three fields—history, psychology, and philosophy. In each of these, a particular convergence of nineteenth-century ideas can be seen as taking the shape of a dialectical spiral and then collectively as giving shape to high modernist literature. In history, the focus will be on the rise of dispensationalism; in psychology, on the extension of psychology to analyses of culture; and in philosophy, on the extension of Hegelian dialectic to notions of knowledge. These strands are chosen for their broad relevance (with variations of course) to literary modernists. The nineteenth- and twentieth-century thinkers targeted for discussion are ones who in demonstrable ways can be seen to have influenced Eliot. The three sections will attend increasingly to Eliot, with the third focused almost entirely on his dialectical imagination.

3

DISPENSATIONALISM AND THE
INVENTION OF HISTORY

In a general sense, all of the essays in this volume are related to the modernist obsession with history. In a more specific sense, the first two essays—"The Dispensations of Art: Mallarmé and the Fallen Reader" and " 'Ole T. E. H.': Pioneer of Modernism"—illustrate the compulsion to analyze history and to associate possibility in art with one's moment and context in history. Modernists tended to break history into large blocks or dispensations, and most felt that they were living at the end of or between periods. Stéphane Mallarmé, to whom both Yeats and Eliot were clearly indebted, formulated an elaborate dispensational analogy between art and religion, claiming that he and his contemporaries were living at the end of an era that would be succeeded by another in which art would supplant Christianity as the religion of the people, with poets as priests. The movement forward would be in one way a movement back, for the new religion of art would be the old religion of Catholicism liberated from its "barbaric" aspects. Mallarmé's ideas in this regard were not unique in the artistic community. In England, Matthew Arnold spoke dispensationally of "criticism in the wilderness" preparing the way for art in the promised land. In Germany, Richard Wagner also thought dispensationally and conceived of himself as a prophet. Opera, he maintained, was the art work of the future, the form that assimilated all of the other arts—music, poetry, painting, dance. To validate itself, however, opera would have to retrieve and reenact the most primitive myths of the Germanic / European psyche.

T. E. Hulme, whom Pound memorialized in the *Cantos* as "Ole T. E. H.," was also a dispensationalist. His theories about the image in poetry, his translations of Henri Bergson's work in metaphysics, and his popularization of Wilhelm Worringer's aesthetics were all born of a conviction that the romantic age had spent itself and was being succeeded by a new classical age. In "Romanticism and Classicism," he presented himself as the prophet of the new classicism. The romantic period began in his view with the Renaissance. The celebration of the human by such giants as Michelangelo and Shakespeare at the dawn of the modern age had ushered in a period of humanism that had led in the nineteenth century to an easy and ungrounded belief in innate goodness and unending progress. Hulme predicted a

4

new age of classicism anchored in a new realism about human nature. The new realism, which was to replace the discredited humanistic view, was the old theological view of Original Sin or its secular equivalent. The way forward into the new dispensation, in another variation of a basic pattern, was the way back. Hulme's dispensational obsession was fed by his immersion in German philosophy, particularly in the brilliantly suggestive work of Worringer in *Abstraction and Empathy*. Worringer, whom Hulme met on his travels in Germany, divided art history into periods, coordinating the spiritual attitudes of each age with the form that appeared in its art. Part of his purpose, like that of many fellow dispensationalists, was to explain and to justify modern art.

The emphasis on the doctrine of Original Sin in this new realism was one version of a widely shared reaction against nineteenth-century liberalism. Hulme, who was not himself a Christian, did not advocate a return to religious belief, but rather an acknowledgment that the religious understanding of human nature was more realistic than the humanistic one. Many of his fellow modernists agreed. The boundary between the Victorian world and the twentieth century, according to W. H. Auden, was the collapse of liberal humanism. Everyone, Wyndham Lewis claimed in *Blasting and Bombadiering*, was sick of the idea that human beings are intrinsically good and capable of infinite progress. Virginia Woolf, in a striking summary of these matters, quipped that in or about the year 1910, human nature changed. The "change in human nature" had been foreshadowed by Nietzsche, with his new (actually pre-Socratic) view of human nature, and by turn-of-the-century social scientists such as Pierre Janet, Freud, Emile Durkheim, and Lucien Lévy-Bruhl.

Woolf's quip about human nature seems too clever to be true, but actually, it identifies one distinguishing characteristic of the period and of the writers called modernist. And 1910, her year for the U-turn on human nature, is also a good working date for the beginning of high modernism in the arts. By 1910, a new day had dawned. In *Heart of Darkness*, Conrad had provided an aerial view linking the most civilized—geographically, politically, psychologically, ethically, spiritually—with the most primitive. In *Les Demoiselles d'Avignon*, Picasso had invented cubism by superimposing the faces of primitive and modern, and in "The Love Song of J. Alfred Prufrock," Eliot intro-

5

duced an intellectual who was nauseated by culture, who identified more with crabs scuttling across the floors of silent seas than with refined ladies strolling across the floors of drawing rooms in Harvard Square. All of Eliot's early writings, in fact, are grounded in a dark view of human nature (in part Christian, in part primitivist), corroborated by an enthusiastic reading of Dostoevsky and Conrad. The poet's realization that human beings cannot be perfected, a basic element in his early classicism, turned out to be compatible with the Augustinian view of human nature, one of many congruences smoothing the road for his midlife journey to the Church.

The modernist convictions about human nature and about history were underscored by the apocalyptic events of the First World War. Paul Valéry argued in 1919 that the war revealed Western civilization to be as fragile as those civilizations "now sunk to the inexplorable bottom of the centuries": just as "Elam, Nineveh, Babylon were vague and lovely names, . . . [so] France, England, Russia . . . would also be lovely names. . . . the abyss of history is large enough for every one."[4] This preoccupation with the beginnings and endings of history is omnipresent in the work of Yeats, Pound, Joyce, and Eliot. Yeats's cyclical theory of history, outlined in *A Vision* and used symbolically in his poetry and plays, is at once representative and eccentric. It has much in common with the ideas of the German historian Oswald Spengler, who argued in *The Decline of the West* (1918) that civilizations are organisms that go through stages of youth, maturity, and decay, and that then, like other organisms, they die. Spengler believed that Western civilization was in an advanced stage of decay and would soon go the way of Babylon, Athens, and Rome. Yeats, whose cycles were organized around lunar models, agreed that apocalypse was near for Western civilization, a vision preserved in chilling clarity in his powerful sonnet "The Second Coming." In "Hugh Selwyn Mauberly," Pound describes Western civilization as an "old bitch gone in the teeth"; and in "Gerontion," Eliot imagines it as an old man gone not only in the teeth, but in the groin and in the brain. Pound's interest in history moved from experiments in retrieving classical and medieval models to an obsession that not only shaped

4. Paul Valéry, "Letters from France: The Spiritual Crisis," *Athenaeum* (11 April 1919): 182.

the *Cantos* but determined most other aspects of his personal destiny. Joyce, with greater detachment, left it to Stephen Daedalus in *Ulysses* to declare that "history is a nightmare from which I am trying to awake."

In Eliot's view, Joyce provided the great example of going forward by turning back. In his use of Homeric materials in *Ulysses*, Joyce had pioneered a method "of controlling, of ordering, of giving a shape and a significance to the immense panorama of futility and anarchy which is contemporary history" (*SP*, 177). Eliot's own dispensationalism is evident in this assessment of *Ulysses* and indeed throughout his work—in his comparative readings of the Greek tragedians and Shakespeare and of the Metaphysical and modern poets, for example, and in his readings of Virgil, Dante, and Blake as representatives of particular dispensations. Eliot's sense of history is at issue in several of the essays in this volume, especially "Common Ground and Collaboration in T. S. Eliot." His defense of classical standards and his appreciation for the advantage of poets and readers sharing religion, language, and culture emerged from a dispensationalist imagination and from an impulse to move forward by assimilating the past. His redefinition of tradition, canonically presented in "Tradition and the Individual Talent," grew out of a serious and continuous meditation on history. The meaning of history, also a major subject in his poetry, is at the heart of "Gerontion," *The Waste Land*, and *Four Quartets*.

The modernist focus on history did not arise from a vacuum. One obvious context is the social sciences. Sir James G. Frazer devoted his entire career to an exploration of the dark abyss of prerecorded history. His double vision of primitive terror and modern assurance is preserved in *The Golden Bough*, arguably the single most important common influence on the modernists. One of his major conclusions was that humanity had evolved from a dispensation based on magic to one based on religion and was moving to a third based on science. An unabashed positivist, Frazer saw science rather than art as the religion of the future, but the structure of his thought was the same as that of Mallarmé. Both believed that going forward involved a recapitulation and reprocessing of ancient forms. Frazer's impact on modernists, especially on Eliot and Joyce, is the subject of one of the essays in this collection, "The Case of the Missing Abstraction." Freud, another undeniable and massive influence, also had a dispen-

7

sational imagination. In *The Future of an Illusion,* he predicted a time in which the "facts" of science would take humanity beyond the "illusions" of Christianity and into a new age of reason, a second enlightenment.

History, according to Eliot's mentor F. H. Bradley, is always invented after the fact. It is always a mental construct, and even in the best of circumstances, it is never disinterested. In part, writing history is an exercise in self-definition. Inventing historical periods and recognizing themselves in the latest enables people both to see themselves as part of history and to distance themselves, morally and aesthetically, from the previous generation. The necessary context for the modernist obsession with history includes the nineteenth-century invention of the "Renaissance," a topic explored in Jeffrey Perl's *Tradition of Return.* Perl's work, to which I am generally indebted, shows that although the Renaissance happened in Italy in the fourteenth and fifteenth centuries, it was invented in France in the early nineteenth (which explains why the word is French rather than Italian). The concept migrated from France to Germany and thence to England. As conceptionalized in Jacob Burckhardt's monumental *Civilization of the Renaissance in Italy,* published in Germany in 1860, and Walter Pater's *Renaissance,* published in England in 1873, the Renaissance became an important and far-reaching reference point in the history of ideas. History was thought of in three large blocks—ancient, medieval, and modern. The third block, defined as a rebirth of the first, begins with the Renaissance. The very idea of the modern, then, includes the idea of a return.[5]

The invention of modernity proved to be convenient for late nineteenth- and early twentieth-century thinkers. It enabled them to distance themselves from their immediate ancestors and to imagine themselves as placed by destiny in the wrong period. Intellectuals like Henry Adams who felt estranged from the modern world of nineteenth-century materialism retreated to the previous block of history, the medieval—preferring the virgin to the dynamo, the garden to the factory, and transcendentalism to materialism. Artists like the Pre-Raphaelites in England and Mallarmé in France who despised

5. Jeffrey Perl, *The Tradition of Return: The Implicit History of Modern Literature* (Princeton: Princeton University Press, 1984). See especially part one, "Ideology and History."

8

the bourgeois also found succor in a premodern period friendly to the idea of cultural elites. Mallarmé's disgust with the bourgeois and his insistence on an intellectual and aesthetic aristocracy are at issue in "The Dispensations of Art: Mallarmé and the Fallen Reader." A similar though less extreme attitude toward readers can be seen in many other writers. Eliot, for example, maintained that a reader should spend at least as much time preparing to read a poem as a barrister spends preparing a brief. His suggestion that readers in this dispensation should prepare themselves for their role derives in part from his conviction that readers are less generally competent due to a religious and educational crisis that has deprived them of shared experiences and values. His belief that great art is contingent on the collaboration of readers is a major subject in "Common Ground and Collaboration in T. S. Eliot." For both Mallarmé and Eliot, it should be noted, the issue of the worthiness of the reader is not related to class, but to competence and to seriousness about art.

According to Perl, Nietzsche is the most influential of the intellectual historians who took the Renaissance for a reference point. Nietzsche was a polemicist, and while the other creators of the Renaissance tended to emphasize the period itself (that is, the thirteenth through the sixteenth centuries in Europe), he emphasized its antecedents (that is, the old world and the primitive values that he thought should be reclaimed). In Nietzsche's opinion, the Renaissance, conceived of as a rebirth of classical antiquity, had stopped short. He argued that the twentieth century should return to the values and the philosophy of the ancient Greeks. He rejected the liberalism of his own century, the rationalism of the previous century, and the Christian views that had dominated the West for eighteen centuries. But unlike most intellectual historians, Nietzsche also rejected the Greek rationalists of the Age of Pericles—Socrates, Plato, and Aristotle. At once radical and reactionary, Nietzsche insisted that cultural health—namely, the health of European civilization—required a return to pre-Socratic virtues and values.

THE MIND OF EUROPE: ANXIETY, CRISIS, AND THERAPY

The analysis of history by such figures as Nietzsche and Frazer into organically related periods is part of the late nineteenth- and early twentieth-century migration of Hegelian idealism and Darwinian science into the human sciences. The fruitfulness of this migration is particularly evident in the field of psychology. Insights gained from the use of philosophy and biology for analyzing the human mind led to major breakthroughs, and these psychological advances were immediately absorbed back into philosophy and science. The work in psychology began with theories of the unconscious, constructed largely on a base of German idealism. The most popular of these theories, outlined by Eduard von Hartmann in *Philosophy of the Unconscious* (1869), became a reference point in the work of the English idealist F. H. Bradley, who in *Appearance and Reality* (1897) brilliantly combined dialectical and evolutionary thinking in a theory of mind supporting both his metaphysics and his epistemology. In America, during the 1880s, William James worked out psychological theories combining biology and philosophy. James expressed the view, as did Pierre Janet and a number of French psychologists, that the mental can ultimately be reduced to the physical. Such philosophic and physiologic theories were incorporated into the work of Freud and other psychoanalytic thinkers. In all of the work in psychology, including Freud's hypothesis regarding the id, ego, and superego, the Darwinian model of continuous and interrelated evolutionary stages is foundational, as is some form of transcendence suggested by philosophic idealism. The mastery and return motif is in psychology a part of recovery, a movement toward mental health.

The developments in psychology are especially important in order to understand literary modernism because the leading modernists adopted psychological models for their analysis of the world in which they found themselves. The psychological theories were appropriated as metaphors for explaining the history of culture, society, religion, and the human race itself. Nietzsche, to take an early example, perceived a psychological pattern in the history of culture. Worringer, in *Abstraction and Empathy*, worked out a psychology of style, with emphasis on the stylistic analogues of spiritual qualities and psychological states. Sociologists followed suit, analyzing social history into blocks comparable to biological and psychological stages. Durkheim argued in *The Elementary Forms of Religious Life* (1915) that there is a collective mind with its own stages, and Lévy-Bruhl argued in *How Natives Think* (1910) that there is a "primitive mind" beneath and behind the "modern mind." Both positions were widely held by other scientists and strongly corroborated by findings in cultural anthropology. Following the example of Nietzsche, cultural historians took up the strain, suggesting that nations and even continents had minds. The mind of Asia, for example, was contrasted with the mind of Europe and the French mind with the English mind. In analyses of the Renaissance, the mind of Italy was contrasted with the mind of Northern Europe.

All of the modernists were aware of these studies in cultural and social psychology, and Eliot was soaked in them. The notes and papers surviving from his doctoral studies show an in-depth grasp of the most important contemporary work in the social sciences and philosophy, and his seminar with Josiah Royce at Harvard University specifically addressed the problem of interpreting the primitive mind.[6] Of highest importance in Eliot's intellectual development was the doctoral dissertation he wrote on Bradley, discussed in this volume in "T. S. Eliot and the Revolt Against Dualism." The Bradleyan concept that Eliot put at the center of his dissertation is explained in this volume's "F. H. Bradley's Doctrine of Experience in *The Waste Land* and *Four Quartets*." Bradley's belief that knowing occurs in stages or levels of immediate, relational, and transcendent experience clearly parallels triadic concepts in psychology. Bradley's essay on immediate experience forms the subject of the first chapter of Eliot's dissertation, and in that essay, the philosopher pays close attention to cultural psychology. For example, Bradley asks: "Was there and is there in the development of the race and the individual a stage at which experience is merely immediate?" He continues by speculating on the extent to which the earlier "stages of mind" recur in the most developed individuals and the most advanced societies.[7] Most of these philosophers and social scientists accepted the idea that the mind of the individual, the society, the culture, and the human race developed in parallel stages. Eliot's interest in theories of social and cultural psychology survived his graduate studies and is

6. Eliot's seminar presentations on this subject are discussed in *Josiah Royce's Seminar, 1913–1914: As Recorded in the Notebooks of Harry T. Costello*, ed. Grover Smith (New Brunswick: Rutgers University Press, 1963).

7. F. H. Bradley, *Essays on Truth and Reality*, 1914 (Oxford: Clarendon Press, 1950), 174.

exhibited in his early book reviews. One of the books he reviewed for the *Monist* in 1918, Wilhelm Wundt's *Review of Elements of Folk Psychology: Outlines of a Psychological History of Mankind,* suggests in its title that humankind itself can be put on the couch and subjected to analysis.

Such studies in cultural and social psychology gave the modernists one of their central metaphors, the mind of Europe. The modernists generally believed that Europe had a mind and that the crisis of their time was the equivalent of a mental collapse. In April 1919, in a revealing passage in the *Athenaeum,* Valéry described the spiritual crisis of war-ravaged Europe as a "mental disorder." Europe, he claimed, had suffered a nervous breakdown. He described her anguish, her anxiety, her desperate attempts to defend her psychological integrity. In his view, cultivated Europe was exhibiting "all the familiar effects of anxiety, the disordered enterprises of the brain which runs from the real to the nightmare, and from the nightmare to the real, like a frenzied rat caught in a trap."[8]

In November and December of the same year, 1919, Eliot referred in the *Egoist* to his own theory of the mind of Europe. In "Tradition and the Individual Talent," he contrasted the mind of the individual poet to the mind of Europe. The poet should never forget that "the mind of Europe—the mind of his own country—a mind which he learns in time to be much more important than his own private mind—is a mind which changes, and that this change is a development which abandons nothing *en route,* which does not superannuate either Shakespeare, or Homer, or the rock drawing of the Magdalenian draughtsmen" (*SE,* 4). Eliot is assuming here that the primitive mind survives behind and beneath the modern, and that health for a poet involves a return, a conscious encounter with the living past. The "really new" is the fruit of this encounter. The profound continuity between the primitive and the modern minds makes it imperative for artists to cultivate the "historical sense," to become conscious of the simultaneity of past and present and of the layers of mind supporting the modern soul. The survival of the primitive in the modern is, in some way, physical; the earlier spiritual and cultural experience survives in the bones of succeeding generations.

8. Valéry, "Letters from France," 182–83.

Poets should cultivate this historical sense, this consciousness that they write with "the whole of the literature of Europe from Homer and within it the whole of the literature of [their] whole country" in their bones (*SE*, 4).

Eliot's reflections about the European mind include a specific diagnosis. The mind of Europe, he maintained, is schizophrenic. In his 1932–33 lectures at Harvard University, he argued that the English mind has been deranged since the time of Shakespeare. The problem is "a splitting up of personality."[9] He had made the same point in his 1926 Clark Lectures at Cambridge University, and even earlier, in his 1921 review of H. J. C. Grierson's anthology of Metaphysical poetry. In the time of Dante and Shakespeare, his argument ran, the mind of Europe had been unified, but beginning in the seventeenth century, that mind fell into two pieces, with the enlightenment and romantic mentalities representing the fragments of a schizoid cultural psyche.

Like Valéry, Eliot argued that the European mind was in desperate need of psychotherapy. Like Freud, he argued that a restoration of health was available through a return to origins and a retrieval of past experience. To renew itself, the European soul would have to return to its cradle. In "Tradition and the Individual Talent," Eliot had suggested as therapy a programmatic revisiting of the past, not because it was the past, but because it was part of the present of which the ordinary person was unaware. Eliot's conviction that some sort of return was essential for the psychological healing of Europe partly motivates his close attention to ancient and modern texts. A few years after the essay on tradition, in one of his commentaries for the *Criterion*, he argued that the retrieval of Greek literature and philosophy is the retrieval of the deepest levels of the modern mind. "The study of Greek is in part a study of our own mind. . . . What analytic psychology attempts to do for the individual mind, the study of history—including language and literature—does for the collective mind."[10] The way forward, in cultural as in mental health, is the way back.

9. T. S. Eliot, *The Use of Poetry and the Use of Criticism* (London: Faber and Faber, 1933), 84, 85. Subsequent references to this volume will be indicated in the text, abbreviated as *UPUC*.

10. T. S. Eliot, "A Commentary," *Criterion* 3, no. 2 (April 1925): 341. Quoted from *The Criterion: 1922–1939* (London: Faber and Faber, 1967).

The most memorable portrayals of the "Age of Anxiety," to use Auden's term for his troubled culture, are to be found in its art. Eliot's early poems are all in one way or another portraits of the mind of Europe. "The Love Song of J. Alfred Prufrock," for example, takes the reader into that mind and reveals a patient etherized upon a table, a paralyzed intellectual whose mind is a prison, a Hell with no exit. But the most focused treatment of the mind of Europe is in "Gerontion," a brilliant poem Eliot wrote in 1919, the very year that Valéry made his remarks on the European soul for the *Athenaeum,* the same year that Eliot himself speculated on the European mind in "Tradition and the Individual Talent." "Gerontion" is an interior monologue, consisting of the thoughts of a dying old man—his memories, desires, fears, hopes. His name, a Greek word suggesting a withered old man, reveals that his cradle was in the cradle of Western civilization. The main structural metaphor in the poem equates Gerontion's brain with a house and his thoughts with its tenants. The coda of the poem is "Tenants of the house, / Thoughts of a dry brain in a dry season." By placing houses within houses, Eliot suggests that the brain of this old intellectual contains the entire history of Europe from the Trojan War to the Treaty of Versailles. Gerontion's mind is, quite simply, the mind of Europe on the very edge of doom. This mind and this poem are the subject of one essay in this volume, "The Structure of Eliot's 'Gerontion': An Interpretation Based on Bradley's Doctrine of the Systematic Nature of Truth."

Eliot once intended to include "Gerontion" as the opening section of *The Waste Land.* Partially in deference to Pound, who objected to that plan, Eliot decided to keep "Gerontion" and *The Waste Land* apart. The impulse to marry the two works, however, is one of many indications that both poems are about the breakdown of the mind of Europe. Eliot compensated for the loss of "Gerontion" by using an epigraph with a parallel figure. The Sibyl of Cumae, who now presides over *The Waste Land,* is an ancient wise woman of Europe now shrivelled to the size of a cricket and imprisoned in a bottle. Like Gerontion and like Tiresias, another ancient and polluted well of European consciousness who appears in *The Waste Land,* the Sibyl is a metaphor for the mind of Europe.

Eliot's interest in cultural psychology is further evidenced by the fact that his original choice for an epigraph for *The Waste Land* includes the dying words of a supreme representative of the European mind, Conrad's Mr. Kurtz in *Heart of Darkness.* "Did he live his life again in every detail of desire, temptation, and surrender during that supreme moment of complete knowledge? He [Mr. Kurtz] cried in a whisper at some image, at some vision—he cried out twice, a cry that was no more than a breath—'The horror! The horror!' "[11] All of Europe, Conrad reveals, went into the making of the brilliant and cultivated Mr. Kurtz. Kurtz is the representative of the mind of Europe as it returns to its origins and relives its history. The words Valéry used to describe the European mind losing consciousness are eerily appropriate for Mr. Kurtz: "at the summons of the same anguish, cultivated Europe has experienced the rapid resuscitation of its innumerable thoughts, . . . it sought refuge . . . in the whole gamut of memories, of inward acts and ancestral attitudes."[12] *The Waste Land,* in one of its many aspects, represents exactly what the discarded epigraph from *The Heart of Darkness* suggests—a deathbed vision of the mind of Europe. "The Case of the Missing Abstraction: Eliot, Frazer, and Modernism," printed in this volume, discusses *The Waste Land* as a repository of fragments of the mind of Europe. Eliot's use of Frazer extends that mind backwards in time as far as human consciousness can go.[13]

Eliot's impulse toward unity is basic to his program of re-collecting and re-viewing primitive, classical, and medieval history and art. The impulse toward unity is also basic in his early and continuous meditation on religion. "Substitutes for Religion in the Early Poetry of T. S. Eliot" surveys his major early experiments for coping with brokenness. This essay begins with his early aestheticism and his Bergsonianism, and it moves to his appropriation of suggestions from Bradley's idealism. His work with myth as he made his way to the ancient Christian position is also reviewed. The myth substantiated by *The Golden Bough* and the early twentieth-century anthropol-

11. Joseph Conrad, "Heart of Darkness," in *Heart of Darkness, Almayer's Folly, The Lagoon: Three Tales* (New York: Dell, 1960), 114

12. Valéry, "Letters from France," 183.

13. A more detailed discussion of *The Waste Land* along the lines suggested in this paragraph can be found in Jewel Spears Brooker and Joseph Bentley, *Reading* The Waste Land: *Modernism and the Limits of Interpretation* (Amherst: University of Massachusetts Press, 1990).

ogists is the myth of the dying and reborn god, a myth that can be seen as corroboration of the central story of the Christian religion. These materials are discussed in the context of readings of "The Love Song of J. Alfred Prufrock," "Gerontion," and *The Waste Land*. Eliot's acceptance of orthodox Christianity continues the pattern of return and retrieval evident in his early work. The Christian religion began and the life of every Christian begins with a rebirth, a renaissance. Nicodemus asked Christ—"Can a man enter the second time into his mother's womb and be born?"—and Christ responded "Ye must be born again." This imperative at once confirms an ancient pattern and anticipates the modern pattern in philosophical, cultural, and psychological discussions.

The pattern of return associated with the recovery of health for the poet and for Europe is the great subject of Eliot's late masterpiece *Four Quartets*. "Keeping Time in Time: Eliot's Struggle with Form in *The Waste Land* and *Four Quartets*" compares and contrasts the formal and thematic focus on mastery and return in the two long poems. In *The Waste Land*, Eliot uses an ancient and comprehensive myth as a reference point; in *Four Quartets*, he allows an ancient pattern to emerge by repeating it in many forms and variations. The sequence moves forward through repetition, recapitulation, circling, echoing, and other versions of looping back. The final quartet recapitulates the other three, completes the abstraction they have generated, and then returns to the first quartet. The knowledge gained in this exploration is the knowledge of the beginning and its ends. "The end of all our exploring / Will be to arrive where we started / And know the place for the first time" ("Little Gidding" V). It is the journey itself that permits the homecoming, the experience gained in the exploration that makes it possible to re-cognize the "first gate."

MASTERY AND ESCAPE: ELIOT'S DIALECTICAL IMAGINATION

The mastery and return motif running throughout Eliot's work derives in part from his studies in philosophy, particularly his doctoral work in nineteenth-century German and British idealism. By the time he began his dissertation in the second decade of this century, dialectical thinking had penetrated into most areas of social and philosophic theory. His graduate studies included close attention to social sciences, and his dissertation was an in-depth examination of Bradley's idealist epistemology. The structure of Bradley's thought is another version of the pattern of mastery and return found in the work of Nietzsche, Frazer, and Freud; and for Eliot, it is the version most carefully studied and most profoundly absorbed. Eliot's philosophic studies thus corroborated and deepened his dialectical tendencies. His graduate work is taken up in several essays in this collection and also in the reviews of books by Piers Gray and Jeffrey Perl. Gray's helpful volume details the influence of nineteenth-century thinkers on Eliot, and Perl's fine study looks at Eliot's intellectual development in the context of literary modernism.

Eliot's Ph.D. dissertation on Bradley's epistemology helps to clarify the intellectual framework for most of his other writings, even those completed before he began the dissertation. An overview of the intellectual context of his dissertation and a chapter-by-chapter reading are contained in "T. S. Eliot and the Revolt Against Dualism: His Dissertation on F. H. Bradley in its Intellectual Context." The most important Bradleyan principle, taken up also in "F. H. Bradley's Doctrine of Experience in T. S. Eliot's *The Waste Land* and *Four Quartets*," is the idea that knowing is a process occurring in stages that may be called immediate experience, relational experience, and transcendent experience. The first is the stage before experience falls into dualistic categories, the second is the dualistic stage, and the third is a stage in which intellectual categories are transcended in a return to the unity of the first stage. The first stage comes before analytical thinking and the last comes after such thinking has been overcome. The first two stages are common to everyone, but the third is one that must be achieved through mastery and discipline.

An understanding of the Bradleyan doctrine of experience as Eliot outlined it in his dissertation clarifies one of the most fundamental principles in his literary criticism and his poetry. From first to last, Eliot was profoundly aware of the dangers of analytical thinking and of the distortion produced by dualistic or binary logic. By its very nature, analysis takes a person from the unity of immediate experience into the fragmentation of dualism, and, furthermore, analytical thinking tends to lock the thinker into the dualistic mode. Immediate experience, a knowing-and-being-in-one before the development of ideas per se, dissolves when the intellect begins to abstract ideas that in turn generate their opposites. Feeding on itself, analytical thinking produces the endless list of opposites—subject and object, mind and matter, real and ideal—that people deal with in their waking lives. Eliot argued that all such oppositions are artificial and that the urge to choose one over the other should be resisted. Binary oppositions, in fact, are mutually dependent and reciprocally defining. Mind, for example, can only exist in relation to matter; moreover, it can only be defined by reference to what it is not, that is, to matter. The appearance of such dualistic categories inevitably invites further analysis and tempts the thinker toward synthesis or an either / or choice. Eliot believed that this sort of thinking is destructive and a parasite upon lived experience.

Eliot's critique of analysis is everywhere evident in his poetry. J. Alfred Prufrock and Gerontion are both victims of "thinking." "Mr. Eliot's Sunday Morning Service" shows the effect of centuries of theological speculation. *The Waste Land* also deals with the destructive effects of knowledge, with the splitting apart of knowledge and values, of thought and feeling, of mind and body. In *Ash-Wednesday,* Eliot explores the possibilities for transcendence through negative mysticism. The attempt to escape dualistic categories through discipline and mastery is, in fact, at the heart of his later verse, especially *Four Quartets.* He readily confesses, as he had long ago acknowledged in his dissertation, that the transcendence of analytical thinking would not be easy; on the contrary, it would be as difficult and as necessary as rebirth. In "Little Gidding," he describes the postanalytical return to unity as a sort of ultimate simplicity costing "not less than everything." This costly simplicity is possible only for those who have consciously held and consciously surrendered intellectual categories.

Eliot's rejection of a binary "either / or" logic of exclusion and his strenuous insistence on a "both / and" logic of complementarity are clearly evident in his literary criticism and his verse. "Tradition and the Individual Talent," for example, is predicated on the conviction that antitheses between past and present, community and individual, and tradition and originality are simply false. For these and other polarities, he substitutes complementarities. The past is part of the present; the community is part of the individual; the tradition is not past and dead, but present and living, and its ever-changing shape includes the new and the individual. Eliot's rejection of binary thinking is also evident in his poetry, with *Four Quartets* providing a textbook example of his complexity, his logic of complementarity, and also of the modernist refusal of synthesis. In this volume, the special mode of complementarity used in *Four Quartets* is explored in "Keeping Time in Time: Eliot's Struggle with Form in *The Waste Land* and *Four Quartets*."

Eliot is often seen by literary historians as personifying a series of conventional oppositions. He is described, for example, as a romantic and a classicist, an elitist and a radical democrat, a reactionary and one of the avant-garde, an American and a European, a Catholic and a Protestant, a skeptic and a believer, an intellectual and an anti-intellectual, and so forth. A number of modern critics, relying instinctively on binary thinking, have insisted on seeing him as one or the other, but in fact, he should be seen as holding in tension both sides of the opposition. Some of these critics, misled by their binary perspectives, have misread the modernists generally and Eliot in particular. Sandra Gilbert and Susan Gubar, for example, read "tradition" and "individual talent" as opposites in their presentation of modernism as a conflict between the sexes. "Tradition and Female Enmity" in this volume is a discussion of modernism and feminism and of Gilbert and Gubar's use of Eliot's criticism in constructing their history of modern literature, particularly in *The War of the Words*. "Modernism and Belligerence," a review of Jeffrey Perl's study of modernist politics, also deals with modernism as a complex of unresolved polarities.

The dialectical spiral at the heart of the mastery and escape motif clearly manifests itself in pedagogy. In many modernist texts, the dynamic move forward by looping back is an unavoidable part of coming to terms with the content. Such texts as *Ulysses* and *The Waste Land*, for example, insist on mastery and return as a condition of basic comprehension. Moreover, in most modernist texts (indeed, in most literary texts), a special version of the dialectical method is operative in the reading process. The reading process, especially as related to modernist texts, is itself a topic in much of Eliot's work. As Brooker and Bentley argue in *Reading The Waste Land*, the poet builds into the text a set of instructions on how to read it. He also gives many indirect suggestions on teaching. Brooker and Bentley abstract from their experience in reading Eliot a principle they name the "hermeneutical loop." They argue that *The Waste Land* sends its readers to many other texts and contexts, all of which prove less satisfactory than the poem itself. The reader then is forced to loop back to the text of the poem, a return that facilitates a much richer understanding of the point from which the hermeneutical journey began.[14] This is a version of the dialectical process as applied to reading, and it functions quite naturally as a principle of pedagogy. Leading students on a journey that takes them away from the text, enables them to explore other worlds, and then returns them to the place from which they started works extremely well in the classroom. Most students will feel that they "know the place for the first time," a deeply satisfying experience made possible by what may have seemed to have been a fruitless journey.

The last two essays in this volume are related to manifestations of the mastery and return motif in pedagogy. The first essay, " 'The Second Coming' and *The Waste Land:* Capstones of the Western Civilization Course," was written to make a case for the usefulness of these ostensibly difficult texts in freshmen survey courses in intellectual history. The recapitulation of texts from Homer to the twentieth century in *The Waste Land* makes that poem ideal as a capstone in Western civilization courses. "The Second Coming" is a powerful companion poem because it gives students an immediate sense of the early twentieth-century crisis in Western culture. The background materials emphasized in this essay are by authors such as Nietzsche, Freud, and Frazer whose ideas also illustrate the dialectical dynamic. The second essay, "When Love Fails: An Approach to Teaching *The Waste Land*," grew out of experiments with teaching this pivotal text to undergraduates in literature courses. Both pedagogical essays illustrate basic features of the return motif: re-covery, re-vision, re-cognition, and re-trieval of texts as part of the attempt to begin to understand Western history and culture.

14. Brooker and Bentley, *Reading* The Waste Land, 154–58.

Dispensationalism and the Invention of History

The Dispensations of Art

Mallarmé and the Fallen Reader

A preoccupation with precisely what happens in the reading of a poem is at the heart of symbolist aesthetics. The quasi-official theoretician of the symbolists, Stéphane Mallarmé, devotes as much attention to creative reading as to creative writing. Obsessed with such matters as the reader's overall function in the aesthetic process and competence to perform that function, Mallarmé refers repeatedly to the situation of poets who find themselves at once in need of and deprived of competent readers.

Mallarmé's references to readers of poetry and to the reading process are, unfortunately, anything but consistent. In one breath, he execrates the reader as a dunderheaded fool; in the next, he honors him as a hidden poet. In one essay, he banishes the general reader from the house of poetry; in another, he welcomes him as a creative participant in a poetry festival. The ostensible contradictions in Mallarmé's theories of reading derive largely from the common assumption that poetry can be read in the same way at all times. Mallarmé maintains, conversely, that poetry must be read dispensationally, or, in other words, that it must be read in one way at one time and in quite another way at another time. Reading must be conceived of in terms of the readers at hand. When they are generally competent, he advocates one method of reading; when they are generally incompetent, he advocates a different method, one that recognizes and attempts to circumvent that incompetence.

The term "dispensation" is borrowed from Christian theology. It refers to a period of time during which one's responsibilities to other people and to God are reckoned according to a special system of divinely ordered principles. Dispensational theology, acknowledging that God deals with people in different ways at different times, is a first principle in hermeneutics, so elementary that the simplest

Bible readers understand it. They may not be able to define "dispensation," much less "hermeneutics," but they know that God dealt with Adam in one way (Dispensation of Innocence: Garden of Eden), with King Saul in another way (Dispensation of Law: Moses to Christ), with Martin Luther in still another way (Dispensation of Grace: Pentecost to the present). Readers also know that this present age will be succeeded by one somewhat like the Age of Innocence. That age, the final one and mirror to the first one, will be the Millennium or the Dispensation of Peace.

Important aspects of dispensationalism emerge through attention to etymology. A *dispensatio* (from Latin *dispensare*, to weigh out or to spend) is an administration, a management of resources. The analogous word in Greek, *oikonomia* (from *oikos*, house; and *nomos*, managing), in English an "economy," is used by New Testament and patristic writers to refer to a divine administration of human history, a period during which the ultimate manager conducts the business of the household of history in a particular way. But an *oikonomia*, a *dispensatio*, is more than a managing; it is a managing without (a meaning preserved in the use of "to dispense with"), a period in which the manager is forced to do away with certain rules, to indulge deficiency. Human deficiency—in theology, the Fall, the definition of humans as fallen and falling creatures—is at the heart of dispensationalism, for dispensations originate in a divine accommodation to human failure. The end of the Dispensation of Innocence (a dispensation only in retrospect, i.e., there was no such thing as a dispensation before the Fall) was brought about by Adam's fall, by his failure in a test situation. Similarly, the end of the Dispensation of Law was due to human failure to keep the law. The new dispensation in each case represents a concession of sorts on the part of God, at least in the sense that God puts aside the failed test and inaugurates a new era with different (always, in one way or another, less demanding) ground rules. God's insistence on inserting Himself between human failure and human banishment, the divine unwillingness to allow people to suffer the consequences of failure (permanent banishment from Paradise and from the divine presence) seems to indicate that the theological imperative for dispensationalism is God's need for some sort of relationship with humankind.

Mallarmé's view of art is analogous in important ways to the dispensationalist's view of history. A dispensation in art may be defined as a period of time during which the relationship between the artist and his audience is managed according to a particular set of principles. Mallarmé speaks of three such dispensations. Rather than giving specific dates or datable events as boundaries of aesthetic dispensations, he simply speaks of the art of the past, that of the present, and that of the future. The constant that exists apart from all three is the artist's absolute need of an audience. Unable to banish the reader entirely, the poet must adjust his principles, must make concessions to accommodate deficient readers. In the past dispensation, artist and audience enjoyed an immediate and creative relationship; in the future dispensation, that perfect relationship will be restored. In the present dispensation, a time of deficiency requiring grace or unmerited favor, the relationship is one of accommodation. But seeing this dispensation, always, as a temporary concession to incompetence, Mallarmé looks backward with nostalgia and forward with hope.

Mallarmé's views about reading (and almost everything else) are difficult to follow, in part because of his prose style. But there is another reason, more treacherous because less obvious. Like most idealists, he uses everyday words to convey eccentric or technical meanings. The word "poem" he sometimes uses to refer to a presence (the text) and sometimes to an absence (an idea). The uninitiated, assuming that a poem is a poem, is bound to be baffled. Because Mallarmé's idea of what a poem is and where it exists is at the center of his dispensational approach to reading, it is necessary to begin with a few rather basic discriminations. Mallarmé's absolute need of a reader, crucial in his dispensational dynamic, derives from his definition of a poem as an edifice existing in the mind of a reader, in part created by that reader. Actually, he speaks of the ideal poem in two distinct ways. His first ideal poem exists *before* expression in the mind of the poet, or in the mind of all poets. The "ideal has obsessed even the most unconscious writers"; it "has been attempted by every writer, even by Geniuses." Associating it with perfection itself, Mallarmé admits with dismay that he as an individual artist will never be able to write it. Still, he will devote his life to an attempt "to reveal and realize a fragment of it . . . and so suggest the rest of it which a single life cannot accomplish."[1] This unrealizable, atemporal poem

1. Stéphane Mallarmé, *Mallarmé: Selected Prose Poems, Essays, & Letters,* trans. Bradford Cook (Baltimore: Johns Hopkins University Press, 1956), 15–16. Subsequent references to this translation will be indicated in the text, abbreviated as Mallarmé 1956.

comprehends as fragments the countless ideal poems in the minds of all poets, both those alive now and those who have been dead for centuries. The poem in the mind of the poet exists apart from any reader.

Mallarmé's second ideal poem, however, is contingent upon the reader, for it exists in the reader's mind. "From time immemorial," Mallarmé explains, "the poet has knowingly placed his verse in the sonnet which he writes upon our minds" (Mallarmé 1956, 27). This poem, existing *after* expression, realized through reading, is analogous to the drama in the mind of the spectator (or reader) of plays. In an 1886 review of *Hamlet*, Mallarmé writes: "This work . . . is so well patterned on the theatre of the mind alone—this being the prototype of all others—that it makes no difference whether or not it is adapted for modern production" (Mallarmé 1956, 58). There are, obviously, as many *Hamlet*s as there are encounters with the text. A play or a poem is not written once and for all; with the collaboration of the reader, it is written anew with every reading. And although sometimes associated with timelessness, the true poem exists in time. Mallarmé's admiration for Emile Verhaeren derives from the Belgian poet's ability to produce poetic texts that initiate a "perpetual creation" of ideal poems.

> What I admire in your book—and in you, my dear fellow—is the perpetual creation of verses which never lose their fluid quality and yet are always perfectly guided. You don't make the mistake (as poets generally have heretofore) of writing them "once and for all." Rather, they are continually re-created, continually different, and yet still themselves—as life is. (Mallarmé 1956, 102)

These ideal poems, like the ideal *Hamlet*s, differ in quality, for the richness of the poem in the mind is contingent on the qualifications and the maturity brought to the occasion by the reader.

Mallarmé's elevation of the reader to a working partner in the creation of poems is explicit in the following compliment to the art of Théodore de Banville.

> Words in all their efficacy are fitted out and joined in a unique and perfect prosody, which asks of the hidden poet (who is Every Reader) that he should sing the song according to the modulations of the sweet or brilliant. Thus, all unaided, that principle springs up which is simply Verse! (Mallarmé 1956, 69)

26

The work of the hidden poet, the collaborator who is "Every Reader," is behind Mallarmé's definition of reading as the mating of a virgin space in the reader's mind with the blank spaces created by the writer's arrangement of words on paper, as a marriage of white and white which results in the birth of the Ideal.

> Reading—
> Is an exercise—
> We must bend our independent minds, page by page, to the blank space which begins each one. . . . Then, in the tiniest and most scattered stopping-points upon the page, when the lines of chance have been vanquished word by word, the blanks unfailingly return; before, they were gratuitous; now, they are essential; and now at last it is clear that nothing lies behind; now silence is genuine and just. (Mallarmé 1956, 33–34)

The distinction between mere blankness and the "essential" blankness that follows the reading of a poem, between mere silence and the "genuine and just" silence that follows the reading, is a key to Mallarmé's conception of art. Mere silence has no content, but the genuine and just silence is a structured silence rich with meaning. The first silence is an absence; the second, a poem in the mind of the reader. The first blankness, Mallarmé goes on to say, is a "virgin space face to face with the lucidity of our matching vision" (Mallarmé 1956, 34); the second, an Idea born of that encounter.

Mallarmé has a special name for the process through which the reader's "consciousness . . . joins the book now here, now there, varies its melodies, guesses its riddles, and even re-creates it unaided" (Mallarmé 1956, 28). This conversion of text into poetry he calls *Transposition*. Regarding the details of *Transposition*, Mallarmé enunciates two seemingly contrary tenets. On the one hand, he imagines a large audience listening to the poem being recited in an auditorium. In this version, the ideal poem is realized in many theaters at once—the literal recital hall, and also the theaters of the mind associated with the individual members of the audience. On the other hand, he sees a solitary aristocratic reader face to face with the text. In this version, the ideal comes into being only in the theater of this one superior mind. These two conceptions have important aspects in common. Both assume the idealist definition of the art work outlined in this essay; both assume the necessity of a competent and creative

27

reader-collaborator. And both are based upon an identification of art and religion, an identification in which the act of reading a poem is seen as an act of worship. But despite the common features, these notions of actualizing a poem remain in important particulars antithetical.

The apparent schizophrenia in Mallarmé's discussions of *Transposition* derives from a distinction he makes regarding the times of poetry. The past and the future are seen as glorious; the present as inglorious.

> I feel that our time is an interregnum for the poet; he should stay out of it; . . . all he can do is work in mystery with an eye to the future or to eternity, and occasionally send his visiting card, a few stanzas, or a sonnet to the "living," so that they won't stone him, should they suspect him of realizing that they do not exist. (Mallarmé 1956, 16–17)

The past dispensation, Mallarmé reveals in "Catholicism," was the Middle Ages; the future, he explains in his revery on Wagner, is a generation or more away.

> The majestic ceremonies of Poetry . . . are incompatible with the flood of banality born along by the arts of our sham civilization. They are the ceremonies of a day which lies unborn within the unsuspecting womb of the people. . . .
>
> Certainly neither this poet nor his contemporaries will be involved in any such ceremony, and therefore his dream need not be troubled by any sense of incapability or by its own distance from reality. (Mallarmé 1956, 72–73)

The reason for Mallarmé's dispensational approach is the deficiency or, to use religious language, the fallenness of the contemporary audience of poetry. Readers of poetry, needed to serve as hidden co-poets, are so base that they are barred from the high office of collaborators in art. The majestic ceremonies of poetry thus are deferred to some millennium "which lies unborn within the unsuspecting womb of the people."

The millennial dispensation, during which the poem in the mind will be generated communally in a public celebration, Mallarmé describes with unusual clarity in "Solemnity."

> I should imagine that when, in the future, we come together for the celebrations which are listed upon the human program, the

cause for doing so will not be the theater, limited as it is and by itself unable to respond to the subtlest of human instincts; nor music, which is in any case an art too fleeting to interest the mob sufficiently; but rather it will be the Ode, assimilating such over-misty, over-palpable elements as the theater and music tend to isolate; it will be dramatized and knowingly divided; heroic scenes will be simply an ode for many voices.

Yes, truly! think, think what that cult could be, which is destined for such celebrations! . . .

[T]his most magnificent of spectacles would be . . . the logical climax and conclusion of the entire artistic surge which was necessarily limited to matters of technical invention during the Renaissance period. Splendid, grandiose, impelling development! This recitation (a term which we must always come back to when poetry is under discussion) will fascinate, instruct, and above all it will astound the People. . . . And so we shall have the Opening of a Jubilee; especially of that figurative jubilee which must conclude a cycle in History and, to this end, must have, I think, the ministry of the Poet. (Mallarmé 1956, 71–72)

In the future dispensation, then, the poet and the people will celebrate together; in the past, the poet and his audience were similarly bound. In this time-between-times, this interregnum, the poet, far from reigning, lives in danger of being stoned by the people. With an eye toward the future, he can only shield himself in mystery until this cycle of history is concluded.

Particularly striking in Mallarmé's aesthetic is the importance attached to the role of the people. In most discussions by literary critics, Mallarmé's name is synonymous with the most perverse disdain of the people. The title of his most famous essay, "Hérésies Artistiques: L'art pour tous," suggests that the idea of art for the people is anathema. Hermeticism in art, however, is not a standard; it is a concession forced by incompetent readers during (as he refers to the present age in "Catholicism") a "dispenser era." Art for all, a heresy in this interregnum when the poet is forced underground, is the sine qua non of the splendid ceremonies associated with better times.

The necessary relationship between artist and audience, perhaps the major point in aesthetic dispensationalism, is a consequence of Mallarmé's identification of art and religion. This identification appears at the beginning of his career in "Hérésies Artistiques" and is elaborated for more than a third of a century in correspondence and essays. Occasionally art is presented as analogous to religion, but typically it is presented as synonymous with religion. The terms are often interchanged, i.e., religion is art, and also art is religion. In *Offices*, for example, Catholicism is the "art" of the past; poetry the "religion" of the future. *Offices*, written at the end of the poet's life, is his most profound meditation on the relationship of art and religion and his most complete description of aesthetic dispensationalism. The three brief essays in this sequence ("Catholicism," "Sequel," and "Sacred Pleasure") are almost universally regarded as Mallarmé's most formidable writings. Bradford Cook's explanation of why he excluded *Offices* from his Mallarmé translations indicates the problems that must be faced.

> However interesting these pieces may be to scholars (exposition of Mallarmé's theories on religion, rite, etc.), they consist generally of a kind of ugly, jagged shorthand highly resistant to clarification. (Mallarmé 1956, xxi)

My purpose in this essay, unfortunately, does not permit me to pass these recalcitrant compositions. "Catholicism" (1895) and "Sacred Pleasure" (1895), in particular, are central to my argument that, in discussions of Mallarmé's ideas and his poetry, art must be approached dispensationally.[2] The theoretical foundation for identifying art and religion, disclosed in "Catholicism," is that both were born in response to a basic and continuing need of the people, a common metaphysical need that Mallarmé calls "exhaling the abyss." "One imagines," he muses, "that religion arises from the juxtaposition of human consciousness and nothingness." A "presumption" born of the need to compensate for the "exterior silence," religion may be defined as a marriage of faith and nothingness or, in the poet's own phrase, "a vibration of certitude and of darkness joined in a meditative unison." He claims that Catholicism, in which certainty

2. The only translation of *Offices* into English that I have been able to locate is: *Stéphane Mallarmé: 1842–1898: A Commemorative Presentation including Translations from his Prose and Verse with Commentaries*, trans. Grange Woolley (Madison, NJ: Drew University, 1942).

Woolley's literal word-for-word translation preserves the difficulties of the French text. My discussion is based on three translations: 1) my own; 2) an unpublished translation by Professor Attilio Rigamonti of the Università di Pavia, Italy; and 3) Woolley's translation. All quotations from *Offices* are from Woolley; subsequent references will be indicated in the text, abbreviated as Woolley.

and darkness were harmonized beautifully, "has ceased," but the human need that generated Catholicism remains. The "honor" of soldering the abyss, of enabling people to cope with fear of the unknown, has been inherited by artists.

> A race, ours, to which befell the honour of lending entrails to the fear . . . which metaphysical and claustral eternity has of itself, and then (to which befell the honour) of exhaling the abyss in some firm baying in the ages. (Woolley, 126)

This explains Mallarmé's merger of art and religion, his identification of the artist with the priest and of the reader (or audience) with the worshipper, and not least, his insistence that the people be involved in art. Artists, then, have a sacred calling—they are to "resume the sombre marvel" (Woolley, 126) which was lost in the great apostasy of the late Middle Ages and the early Renaissance; they have an awesome responsibility: the construction of an alternative religion that will facilitate the "common functioning." In their ministry to the common need, artists must draw inspiration from their "own resources." The divinity they must take as a "point of departure" can be tapped only by descending into the self, or, as Mallarmé puts it, by "visiting" one's own "unconsciousness" and then ascending "with the ignorance of the secret" (Woolley, 126).

Mallarmé's dispensationalism is obvious in "Catholicism." The essay is based on a comparison between two great periods in which the religious needs of the people have been / will be satisfactorily met. The first period, in which Catholicism served as the religion, the poet identifies as the Middle Ages; the second, in which poetry will serve, he associates with an unspecified future age. Confessing that he retains a sympathy for Catholicism, Mallarmé discloses that he wishes to lean his aesthetic religion of the future upon its remains. His own words are that he wishes "to lean the Dream on the altar against the refound tomb—its feet like posts in ashes" (Woolley, 130).

In regard to the ceremony of this new religion, the "mind" of the poet "disdains syntheses," i.e., rejects the idea of doing research and then formulating from several sources a synthetic ritual. It prefers instead "to lead astray a research" that has become "empty" because it is no longer appropriate that the "bewildered, the banal and vast public place also yield to injunctions of salvation" (Woolley, 126). Presumably, this means that since Christian ritual has been disembowelled, it should be diverted, or led astray, from the use intended by such researchers as Aquinas. As a modern Aquinas formulating a successor to Catholicism, Mallarmé desires to project holiness into future centuries as Aquinas projected it into the nineteenth, but he is afraid lest his own "projection of holiness should not suffice and should fall short." To guard against falling short, he will resist the present mania for "dispensing" with tradition; he will, rather, salvage any part of the Catholic ritual that can be adapted for use in his new religion of art.[3]

Mallarmé then asks whether the ritual of the Mass can be saved by being "exteriorized" from its present use, or whether it must perish by becoming merely a grandiose kind of entertainment. He suggests that the ritual can be saved if the artist will adapt it for the new religion, allowing it to become an "intrusion in future festivals." These future festivals can be imagined if one is able to "suspend as his vision, the heavy chandelier, multiple evoker of motives" (Woolley, 128). The chandelier, reflecting light in many facets of cut glass, is one of Mallarmé's metaphors for the symbol.

At this point in the divagation, Mallarmé tries to evoke the festival of the millennial dispensation by suspending one of his favorite symbols—a bird. He envisions the audience distributing itself into two great wing-shaped groups of brooding humanity. "The multitude bifurcates to some amphitheatre, like a wing of human infinity, terrified before the brusque abyss" (Woolley, 128). The function of true religion, appeasing the terror of the masses huddled on the precipice overlooking nonbeing or death, will in the future dispensation be the responsibility of artists. In discharging this responsibility, artists will turn to music. In "Solemnity," Mallarmé maintains that the future festival will feature neither music nor drama but an "ode for many voices." But here in "Catholicism," he envisions a "performance with concert," perhaps a Wagnerian music-drama.[4] The music is important because it miraculously induces an interpenetration, "in

3. For another discussion of Mallarmé's analogy of poetry and Catholic ritual, see chapter 9, "The Poet as Ritualist," in Wallace Fowlie, *Mallarmé* (Chicago: University of Chicago Press, 1953).

4. This is, I believe, a running contradiction in his essays and letters. Sometimes he admits only poetry to his millennium; at other times, he admits poetry, drama, and music, or their combination in a Wagnerian synthesis.

reciprocity, of the myth and the concert hall." This reciprocity, uniting the orchestra, the audience, and the hero, is crucial in relieving the terror of the people.

> The orchestra floats, swells, and the action, taking place, does not isolate itself as something foreign and we do not remain (merely) witnesses: but, from each seat, through the terrors and the brilliance, in turn, we are circularly the hero—suffering not to attain to himself except by storms of sounds and emotions displaced on his gesture and our invisible afflux. He is Nobody, according to the rustling, diaphanous curtain of symbols, or rhythms, which he opens on his statue, to all. (Woolley, 128)

The actor on stage is cloaked in a diaphanous curtain of symbols that nullifies his particularity, transforming him into Nobody, the hero of the Ideal Drama. The spectators are at once witnesses to and actors in this drama. Participating in the hero's suffering, each spectator is transformed into Nobody. This participation is achieved through contemplation—"whosoever contemplates it [becomes] an unconscious protagonist" (Woolley, 129). The afflux of the witness/hero is invisible, making possible the appropriation of the sounds and movements of the figure on stage by many spectators simultaneously.

But this performance is more than a *pièce*, or play; it is also an *office*, or religious service. Mallarmé predicts that "the obsession, which the mind has for the theatre, shall grow in temple majesty" if the audience will recognize in the drama a communion service celebrating not the Passion, which is the "pompous aesthetics of the church," but the birth-death-rebirth cycle of the seasons. This ritual, purged of the barbarous idea of cannibalism, will relieve terror and effect unity just as the Mass did.

> Our communion or part of one to all and of all to one, thus, liberated from the barbarous meal that the sacrament designates—in the consecration of the host, nevertheless affirms itself, prototype of ceremonials, in spite of the difference from an art tradition, the Mass. (Woolley, 129)

An understanding of the Communion Service is one key to making sense of Mallarmé's discussion in this cryptic essay, for what happens in the Communion Service is what he says will happen in the communion ritual of his millennial dispensation. Of special importance is the fact that the Mass is commemorative, that it reenacts a momentous event of the past, the sacrificial death and resurrection of Christ. The past event features a being at once human and divine whose solitary death is a never-to-be-repeated sacrifice; he dies once and for all (for all people and for all time). The reenactment features human suppliants who identify in that death and resurrection. The reenactment is communal rather than solitary, and it is repeated every time the Mass or Communion Service is consummated.

In Mallarmé's aesthetic, writing a poem is analogous to Christ's Passion, and reading a poem to the ceremony of the Mass. The first, which features the poet, is essentially lonely and culminates in death. The second, which features primarily the audience, is essentially communal and culminates in rebirth. The analogy of Christ and the poet, of the Passion and the creation of a poetic text, is described many times in Mallarmé's letters to friends. To Théodore Aubanel, he writes about the suffering a poet must undergo in order to write a great work; and he confesses, "I died, and I have risen from the dead with the key to the jewelled treasure of my last spiritual casket" (Mallarmé 1956, 90). To Villiers de l'Isle-Adam, he writes that in order to purify poetry and link a poem to the "Idea of the Universe," he has endured indescribable nights of horror, culminating in death.

> And yet the irony and Tantalian torture is that, if my body is to rise from the dead, I must remain powerless to write them for a long time. For I am in the last stage of nervous exhaustion; my mind is so evilly, so perfectly afflicted that I am often unable to understand even the most banal conversation. (Mallarmé 1956, 92)

And as Golgotha was preceded by Gethsemane, Mallarmé insists that the death of the poet is preceded by *agonie*, a severe anguish preparing him for the sacrificial act that will redeem the text from nothingness. The most vivid accounts of both his Gethsemane and his Golgotha are preserved in letters to Henry Cazalis. The agony, the death, the descent to hell are described in the following lines from a letter of 1867.

> These last months have been terrifying. My Thought has thought itself through and reached a Pure Idea. What the rest of me has suffered during that long agony, is indescribable. But, fortunately, I am quite dead now, and Eternity Itself is the least pure of all the

regions where my Mind can wander. . . . I struggled with that
creature of ancient and evil plumage—God—whom I fortunately
defeated and threw to earth. But I had waged that battle on His
boney wing, and in a final burst of agony greater than I should
have expected from Him, He bore me off again among the Shad-
ows. . . . the price of my victory is so high that I still need to see
myself in this mirror in order to think; and that if it were not in
front of me here on this table as I write you, I would become
Nothingness again. (Mallarmé 1956, 93–94)

But death is followed by resurrection, for the poet is resurrected in
the reader's communion service. Mallarmé claims that this ritual will
have effects comparable to those formerly associated with the distribution of the "real presence."

[T]his devotee demands a fact—at least the credence to this fact in
the name of results. "Real presence:" or, let the God be there,
diffused, total, mimicked from afar by the effaced actor, understood by us trembling. (Woolley, 129)

The actor, like the priest in Catholicism, is a surrogate figure who
appears only to efface himself in favor of the hidden god. The god
resurrected in this ceremony is the poet who sacrificed himself in the
creation of the poetic text. Art's splendid ceremonies, bearing a "far-
off resemblance with grave things of the past, darkened in memory,"
will elevate the theater, "that which rumour denominates a social
edifice," into the temple.

The Passion and the Mass, both in Mallarmé's theory and in Christian thought, are interdependent. Neither has meaning in itself. The
theology at issue here, discussed at length in both Romans and Hebrews, revolves around the marriage of two of God's essential attributes, justice and mercy. Since all have sinned and since divine
justice requires death for sin, divine mercy seems to be precluded.
The dilemma is resolved in a way that perfectly satisfies justice without impeding mercy. Because Christ remained sinless, his death, in
itself, was a meaningless event, a punishment without a crime. It
gains meaning—as satisfaction of divine justice, as channel of divine
mercy—when sinful beings ritualistically appropriate it as their own
punishment. This appropriation happens in the ceremony of the
Mass. In eating the broken body and drinking the spilt blood, suppliants not only identify with the death of Christ but also give mean-

ing to that death. The Passion and the Mass, then, like writing a poem and reading one, are reciprocally related. If the Mass is a sham, the Passion signifies nothing; more apparent, if the Passion is a sham, the Mass becomes a tale told by an idiot.

Mallarmé concludes his essay on Catholicism by predicting that his new religion will rival in splendor Aquinas's old religion which has declined to a mere shadow. Again, his language is memorable: "A magnificence shall spread itself out . . . analogous to the Shadow of long ago" (Woolley, 130). That Shadow, Catholicism, and its sacrament, the Mass, now denominated as an *art* tradition, will be known only to scholars; but this magnificence, the art work of the future, and its sacrament, the performance, will be denominated the true religion and will be embraced by the people.

In this notion of *Transposition,* then, the poem in the mind is generated communally, ceremonially, in a magnificent public celebration. But the poem in the mind, as suggested earlier, is sometimes generated in a manner that seems to be the antithesis of this Catholic performance. In this alternative realization, a solitary, predestined, aristocrat retires to his closet, and through contemplation he or she constructs, beyond the text, in the sanctuary of the mind, a superior silence that is the ideal poem. In the spirit of evocative imprecision which Mallarmé admired (attempting to avoid mere imprecision, which he despised), I christen this notion of *Transposition* as Calvinist. The Catholic notion applies in past and future dispensations; the Calvinist in the present one. The Catholic notion assumes a public worthy because it collaborates in actualizing the poem; the Calvinist notion, a public degenerate because it is unfit to collaborate with the poet. The Calvinist notion is compelled by the fact that the present general reader is, to use the theological term, fallen; it is an expediency that makes poetry possible for a few competent readers and poets in what Mallarmé scornfully refers to as "our make-everything-clear-and-easy era" (Mallarmé 1956, 28).

It is arguable that Mallarmé himself would have disapproved, on general principles, of the association of his aesthetic with the theology of France's brilliant logician, John Calvin. But the major intellectual strains in his view of the solitary reader actualizing a text are analogous to the major doctrines of Calvinist theology. These ideas include human depravity, the predestination of saints, the rejection of mediators between the divine and the human, the emphasis on the

individual Christian rather than the community of saints, the autonomy of the Bible, and the focus on an explication de texte (a sermon)
rather than the Mass as the center of worship.

The Calvinist notion of *Transposition* may be illuminated by reference to Mallarmé's famous essay "Hérésies Artistiques: L'art pour
tous," first published in the 15 September 1862 issue of *L'Artiste*.[5]
Although written when Mallarmé was only twenty years old, this
essay is generally considered "a key to his entire work,"[6] roughly
equivalent in his thought to "Tradition and the Individual Talent" in
T. S. Eliot's thought. The main ideas are suggested in the title. The
first concerns the nature of art; the second, the audience of art. In
using the term "hérésies artistiques," Mallarmé is saying that art is a
religion. In defining the heresy as "l'art pour tous," he is saying that
art is for a minority audience; to use religious language, art is only for
the elect. The idea of the sanctity of art is important in both the
Calvinist and the Catholic conceptions of *Transposition*, but the idea
of hermeticism, really the main subject of this early essay, belongs
primarily to the Calvinist view. For reasons already discussed, art for
all is not a heresy in the Catholic view.

At the center of the Calvinist view of *Transposition* is the fallenness,
the depravity, of the reader. Mallarmé is infamous for the scorn he
heaps upon the reading public. In "Hérésies Artistiques," he refers to
the masses as the mob, as packs of baying hounds, as buffoons smell-
ing of the gutter, as Philistines, as irksome intruders. With devastating irony, he refers to the masses as "citizens," members of the
so-called reading public, "on whom modern vanity, being short of
flattering titles, has conferred the empty title of citizen."[7] Mallarmé
argues that poetry has been defiled by multitudes of citizens who,
with "the stupidity characteristic of the masses,"[8] rush into sanctu-
aries that angels would fear to enter. It is as if those hoards of tourists

---

5. Stéphane Mallarmé, "Hérésies Artistiques: L'art pour tous," in *Oeuvres Complètes*,
ed. Henri Mondon et G. Jean-Aubry (Paris: Editions Gallimard, 1945), 257–60. Translations into English are my own. The French text is given in footnotes.

6. Guy Michaud, *Mallarmé*, trans. Marie Collins and Bertha Humez (New York: New
York University Press, 1965), 15. Most scholars consider this essay as the most com-
plete statement of the poet's aesthetics. For example, see Fowlie, 233; and Norman
Paxton, *The Development of Mallarmé's Prose Style* (Genève: Librairie Droz, 1968), 43.

7. " . . . un de ces hommes pour qui la vanité moderne, à court d'appellations
flatteuses, a évoqué le titre vide de citoyen . . ." (Mallarmé 1945, 258).

8. " . . . une sottise qui est le lot de la majorité . . ." (Mallarmé 1945, 260).

who visit Notre Dame each summer should stroll up to the altar during Mass and take a bite of the bread or a sip of the wine. This early essay concludes with a ringing exhortation to fellow poets: "Let the masses read books on morals, but for goodness sake, do not give them our poetry to corrupt."[9]

The doctrine of depravity is balanced in Mallarmé as in Calvin by the doctrine of predestination or election. Poetry, says Mallarmé, is a "mystery accessible only to a few rare individuals."[10] The analogy with religion is explicit: "Religions take refuge behind secrets unveiled only to the elect; art has its own elect."[11] The high standing of predestined readers is underscored by Mallarmé's reference to them as members of the "*sandhédrin de l'art.*" The Sanhedrin was, until its dissolution in the destruction of Jerusalem in A.D. 70, the supreme council of the Jewish people. Although it included a few distinguished elders and scribes, it was composed primarily of hereditary priests—the High Priest, living former High Priests, and outstanding members of the larger family of priests. By demanding a reader who belongs to the "*sandhédrin de l'art,*" Mallarmé demands that the reader be holy and learned, competent and aristocratic.

Mallarmé, then, calls competent readers in the present dispensation "patient predestined ones." Because such readers are hidden poets, this doctrine not surprisingly can be reduced to the proposition that only poets can read poetry. In one of his letters to Cazalis, he is perfectly clear: "What you say about your aunt's and sister's reactions saddens me but doesn't surprise me, for I am utterly convinced that art is for artists alone" (Mallarmé 1956, 86). This does not mean that readers must have published or even written a line of verse; it means that they must have the capability to take a text and, collaborating with the writer of that text, create a poem. Intelligent reading of a text makes a poet just as surely as intelligent writing makes one.

Mallarmé's elevation of hermeticism from an incidental to a fundamental feature of art often is considered the ultimate perversity, especially today when many critics are militantly egalitarian. But the

9. "Que les masses lisent la morale, mais de grâce ne leur donnez pas notre poésie à gâter" (Mallarmé 1945, 260).

10. " . . . un mystère accessible à de rares individualités" (Mallarmé 1945, 259).

11. "Les religions se retranchent à l'abri d'arcanes dévoilés au seul prédestiné: l'art a les siens" (Mallarmé 1945, 257).

deliberate exclusion of the general reader is neither perverse nor un-reasonable. The attempt of the modern state to bring about universal literacy has generated a huge reading public, Mallarmé's "citizens," that has a severely limited understanding of the complexities and the beauties of language. By forcing the medium of poetry upon every school child, well-meaning though unintelligent bureaucrats have produced a crisis for poetry. Its language, laments Mallarmé, "con-tains no mystery to shield it from hypocritical curiosity, imparts no terror to shield it from impieties or from the smiles and grimaces of the ignorant and the hostile."[12] Baudelaire's *Les Fleurs du Mal*, for example, is written "in letters which, with each dawn, bloom and embellish the flowerbeds of utilitarian prose."[13] And his immortal poems contain the same words as the poems of hacks. This linguistic democracy has led to the nearly universal misconception that the mere ability to read words qualifies one to read Baudelaire. Mallarmé complains that the most insensitive blockheads in France approach this great poet boldly, presenting "in lieu of a ticket, a page of the ABC book from which they learned to read."[14] "Let us chance to whisper softly the names of Shakespeare or Goethe: immediately this buffoon lifts up his head with an air which implies 'Now this is my spe-cialty.'"[15] As a remedy for this situation, Mallarmé suggests that poets invent for their exclusive use "an immaculate language— priestly formulae the arid study of which would blind the profane but would stimulate the patient predestined ones."[16] And, of course, not only language, but many other facets of the strenuous poetry of the best artists in the present dispensation derive from the poet's awareness that most of his contemporaries do not know how to read.

12. "Celui-là est sans mystère contre les curiosités hypocrites, sans terreur contres les impiétés, ou sous le sourire et la grimace de l'ignorant et de l'ennemi" (Mallarmé 1945, 257).

13. "Les *Fleurs du Mal,* par exemple, sont imprimées avec des caractères dont l'épanouissement fleurit à chaque aurore les plates-bandes d'une tirade utilitaire . . ." (Mallarmé 1945, 257).

14. " . . . ces intrus tiennent en façon de carte d'entrée une page de l'alphabet où ils ont appris à lire!" (Mallarmé 1945, 257).

15. "Hasardons, en le murmurant aussi bas que nous pourrons, les noms de Shake-speare ou de Goethe : ce drôle redresse la tête d'un air qui signifie : 'Ceci rentre dans mon domaine.'" (Mallarmé 1945, 258).

16. "une langue immaculée,—des formules hiératiques dont l 'étude aride aveugle le profane et aiguillonne le patient fatal . . ." (Mallarmé 1945, 257).

Mallarmé's Calvinist notion of reading is further distinguished in that it focuses on the reader as a solitary individual. A shift of emphasis from the common to the unique, from the community to the individual, is a major concomitant of the Reformation. Calvin's break with the medieval world centers in his insistence on the importance of the individual's responsibility to God. Vertical relationships (human to divine) assume greater importance than horizontal ones (person to person). The Communion Service, traditionally the core of the Christian service, loses its priority to the sermon. In Mallarmé, the Calvinist notion of reading features a solitary reader. Speaking of himself in the third person, Mallarmé opens one essay with these words: "A contemporary French poet who, for several reasons, takes no part in official displays of beauty, would like now to continue along the lines of his daily task (which is the mysterious polishing of verse for lonely Celebrations)" (Mallarmé 1956, 72). The lonely celebrants are individual readers; they admit neither priest nor fellow communicants to their services.

Another analogy between Calvin's concept of worship and Mallarmé's concept of reading is the relative unimportance of place. The lonely celebrations can occur in a closet as well as (or better than) in a cathedral. In both the poet and the theologian, this seeming indifference to place is actually an internalization of place. Calvin's temple is the heart of the believer; Mallarmé's theater, the mind of the reader. In an 1898 letter to the gifted Belgian poet Emile Verhaeren, Mallarmé describes this ideal sanctuary.

> I thought I would be seeing your *Dawns* on the Parisian stage this winter. But how glad I am now that the performance will be limited to the spiritual theater within ourselves, where the combination of our inner love of pomp and the splendid vigilance of our thought will present it in its most magnificent form. (Mallarmé 1956, 105–6)

This theater of the mind, he says in the *Hamlet* review, is the prototype of all others. It is here that the solitary, anonymous, predestined reader in this present dispensation is able to experience the religious consolation available through poetry.

The Calvinist notion of *Transposition* is also distinguished by special emphasis on the text. "If his [the reader's] connection with that divinity is to be made clear, it can be expressed only by the pages of the open book in front of him" (Mallarmé 1956, 27). Mallarmé was obsessed with the physical text for the same reason that the Reformers were obsessed with the text of the Bible; the text was the spiritual instrument that could lead an individual to the ideal or to God. Mallarmé was even attentive to such matters as how words should be placed on a page and how pages should be folded. The text must be prepared with such care that the reader can "knowingly imagine that a given motif has been properly placed at a certain height on the page, according to its own or to the book's distribution of light" (Mallarmé 1956, 27). A famous application of these ideas occurs in "Un coup de dés," a stunning poem that integrates typography into other elements of meaning. Mallarmé's impulse to elevate the text is comparable to that of the Reformers who insisted on the textual autonomy of the Bible. They claimed verbal sufficiency, verbal inerrancy, and specific rather than general inspiration. They privileged no interpreter as mediator between an individual and the Bible. Such claims are related to the priority of the individual over the common, for to claim textual autonomy is, from one point of view, to vest authority in individual rather than in communal (or traditional, or institutional) readings.

A final feature of the Calvinist notion of *Transposition* is that it does away with ceremonies, rituals, and performances. The lonely celebration in the sanctuary of the mind consists entirely of reading and meditation. Only in meditation, which Mallarmé calls contemplation, are the essences available through art distilled and embodied in Idea. In "Hérésies Artistiques," even music, which technically speaking requires a performance, is spoken of in terms of a reading. There is no conductor, no orchestra; there is only the reader and the score. That this reader must be a specialist in an esoteric language has spared music the desecration that has been visited upon poetry.

> Let us casually open Mozart, Beethoven, or Wagner; let us cast an indifferent eye upon the first page of their work: we are seized by a religious wonder at the sight of these macabre processions of austere, pure, unknown symbols. And we close the missel which remains uncontaminated by any defiling thoughts.[17]

17. "Ouvrons à la légère Mozart, Beethoven ou Wagner, jetons sur la première page de leur oeuvre un oeil indifférent, nous sommes pris d'un religieux étonnement à la vue de ces processions macabres de signes, sévères, chastes, inconnus. Et nous refermons le missel vierge d'aucune pensée profanatrice" (Mallarmé 1945, 257).

41

Later in this essay, he compares reading poetry to "sight-reading" Verdi. Interestingly, most of Mallarmé's published comments on Wagnerian opera, including the famous "Revery" of 1885, were written from knowledge gained entirely through reading. According to Bradford Cook, "Only in the years following 1885 did he attend performances of Wagnerian opera and thus familiarize himself with the 'Master's' actual accomplishment" (Mallarmé 1956, 146). And, of course, in those remarks about seeing *Hamlet* and *Dawns* in the theater of his mind, Mallarmé is speaking of reading the texts of those plays, in solitude, without distraction. There are no actors, there is no performance, except within the mind of the reader. The Calvinist notion of *Transposition*, this expediency compelled by the fallenness of the reader in the present dispensation, does not conflict with the Catholic notion of reading outlined earlier in this paper. In truth, these views are complementary; and both are embedded in the analogies between poetry and religion that run throughout his career.

Two generalizations emerge from a consideration of Mallarmé's scattered references to these analogies. The first is that the early discussions focus on the Calvinist view of *Transposition;* the late discussions, ostensibly contradicting but not disowning the Calvinist view, focus on the Catholic view. This shift corresponds to Mallarmé's struggle in his earlier discussions with the practical problems of a poet in the present age; whereas he becomes in the later discussions more and more interested in the ideal, realized in the past and potentially realizable in the future. A second generalization is that the earlier references to the analogies tend to assimilate both the other arts and religion into poetry (performance into nonperformance), whereas the later references tend to assimilate poetry into the performing arts and religion (nonperformance into performance). In other words, the Calvinist view treats music, drama, and religion as if they were poems to be read, but the Catholic view treats poetry as if it were a spectacle or a ritual to be performed.

That poetry can exist in the present dispensation only as a minority religion practiced by aristocrats troubled Mallarmé deeply. Art's raison d'être is that it follows Catholicism in enabling the masses to cope with the "exterior silence," with death and nonexistence. The survival tactics of the poet in this "make-everything-clear-and-easy era" bypass the common needs that not only gave birth to religion but justify its continuance. But even in this great "Between," as Heidegger calls an era between the demise of the traditional god and the advent of his successor, the needs of the people persist. Mallarmé suggests that these needs can presently be satisfied through drama and music. His admiration for Wagnerian opera with its marriage of myth and music is based on the conviction that it can serve in the present as a religion for the people. His revery on Wagner begins with the reflection that, although poetry with her majestic ceremonies is in the present a "Chimaera-Who-Cannot-Be," Wagnerian opera is already a reality and is meeting the needs of the people.

> For the second time in history, the people (first Greek and now German) can borrow sacred feelings from the past and look upon the secret of their origins, even as that secret is being acted out. Some strange, new, primitive happiness keeps them seated there before that mobile veil of orchestral delicacy, before that magnificence which adorns their genesis. Thus, all things are restrengthened in the primitive stream. (Mallarmé 1956, 76)

In France, too, Mallarmé suggests in "Sacred Pleasure" (*Offices*), music is satisfying the religious needs of the people. The Sunday afternoon concert is taking the place of the Catholic Mass for many Parisians.

Wagnerian opera and the symphony can minister to audiences that poetry cannot reach, Mallarmé explains in "Sacred Pleasure," because collaboration in music requires less "lucidity" on the part of the audience.

> The sovereign-bow beating the first measure would never fall were it necessary that at this special instant of the year the chandelier in the concert hall should represent by its multiple facets a lucidity of the public relative to what is about to take place. (Woolley, 114)

At these Sunday concerts, Mallarmé is primarily an investigator of religious possibility. He is aware of himself as an outside observer, as a "poet" and "verbal artist." As an artist whose work, despite its innate superiority, is incomprehensible to the people, Mallarmé finds himself "caught by a doubt, a single extraordinary one." Why do the newspaper-moulded citizens bother to attend these wonderful concerts?

43

> The multitude satisfied by the insignificant play of existence, en-
> larged into politics, as the newspapers daily designate it, how
> does it happen—is it true it is due to some instinct, that, crossing
> over the literary intervals, this multitude should have need of
> finding itself face to face with the . . . poetry without words?
> (Woolley, 115)

This audience, possessing little verbal or literary intelligence, seems
to be drawn into the performance by instinct. But does instinct qualify its members for collaboration in art? Do they actually take part in
this religious service?

> The idea haunts one, very much like an instance of enormous and
> superior reporting: of verifying to what degree on Sundays, an
> audience takes part in the pleasure which it elects, yes, whether
> the concert takes place for anyone. (Woolley, 115)

If these people had assembled to hear him read his poetry, they
would be unable to take any part. The reading would be no more
than "a pouring forth in inanity in absence." But to Mallarmé's astonishment, this audience that is incapable of any deep understanding of words and meanings can participate in the ceremony of a
musical concert.

> Behold eyes, lost, ecstatically, outside their curiosity! . . . A little
> of the even uncomprehended sentiment, with which one's ex-
> pressions harmonize, makes an internal impression. It is an hon-
> ourable attitude, and is a participation, according to the pretext
> agreed upon, in the configuration of the divine.
>   Seriously.
>   The public which begins to surprise us so much as virgin ele-
> ment, or ourselves, fulfills in regard to the sounds, its function *par
> excellence* of guardian of the mystery! Its own! It confronts the
> orchestra with its rich silence, where dwells the collective great-
> ness. (Woolley, 115–16)

These citizens, who in other contexts Mallarmé calls mindless, stu-
pid, vague, profane, become at the symphony concert worthy collaborators in mystery. Mallarmé describes what happens to these citizens in the following words: "An initiation beneath illuminates, like
the dominical washing of banality" (Woolley, 116).

Mallarmé's ideas on art and religion can now be expanded to in-

44

clude music (and/or drama), the religion of the present which, in contrast to poetry, is able to facilitate the "common functioning." These ideas are not, in the main, contradictory. When he execrates the general reader and calls art for all a heresy, he is speaking of this present dispensation. When he exalts the reader and calls art a splendid public ceremony, he is speaking of the future dispensation. When he turns from poetry to music, he is searching for a religion that will work in the present.

An elucidation of Mallarmé's ideas about art is helpful for deciphering his poems. "Prose pour des Esseintes," for example, is at once an illustration and a description of some of the ideas presented here. But a clarification of Mallarmé's views is valuable far beyond any light it sheds on his own poetry. His influence on modern European art in all media but particularly on poetry is enormous. Without Mallarmé, the finest poets of this century—Valéry, Rilke, Yeats, and Eliot—would have been, as we know them, inconceivable. The interesting fact, however, as Eliot has pointed out, is that the great modern poets were not greatly influenced by Mallarmé's poetry but by his attitude toward poetry. If this dispensational reading of his aesthetic is valid, then a basic aspect of his thought has been ignored or misunderstood. In particular, Mallarmé's reputation as an elitist, based on what I have called his Calvinist expediency, has obscured the fact that at the heart of his aesthetic is an obsessive interest in what he calls the "common functioning." Many of his techniques (e.g., allusiveness, discontinuity) derive from his attempt to deal with incompetent or fallen readers. The "immaculate language" for which he is famous (or infamous) was especially designed for double duty—to seduce competent readers and to repel incompetent ones. His ritualism derives from his conviction that art must ultimately be justified in terms of the "common functioning." An understanding of his attitude in these matters enlarges one's understanding not only of modern poetry, not only of romantic poetry, but of the possibilities and limitations of all art.

"Ole T. E. H.": Pioneer of Modernism

"The *point de repère* usually and conveniently taken as the starting-point of modern poetry," according to T. S. Eliot, "is the group denominated 'imagists' in London about 1910.[1] The ringleader of this group, its philosopher and one of its representative poets, was T. E. Hulme. Through his own work and even more through the work of major poets such as T. S. Eliot and Ezra Pound who learned from him, Hulme contributed immeasurably to poetry in the twentieth century. But he was more than one of the founding fathers of modern poetry; in all the arts, he was a prophet of and an advocate for modernism. Nothing was more important in the development of modern art than the consciousness, shared by major artists in all media in the decade before World War I, that a major dispensation in the history of art, a dispensation reaching back hundreds of years to the early Renaissance, was coming to an end; and that a new dispensation, with themselves as pioneers, was beginning. And no one person was more instrumental in generating this consciousness than Hulme. The old dispensation, he named romanticism; the new, he called classicism. By announcing the new age, by endlessly reiterating it as a fact to the brightest minds of his generation, he armed them with the conviction that they were the makers of a new renaissance; and thus armed, they systematically broke conventions of form honored by centuries, and they established conventions that have become the hallmarks of twentieth-century art. Hulme was not, as he himself freely and frequently admitted, an original philosopher, but in serving as a conduit for Continental thinkers such as Henri Bergson and Wilhelm Worringer, whose ideas are basic in modern thought, he

1. T. S. Eliot, "American Literature and the American Language," in *To Criticize the Critic and Other Writings* (London: Faber and Faber, 1965), 58. Subsequent references to *To Criticize the Critic* will be indicated in the text, abbreviated as *TCTC*.

contributed much to the shape of the twentieth-century mind. He was, moreover, a representative of that mind. When Hulme's essays were published in 1924, Eliot wrote in his April "Commentary" for the *Criterion* that Hulme

> appears as the forerunner of a new attitude of mind, which should be the twentieth-century mind, if the twentieth century is to have a mind of its own. Hulme is classical, reactionary, and revolutionary; he is the antipodes of the eclectic, tolerant, and democratic mind of the end of the last century.[2]

Hulme was killed in World War I at the age of thirty-four—most of his promise unfulfilled, most of his writing still in the early draft stage. Even so, as poet and quasi philosopher, as prophet and propagandist, he had left such a mark on his generation that by the 1930s he had become the focus of a myth.

Thomas Ernest Hulme was born 16 September 1883 at Gratton Hall in the village of Endon in North Staffordshire, origins he used much later in constructing his journalistic pseudonyms—Thomas Gratton and North Staffs.[3] His father, Thomas Ernest Hulme, was a farmer and ceramic-transfer manufacturer. In February 1902, he went up to Cambridge, where he distinguished himself in mathematics and gained a reputation as a fluent and intelligent talker and debater, especially about philosophy and art. In 1904, Hulme was sent down from Cambridge for a sophomoric misdemeanor: in most accounts he is said to have indulged in a brawl and hit a policeman. His reputation as Cambridge wit and chief debunker, remarked by many of his contemporaries at St. John's College, secured him a hero's send-off. J. C. Squire recalls in *The Honeysuckle and the Bee* that Hulme was given the longest mock funeral ever seen in Cambridge, complete with a hearse bearing the young martyr and a procession of disciples mourning alongside.[4] For the next two years, Hulme studied science at University College, London. But philosophy was his first love. Neither his studies in London nor his dismissal from Cambridge was sufficient to keep him from attending Cambridge lectures in philosophy. The scientific and philosophic studies of these two years were to provide the foundation of his mature thought.

2. T. S. Eliot, "A Commentary," *Criterion* 2, no. 7 (April 1924): 231.

3. For a fuller biographical account, see Michael Roberts, *T. E. Hulme* (London: Faber and Faber, 1938).

4. J. C. Squire, *The Honeysuckle and the Bee* (London: Heinemann, 1937), 155–56.

In July 1906, Hulme went to Canada, where for eight months he supported himself as a laborer. The Canadian experience, though shrouded in mystery, seems to have been formative. In later years, he associated both his taste in art and his convictions in philosophy with his solitary experience on the great prairies of Canada. He returned to England in 1907 but stayed only a few weeks before moving on to Brussels. For the next seven months, teaching English to support himself, he worked hard to perfect his French, to learn German, and to acquire a firsthand knowledge of contemporary French poetry and philosophy. He continued to be most captivated by philosophy, particularly by the ideas of the French vitalist, Henri Bergson. Hulme knew, presumably, Bergson's *Matière et mémoire* (1896) from his courses at Cambridge. In 1907, according to his friend F. S. Flint, he read Bergson's *Essai sur les données immédiates de la conscience* (1889); and also in 1907, for the first time, he met with Bergson in Paris. Hulme evidently was profoundly moved by the meeting, for he later gave much energy to explaining and defending Bergson in England.

In 1908, Hulme left Belgium to resettle in England. Within a year of his return, he had made a lasting contribution to the development of English poetry. Soon after his arrival in London, he, Henry Simpson, and others banded together to form what they called the Poets' Club. As its first secretary, Hulme composed and circulated a charter statement that he called "Rules 1908." The Poets' Club met once a month (July, August, and September excepted) for dinner, for readings of original verse by members, and for twenty-minute papers by members or guests. Some of those original verses read by members in 1908 were collected at the end of the year into a little volume called *For Christmas MDCCCCVIII;* two of them, "Autumn" and "A City Sunset," both by Hulme, are vintage examples of what later came to be called imagism. And one of those twenty-minute papers presented in 1908 or very early in 1909, Hulme's "Lecture on Modern Poetry," outlines the general principles publicized a few years later as the doctrines of imagism. Hulme's miscellaneous notations of this period, edited by Herbert Read as "Notes on Language and Style," express in essence the aesthetic of some of the best poets of this century.[5]

5. Hulme's "Lecture on Modern Poetry" and "Notes on Language and Style" are

Herbert Read, Hulme's editor and an authoritative spokesman for modernism in all the arts, offers the opinion in *The True Voice of Feeling* (1953) that the most alert mind in England during the decade before the war was that of T. E. Hulme. One thing is certain: Hulme did bring special intelligence and energy to the Poets' Club in 1908. He brought, first of all, an understanding of the watershed situation in contemporary science and philosophy. Knowing that he and his contemporaries stood on the terra incognita between major dispensations in the history of thought, he brought to the Poets' Club a quasi-fanatical opinion that the new age demanded a new poetry consonant with the new physics and the new philosophy. He brought, moreover, very definite ideas about what the new poetry should be like. Specifically, from French psychologists and from Bergson, he brought a special concept of the image. And from Gustave Kahn, the French poet and critic who more than any other is credited with the invention of vers libre, he brought an insistence on formal experimentation and on organic form. Hulme's concept of *l'image,* as Wallace Martin has demonstrated, owes much to the definitions of the term by nineteenth-century psychologists, in particular, Hippolyte Taine and Theodule Ribot.[6] In the epistemology of these psychologists, *l'image* was a technical term referring to the immediate data of sensory experience, the raw material, so to speak, of consciousness that exists prior to thought, prior to language. As synonyms of *image,* the words *impression* and *picture* were frequently given; as an antonym, the word *idea* was most frequently used. Babies and animals, these psychologists suggested, think in terms of sharp, visual images (*impressions*), but adults normally convert the immediately given image into ideas and then into words. This conversion, a filtering of images through the mind, blurs or destroys the sharp, visual element, leaving a mere word, an abstraction that can be moved about in the mind or on paper without being visualized.

Hulme picked up these ideas and recorded them in his notes. His pet words, *image* and *impression,* are actually technical words used more or less as defined above. The image, he insists, is prior to ideas.

---

collected in *Further Speculations,* ed. Sam Hynes (1955; rpt. Lincoln: University of Nebraska Press, 1962).

6. Wallace Martin, "The Sources of the Imagist Aesthetic," *PMLA* 85 (March 1970): 196–204.

He suggests more than once that the world is most accurately known if "judged" from "the status of animals, leaving out 'Truth.'"[7] He told the Poets' Club in 1908 that as modern poets, they must attempt to arrest the mind with a picture, not let it race along to a conclusion. Hulme finds "an analogous change in painting," and adds, "where the old endeavored to tell a story, the modern attempts to fix an impression" (Hulme 1962, 72). The intellectualization of images, he argues, is reductive because it requires a radical simplification of the rich complexity of experience. In this conviction, as in many others, Hulme is in step with the greatest of his contemporaries. Major poets such as Yeats and Eliot, major philosophers such as Bradley and Bergson, even major scientists such as Bohr and Heisenberg, were anti-intellectual in the sense that they were aware of the inherent limitations of discursive thought.

Although rooted in nineteenth-century psychology, Hulme's idea of the image was modified, as Wallace Martin points out, by his assimilation of Bergson. Briefly stated, Bergson's epistemology is that there are two ways of knowing, one based on the intellect and one based on intuition. The first, oriented toward action, reduces the unity that is reality into parts that can be used in practical ways, or as Bergson would put it, in the service of life. Intuition, on the other hand, is not oriented toward action or use. It apprehends simply for the sake of apprehending and involves a participation in rather than a dissection of reality. Life and its meaning, Bergson asserts, can be grasped only through intuition. And intuition, he explains in *Matière et mémoire* and *Introduction à la metaphysique* (which Hulme translated), is inseparable from a sensuous reception of images. Poets, insofar as they are disinterested in using reality in a practical way, are especially open to the essential truth that comes via intuition. This need to discover truth through intuition explains in part why Hulme, whose basic interest was philosophy, was so intent on formulating a theory of poetry and on composing exemplary poems. He argues that poetry

> is a compromise for a language of intuition which would hand over sensations bodily. It always endeavours to arrest you, and to

7. T. E. Hulme, *Speculations: Essays on Humanism and the Philosophy of Art*, ed. Herbert Read, with Frontispiece and Foreword by Jacob Epstein (London: Routledge & Kegan Paul, 1924), 229.

make you continuously see a physical thing, to prevent you glid-
ing through an abstract process. (Hulme 1924, 134)

Poetry, in other words, catches the reader between the immediate
sensuous apprehension of reality and its reduction to abstractions.
Hulme further argues that "Images in verse are not mere decoration,
but the very essence of an intuitive language" (Hulme 1924, 135).

The aesthetic brought by Hulme to the Poets' Club in 1908 has
another aspect—its concept of structure in art—that descends directly
from his emerging epistemology. Images in reality do not occur in
logical sequence. The presence of logical sequence, in fact, is evidence that images are at least one step removed from reality, that they
have been filtered through mind. Images in poetry, likewise, should
not be connected by any sort of transitional devices; especially, they
should not be related intellectually or logically. In his early notes,
Hulme writes again and again that images must simply be juxtaposed, simply set side by side. The best art, he claims, does not
consist of a flowing-on of words, but of the simultaneous presentation of two different images. In lines that anticipate Eliot's "Preludes," Hulme remarks:

> Say the poet is moved by a certain landscape, he selects from that
> certain images which, put into juxtaposition in separate lines,
> serve to suggest and to evoke the state he feels. . . . They unite to
> suggest an image which is different to both. (Hulme 1962, 73)

The poem does not exist in either image, or even in both images,
but in the spark that is generated between them in the mind of the
reader. A poem, then, is a happening generated by a succession of
visual images, a unity "forced by the coming together of many different thoughts, and generated by their contact. Fire struck between
stones" (Hulme 1962, 80). The idea of poetry as "fire struck between
stones," anticipating Ezra Pound's "ideogrammic method," is basic
to the modern sense of poetic structure. As Hulme predicted, the
principle of logical or rhetorical continuity which worked for poets in
the nineteenth century will not do for the present age; the present age
requires an elaboration of the principle of discontinuity.

The concept of the image brought by Hulme to the Poets' Club in
1908 is arguably his major theoretical contribution to modern poetry.
But he also brought a concept of verse form from the French symbolist poets, and this concept complements the idea of the image worked

51

out from his understanding of French philosophers. His concept of the image itself owes very little to the symbolists, for they emphasized soft, vague images and he hard, precise ones. His concept of verse form, however, owes much to the symbolist poet Gustave Kahn, the first poet to write about vers libre. Kahn's *Premiers poèmes* (1897) contains a short essay consisting of *"une étude sur le vers libre."* In his 1908 address to the Poets' Club, Hulme says that

> The new technique was first definitely stated by Kahn. It consisted in a denial of a regular number of syllables as the basis of versification. The length of the line is long and short, oscillating with the images used by the poet; it follows the contours of his thoughts and is free rather than regular; to use a rough analogy, it is clothes made to order, rather than ready-made clothes. (Hulme 1962, 70)

Later in the speech, he puts this idea in other words.

> Regular metre . . . is cramping, jangling, meaningless. . . . Into the delicate pattern of images and colour it introduces the heavy, crude pattern of rhetorical verse. . . . It is a delicate and difficult art, that of evoking an image, of fitting the rhythm to the idea, and one is tempted to fall back to the comforting and easy arms of the old, regular metre, which takes away all the trouble for us. (Hulme 1962, 74)

The principle that form in verse should follow the contours of the image rather than the formulae of rhetoric or of meter, then, was basic in Hulme's 1908 program for modernizing poetry.

Part of Hulme's success in propagating his theories derived from an ability to convey his ideas compactly through catchwords. He predicted, for example, that the new poetry for the new age would be dry, hard, small, physical, direct, and classical. By dry, which he opposed to damp, he meant unsentimental in regard to its subject: "I object to the sloppiness which doesn't consider that a poem is a poem unless it is moaning or whining about something" (Hulme 1924, 126). He also advocated an unsentimental attitude toward art itself. He begins the 1908 lecture by saying, "I want to speak of verse in a plain way as I would of pigs: that is the only honest way" (Hulme 1962, 67). By hard, which he opposed to soft, he meant concrete, precise, definite, with no vagueness or blurring of outlines. Hard verse is composed entirely of images with no explanations or comments added. By small, which he opposed to big, he meant nonheroic:

> The old poetry dealt essentially with big things . . . but the modern is the exact opposite of this, it no longer deals with heroic action, it has become definitely and finally introspective and deals with expression and communication of momentary phases in the poet's mind. (Hulme 1962, 72)

By physical, which he opposed to intellectual, he meant that poetry should be based in feeling rather than in thought: "All poetry is an affair of the body" (Hulme 1924, 242). By direct, he meant almost the same. The images of direct poetry are images caught before the mind goes to work on them. Once they have been conducted through the passageways of the brain, they become indirect. By classical, which he opposed to romantic, he meant restrained or limited by an awareness of humanness. Modern poets, even in their most imaginative moments, will remain aware of finitude, will remain faithful to the idea of limits.

Hulme's ability to organize his fellows and his way of synthesizing Continental psychology, philosophy, and aesthetics into simple Anglo-Saxon catchwords might have counted for little but that he also brought considerable talent as a poet. His poems, almost all dating from 1908 and 1909 and composed as blackboard exercises for his friends, are elegant and beautiful, probably the best of all the poems associated with the imagist movement. "Autumn," which appeared in the 1908 Christmas anthology, is the most famous imagist poem:

> A touch of cold in the Autumn night—
> I walked abroad.
> And saw the ruddy moon lean over a hedge
> Like a red-faced farmer.
> I did not stop to speak, but nodded,
> And round about were the wistful stars
> With white faces like town children.[8]

Hulme deals with phenomena, such as the moon, that are the stock-in-trade of the romantics. But he achieves a different effect. Instead

---

8. Hulme's poems are quoted from "Appendix C" in his *Speculations.*

of projecting the familiar and the human into the great beyond, he brings the large and impressive back into the realm of the everyday. The moon, for example, he compares with a "red-faced farmer," or in "Above the Dock," with a child's toy caught in a boat's mast:

> Above the quiet dock in midnight,
> Tangled in the tall mast's corded height
> Hangs the moon. What seemed so far away
> Is but a child's balloon, forgotten after play.

Eliot admired these poems. In "The Function of Criticism," he noted that "the poems of T. E. Hulme only needed to be read aloud to have immediate effect" (*SE*, 21). In "Reflections on *Vers Libre*," he quotes "for its beauty" Hulme's "The Embankment: The fantasia of a fallen gentleman on a cold, bitter night," a poem that had appeared in the 1909 anthology of the Poets' Club (*TCTC*, 185–86).

> Once, in finesse of fiddles found I ecstasy,
> In a flash of gold heels on the hard pavement.
> Now see I
> That warmth's the very stuff of poesy.
> Oh, God, make small
> The old star-eaten blanket of the sky,
> That I may fold it round me and in comfort lie.

This delicate poem was remembered more than half a century after Hulme's death when, in 1968, Ezra Pound praised it in an interview.[9]

By February 1909, the Poets' Club had come to the attention of F. S. Flint, a young scholar-poet who had been publishing a series of articles on recent books of verse for the *New Age*. In the 11 February issue, Flint attacked *For Christmas MDCCCCVIII*, comparing it unfavorably with the work of recent French poets. As secretary for the club, Hulme answered, calling Flint a "belated romantic." The spat with Flint developed, oddly enough, into a friendship that has entered the annals of literary history. Hulme had become bored with the Poets' Club, and as Flint tells the story, Hulme "proposed that he should get together a few congenial spirits, and that we should have weekly meetings in a Soho restaurant." The first meeting of Hulme's new group took place on 25 March 1909, with subsequent

---

9. Daniel Cory, "Ezra Pound," *Encounter* 30, no. 5 (May 1968): 38.

meetings every Wednesday evening, at Café Tour d'Eiffel. The congenial spirits Hulme rounded up included Edward Storer, Francis W. Tancred, Joseph Campbell, and Florence Farr. Flint's account of this lively group is instructive: "What brought the real nucleus of this group together was a dissatisfaction with English Poetry as it was then (and is still, alas!) being written." Their goal was to replace contemporary poetry with a new art forged from several ancient and modern sources:

> We proposed at various times to replace it by pure *vers libre*; by the Japanese *tanka* and *haikai*, . . . by poems in a sacred Hebrew form, . . . by rhymeless poems like Hulme's "Autumn" and so on. . . . there was also a lot of talk and practice among us . . . of what we called the Image. We were very much influenced by modern French symbolist poetry.

And Hulme, Flint makes very clear, was the man in charge: "In all this, Hulme was ringleader. He insisted too on absolutely accurate presentation and no verbiage." Flint reports that the group spent much of their time together trying to write specimens of what they conceived to be up-to-date poems. They all wrote dozens of haikus for amusement, and Hulme and Tancred were wont to spend several hours a day searching for just the right phrase.[10]

On 22 April 1909, some weeks into the Café Tour d'Eiffel meetings, Ezra Pound was introduced to the Hulme group. His appearance was characteristically dramatic. With flowing cape, flaming-red beard, and flashing eyes, he boomed out his "Sestina: Altaforte" in such tones that waiters rushed over to screen off this colorful group from their other customers. According to Flint, Pound was anything but modern in his taste:

> He could not be made to believe that there was any French poetry after Ronsard. He was very full of his *troubadours;* but I do not remember that he did more than attempt to illustrate (or refute) our theories occasionally with their example. (Flint 1915, 71)

The fact is that Pound's dissatisfaction in 1909 and for a while afterward was not centered on the poetry of Edwardian London but on that of his Café Tour d'Eiffel associates. The morning after his

10. F. S. Flint, "The History of Imagism," *Egoist,* no. 2 (1 May 1915): 70–71.

first meeting with them, greatly annoyed by what he considered their "cheap irreverence," he composed "The Ballad of the Goodly Fere" to reassert his dedication to contemporary taste in literature. In "How I Began," he gives the details:

> In the case of the "Goodly Fere" I was not excited until some hours after I had written it. I had been the evening before in the "Turkish Coffee" café in Soho. I had been made very angry by a certain sort of cheap irreverence which was new to me. I had lain awake most of the night. I got up rather late in the morning and started for the Museum with the first four lines in my head. I wrote the rest of the poem at a sitting. . . . I began to realize that for the first time in my life I had written something that "everyone could understand," and I wanted it to go to the people.[11]

Hulme, on the other hand, had no expectation that people in the street would appreciate his poetry. He argued that although the romantic tradition had run dry, the frame of mind that demanded romantic qualities in poetry still prevailed. Good contemporary verse would not be understood by critics, much less by "the people."

In view of the discussion Ezra Pound later generated over the origins of imagist ideas, it is worth noting that in 1909 and for a short time thereafter, he approved of verse as it was then written. On 21 May 1909, a month after his meeting with Hulme and his malcontents and having already assumed the role of master to the up-and-coming, Pound wrote William Carlos Williams a letter that simply oozes enchantment with Edwardian London.

> If you were in London and saw the stream of current poetry, I wonder how much of it [Williams's own poetry] you would have printed? . . . There is no town like London to make one feel the vanity of all art except the highest. . . . If you'll read Yeats and Browning and Francis Thompson and Swinburne and Rossetti you'll learn something about the progress of Eng. poetry in the last century.[12]

Pound continued to meet with Hulme and his friends, but by his own testimony, he never felt at home with these poets. Noel Stock admits

11. Ezra Pound, "How I Began," quoted in Noel Stock, *The Life Of Ezra Pound* (New York: Random House, 1970), 100.

12. Ezra Pound, *Selected Letters of Ezra Pound 1907–1941*, ed. D. D. Paige (New York: New Directions, 1950), 7–8.

that although Pound learned much from these meetings, "it was several years before he was able to bring the lessons of 1909 fully into line with his own technical and theoretical interests (Stock 1970, 100). At the end of 1909, the Poets' Club published a second Christmas anthology, this time with not only Hulme but Flint and Pound among the contributors. Hulme's enthusiasm shifted back to philosophy in 1909, and the Café Tour d'Eiffel group gradually fell apart. Flint's *Egoist* history reports that it "died a lingering death at the end of its second winter" (Flint 1915, 71).

Hulme's interest in writing poetry, by all reports, ended in 1910. Most commentators agree with Jacob Epstein that Hulme was simply bored.

> At one time, in company with a group of "imagists," Hulme "composed some short poems with which, had he gone on, he would have made what we called a literary "success." But this seemed to him too facile.[13]

To punctuate his career as poet, Hulme allowed five short poems from his many exercises to be published in the 25 January 1912 *New Age* as "The Complete Poetical Works of T. E. Hulme." In October of the same year these same lyrics with the same wry title were re-published, this time as an appendix to Ezra Pound's *Ripostes.*

The appearance of Hulme's poems in *Ripostes* is usually taken as the official beginning of the imagist movement in modern poetry. Pound included a note explaining that he was including the poems "for good fellowship, for good custom, . . . and for good memory, seeing that they recall certain evenings and meetings of two years gone." He refers to Hulme and his Café Tour d'Eiffel friends as "the 'School of Images,' which may or may not have existed," and adds, "As for the future, *Les Imagistes,* descendants of the forgotten school of 1909, have that in their keeping."[14] Pound lost no time in rounding up some "descendants" of the forgotten "School of Images." His 1912 discoveries included his American friend Hilda Doolittle (H. D.) and her British friend Richard Aldington. In March 1913, Pound published in *Poetry* magazine the manifesto of the new movement. Sup-

13. Jacob Epstein, "Foreword," in Hulme, *Speculations,* viii.
14. Ezra Pound, in *Personae: The Collected Shorter Poems of Ezra Pound* (New York: New Directions, 1949), 251.

posedly as a response to questions put by F. S. Flint in an interview, Pound lists three principles of imagism:

> 1. Direct treatment of the "thing," whether subjective or objective.
> 2. To use absolutely no word that did not contribute to the presentation.
> 3. As regarding rhythm: to compose in sequence of the musical phrase, not in sequence of a metronome.[15]

Except for the insertion of the word *musical,* these rules, almost in these very words, had been repeatedly enunciated by their old friend Hulme. He was not mentioned in the *Poetry* article, but in the history of imagism that Flint wrote for the *Egoist* in 1915, Hulme is given credit for coming up with imagist theory and the first imagist poems in 1909, and Pound is given credit for launching the movement in 1912.

For a number of reasons, some obscure, some related to the appearance of Amy Lowell in the imagist group, some related to personal animosity toward Hulme, Pound began to assume a proprietary attitude regarding imagist doctrines. This was evidently a matter of indifference to Hulme, who seems to have viewed both Pound and imagism with amusement and slight contempt, but to most of the other imagists, such as Flint and Aldington, Pound's insistence on gaining credit for another man's ideas was a cause of resentment. Pound's generosity toward his fellows in art is legendary, and rightly so, but in the case of Hulme, a man to whom he owed much, he was less than generous. Long after Hulme's death, Pound continued his personal campaign to deny Hulme a place in the history of modern poetry. In 1937, in response to an inquiry from Michael Roberts, he wrote to warn against the view that Hulme "invented the moon and preceded Galileo's use of the telescope":

> What I am trying to get into yr. head is the *proportion* of ole T. E. H. to London 1908 to 1910, '12, '14. Hulme wasn't hated and loathed by the ole bastards, because they didn't know he was there.[16]

In January 1939, Pound wrote an article for *The Townsman* "to correct a distortion which can be found even in portly works of reference.

---

15. F. S. Flint and Ezra Pound, "Imagisme" (1913), in *Ezra Pound: A Critical Anthology*, ed. J. P. Sullivan (Baltimore: Penguin, 1970), 198–206; 41.

16. Ezra Pound, *Selected Letters,* 296.

The critical LIGHT during the years immediately pre-war in London shone not from Hulme but from [Ford Madox] Ford."[17] The strident tone of Pound's railing against the dead, not surprisingly, underscores rather than undermines Hulme's importance in prewar London.

The most astonishing of Pound's comments on Hulme is the repeated statement that Hulme was a nonentity in prewar London. From 1911 until the war, Hulme presided over a salon attended by a glittering assortment of luminaries in art and literature, in philosophy and politics. Hulme's salon was held on Tuesday evenings in a magnificent house at 67 Frith Street in the very heart of London. This house, which had once been the Venetian embassy and was in 1911 the residence of his close friend Ethel Kibblewhite, became in 1911 the center of Hulme's activities and remained so until his death. His salon was the scene of legendary arguments and has been described by many who attended from week to week. The painter C. R. W. Nevinson recalls that in 1911 and 1912 Hulme,

> a brilliant mathematician and philosopher, . . . was gathering round him a remarkable salon, the equal of which I have never seen. . . . [Hulme] had the most wonderful gift of knowing everyone and mixing everyone. . . . Here I used to meet [Jacob] Epstein, [J. C.] Squire, [Henri] Gaudier-Brzeska, W. L. George, Douglas Ainslie, Rupert Brooke—something of a dandy—Ashley Dukes, [A. R.] Orage, Mrs. Hastings, Eddie [Sir Edward] Marsh, [Robert] Bevan, Harold Monro, and [F. S.] Flint; Germans, Frenchmen, Italians, and Spaniards, including the philosopher Maestro, who 'they say,' was shot in the Spanish upheaval. There were journalists, writers, poets, painters, politicians of all sorts, from Conservatives to New Age Socialists, Fabians, Irish yaps, American bums, and Labour leaders such as Cook and Larkin.[18]

The sculptor Jacob Epstein describes Hulme's Tuesdays in similar terms, claiming that he was greatly entertained by the "many violent discussions in Frith Street," including one that he had with the painter Stanley Spencer concerning a statue of Buddha. Epstein's list of those who frequented Hulme's salon includes, in addition to those mentioned by Nevinson,

---

17. Ezra Pound, "This Hulme Business," *Townsman* 2 (5 January 1939): 15.
18. C. R. W. Nevinson, *Paint and Prejudice* (New York: Harcourt, Brace, 1938), 85.

> Ford Madox Ford (I remember him as a very pontifical per-
> son), . . . Richard Curle, . . . Wyndham Lewis, Ezra Pound, Rich-
> ard Aldington, Ramiro de Maeztu, who later became Spanish
> Ambassador to the Argentine, . . . Among Artists, Charles Gin-
> ner, Harold Gilman, . . . Spencer Gore, Madame Karlowska, . . .
> and Stanley Spencer. . . . Hulme, to attract so large and varied a
> company of men, must have had a quality, . . . of great urbanity,
> and his broad-mindedness . . . only ceased when he met humbug
> and pretentiousness.[19]

Epstein's account of Hulme's manner is corroborated by that of another guest, D. L. Murray of the Aristotelian Society. Hulme's

> character, at once authoritative and genial, made him an ideal
> leader of such assemblies. His resemblance to the early portraits
> of Henry VIII before that monarch's corpulent days was often
> remarked upon, and he certainly had a most dominating person-
> ality, by means of which, however, he used to draw out the opin-
> ions of his guests and stimulate debate rather than to impose his
> own views. The truth is that, however rigid and narrowly defined
> his own philosophy was, he never lost his intellectual interest
> in all manner of systems, beliefs, art theories and personalities,
> loved listening to ideas the most opposed to his own, and de-
> molishing them with a ferocity too jovial to give offence to the
> victims.[20]

Ezra Pound, in his article for *The Townsman*, also comments on
Hulme's salon: "His evenings were diluted with crap like Bergson
and it became necessary to use another evening a week if one wanted
to discuss our own experiments or other current minor events in
verse writing" (Pound 1939, 15). One of Epstein's memories regards
Pound:

> Someone once asked him [Hulme] how long he would tolerate
> Ezra Pound, and Hulme thought for a moment and then said that
> he knew already exactly when he would have to kick him down-
> stairs. (Epstein 1955, 60)

Pound's colorful report that Hulme's Tuesdays were "diluted"
with Bergson rings true. Hulme had visited Bergson again in Paris in

19. Jacob Epstein, *Epstein: An Autobiography* (New York: Dutton, 1955), 59–60.
20. Alun R. Jones, *The Life and Opinions of T. E. Hulme* (London: Victor Gollancz,
1960), 92–93.

July 1910. In April 1911, as a representative of the Aristotelian Society, he had gone to a philosophical congress in Bologna where he had again met Bergson and heard him lecture once more on intuition and the image. Back in England, he contributed a series of articles on Bergson to the *New Age* and gave a series of lectures on Bergson at the London home of Mrs. Franz Liebich. In 1912, Hulme applied for readmission to Cambridge and was successful in part because of a warm recommendation from the famous Frenchman. In 1912, he translated Bergson's *Revue et Métaphysique et de Morale* (1903) into English, and according to the notes left among his papers, was planning a book on Bergson's ideas.

Bergsonian vitalism, however, was a mere adjective at Hulme's salon. The noun was Hulme's conviction that a four-hundred-year-old dispensation in thought was ending and a new dispensation beginning. Both in the technical sense of a forth-teller, one who explains an age to itself, and in the popular sense of a foreteller, one who explains the future, Hulme was a prophet. He brought to the Frith Street salon an understanding of the watershed situation in contemporary science and philosophy—namely of the twentieth-century mind revolting against the seventeenth; basically, as A. O. Lovejoy has pointed out, a revolt against dualism. Bergson is part of this revolt in philosophy—his theory of intuition and his concept of the image as a mediator between mind and matter are inseparable from his attempt to overcome the dualism inherent in Cartesian epistemology. Hulme maintained that the previous age had begun with the glorification of the human in the Renaissance, had descended to the deification of the human in Rousseau, and had hit bottom in the confusion that resulted from adding Darwinian notions of progress to nineteenth-century notions of secular humanism. That passing age was characterized, then, by an uncritical belief in human goodness. The new age, just beginning with him and his contemporaries, was characterized by a collapse of faith in human innate goodness and in the inevitability of progress. The mentality of the previous age emerged from a working out of the principle of continuity; that of the present would emerge from a working out of the principle of discontinuity—in science, in philosophy, in religion, and in art.

Hulme's conviction that the difference in the previous and the present dispensation is at bottom a difference in one's attitude toward human nature led him to emphasize the importance of the theological doctrine of Original Sin. Against the common humanistic view that people are intrinsically good but spoiled by circumstance, he urged the classical religious view that they are intrinsically limited but ennobled by discipline and order. Hulme's position on human nature led Wyndham Lewis to dub him "Hulme of Original Sin," explaining that although everyone in England was getting a bit sick of the idea that people are like gods and capable of infinite progress, none of them, theologians included, had ever heard of the idea of Original Sin, nor would have had it not been for Hulme. In discovering it, Lewis concludes, Hulme did everyone a good turn and proved himself a genius.[21]

Hulme's dispensational obsession was fed by his immersion in contemporary German philosophy. He knew the German language and was well read in such philosophers as Immanuel Kant and Edmund Husserl. In November 1912, this man who had once remarked that life's ultimate pleasure consisted in reading Kant in German while submerged in a tub of warm water went to Berlin to spend six months studying philosophy and to attend the Berlin Congress of Aesthetics. While there, he met Wilhelm Worringer whose speculations on historical crises and artistic form in *Abstraction and Empathy* (1908) are central in the elucidation of modern art. Hulme attended Worringer's lectures and found in them a substantiation of his own ideas about history and art. Worringer, like Hulme, believed that there was an intimate connection in every age between form in art and attitudes in religion and philosophy.[22] By the time Hulme returned to England, he had assimilated Worringer's thesis into his own dispensational preoccupation, and on 22 January 1914, he presented a clear exposition of Worringer's views to the "Quest Society." Hulme was, in fact, very close to developments in modern art. The "London Group," including not only Walter Sickert, Britain's leading impressionist, but also Wyndham Lewis, one of the more outrageous of the vorticists, was born in the Frith Street salon. C. R. W. Nevinson, one of the original members, reports that

21. Wyndham Lewis, *Blasting and Bombardiering* (London: Eyre & Spottiswoode, 1937), 101.

22. See Wilhelm Worringer, *Abstraction and Empathy: A Contribution to the Psychology of Style*, trans. Michael Bullock (1908; rpt. New York: International Universities Press, 1963).

> [Harold] Gilman was the motive force. Slowly but surely with the help of [Hulme] he gathered all the warring elements of Impressionists, Post-Impressionists, Neo-Primitives, Vorticists, Cubists, and Futurists. (Nevinson 1938, 85)

And from the gathering of these artists at Hulme's Tuesdays, the London Group originated.

In August 1914, Britain entered World War I. Hulme was not, as is often asserted, a militarist, but he believed that certain values are worth dying for. Accordingly, he joined the Honourable Artillery Company and shortly after Christmas found himself in France in the trenches. In the spring of 1915, a bullet passed through his arm, killed the man with him, and earned Hulme a place in Pound's "Canto XVI":

> And ole T.E.H. he went to it,
> With a lot of books from the library,
> London Library, and a shell buried 'em in a dugout,
> And the Library expressed its annoyance.
>   And a bullet hit him on the elbow
> . . . gone through the fellow in front of him,
> And he read Kant in the Hospital, in Wimbledon,
> in the original,
> And the hospital staff didn't like it.[23]

Throughout the war, Hulme kept up his journalistic activity, writing mainly on war subjects. On 28 September 1917, not long after his thirty-fourth birthday, he was killed near Nieuport by a sudden burst of shellfire. Wyndham Lewis, serving less than a quarter of a mile away, witnessed the hit: "From the black fountains of earth that sprouted up, in breathless succession, occasional debris hurtled around us" (Lewis 1937, 99). A splintered piece of wood from the explosion sailed over Lewis's head, hitting the dugout at his back. Jacob Epstein, one of the many artists who admired Hulme, reported that his death caused great sadness in London.

It is sometimes said that Hulme's influence on modern thought dates from the publication of *Speculations* in 1924. But that is simply not true. There is irrefutable evidence of a profound influence on the poets who met at the Café Tour d'Eiffel and on the poets and artists

---

23. Ezra Pound, *Selected Cantos of Ezra Pound* (New York: New Directions, 1934), 31.

who came to Frith Street, men like Pound and Lewis who survived the war and helped to shape the postwar world. And there is evidence, outlined by Ronald Schuchard, of an early (1916) influence on T. S. Eliot, a man without whose art the twentieth century would not be itself.[24] The dry elegance of Eliot's revolutionary poetry had been predicted by Hulme; the social and religious threads woven together in Eliot's *Idea of a Christian Society* (1939) and other essays had been adumbrated by Hulme before the war. As poet, as propagandist, as prophet, as representative of his age, T. E. Hulme was one of those most responsible for giving a shape and a direction to the intellectual discontent of prewar London. And that discontent, certainly, is part of the foundation of the twentieth-century mind.

24. Ronald Schuchard, "Eliot and Hulme in 1916: Toward A Revaluation of Eliot's Critical and Spiritual Development," PMLA 88 (October 1973): 1083–94.

Common Ground and Collaboration in T. S. Eliot

The working man who went to the music-hall and saw Marie Lloyd and joined in the chorus was himself performing part of the act; he was engaged in that collaboration of the audience with the artist which is necessary in all art.—*T. S. Eliot (SE, 407)*

T. S. Eliot is generally regarded as an elitist. Long associated with intellectual coteries, he flaunted in the early poems such polysyllabic monstrosities as "polyphiloprogenitive." Complex poems like "Gerontion" and *The Waste Land,* though providing fodder for generations of voracious critics, seemed inaccessible to ordinary readers. Not surprisingly, Eliot has often been accused of a deliberate attempt to outrage the common reader by cultivating complexity for its own sake. The conspicuous cerebration in his poetry, the sometimes pontifical tone of his literary and social criticism, his distrust for majoritarianism and modern democracy, his identification with the Anglican church, even (or especially) his ubiquitous umbrella and his elegant weariness—all these and more are part of the elitist image of this connoisseur of Stilton cheese and Cheshire cats.

Eliot's reputation as an elitist has obscured one of the most significant features of his thought. At the bottom of everything he wrote, including his greatest poems, is his search for common ground. The word "common" is repeated over and over in his essays. As Eliot uses it, "common" has no pejorative connotations; it carries, rather, the standard dictionary meaning of "shared" or of "belonging to several or many." Eliot's influential critical doctrines, e.g., tradition, classicism, impersonality, wholeness, orthodoxy, are without exception a celebration of commonality; his great poems, from "The Love Song of J. Alfred Prufrock" to *Four Quartets,* constitute a pursuit of what is common. His innovations in poetic form are integrally related to a desperate attempt to secure common ground. Many other aspects of his life, e.g., his attraction to the theater and his affiliation with the Church of England, are explicable in terms of his appreciation for what can be meaningfully shared with human beings of every class in his culture. The 1929 essay on Dante, pivotal in Eliot's career as thinker and artist, is a good starting point for exploring his insistence on commonness.

Eliot's deep esteem for Dante is based on his conviction that the Florentine "is the most *universal* of poets" (*SE*, 200). While the concept of universality is too complex to be captured in a synonym, or even in an essay, there can be no doubt that the simple idea of commonness is the core of Eliot's meaning. Dante's achievement was possible because his poetic medium, medieval Italian, was extremely close to "universal Latin," and thus, for practical purposes, a common language throughout Europe. "The language of each great English poet is his own language; the language of Dante is the perfection of a common language" (*SE*, 213). The common language (or universal language, since Eliot interchanges the adjectives) made possible a common mind. Dante "thought in a way in which every man of his culture in the whole of Europe then thought" (*SE*, 203). This common mind greatly diluted national and/or racial mentalities because it "tended to concentrate on what men of various races and lands could think together" (*SE*, 201). Inseparable from this common language and common mind was a common culture. "The culture of Dante was not of one European country but of Europe" (*SE*, 201).

In reference to literary form, Dante benefited from access to a "method which was common and commonly understood throughout Europe" (*SE*, 203). This method is allegory, "not a local Italian custom, but a universal European method" (*SE*, 205). Allegory, of course, is contingent on the poet and his reader sharing certain unstated knowledge. The association of Dante's genius with his appropriation of common ground continues in Eliot's discussion of Dante's visual imagination. The surface level of Dante's poetry is consistently an appeal to what human beings have in common, i.e., the senses. This makes Dante more universal because, in Eliot's words, "our eyes are all the same" (*SE*, 205). The sense behind the nonsense in Eliot's often ridiculed view that "Genuine poetry can communicate before it is understood" (*SE*, 200) is related to the universality of the senses. "We can see and feel the situation of the two lost lovers

[Paolo and Francesca], though we do not yet understand the meaning which Dante gives it" (*SE*, 206). Appealing to this perfect common ground, Dante quickly establishes contact with his reader and then easily sustains that communion until the ideas on which the allegory has been built are understood.

The most important common ground connecting Dante and his international audience was the Christian religion, particularly the Catholic ideational system which culminated in St. Thomas Aquinas's synthesis of Aristotle, St. Paul, and the church fathers. Eliot's principal position on the relation of art and belief is that although readers need not endorse the beliefs embodied in a poem, they must at least "understand" them. Less than belief, but more than knowledge, to understand is to accept the ideas in a poem as coherent and as possible.

> When I speak of understanding, I do not mean merely knowledge of books or words, any more than I mean belief; I mean a state of mind in which one sees certain beliefs, as the order of the deadly sins, in which treachery and pride are greater than lust, and despair the greatest, as possible. (*SE*, 220)

Dante's incomparable advantage was that his audience went beyond understanding; like the poet himself, they believed in the great doctrines of Christianity.

The importance of common ground in Eliot's thought can also be illustrated from "What is a Classic?"—his 1944 Presidential Address to the Virgil Society. Eliot begins by trying to reclaim the word "classic" from the semantic quagmire created by centuries of cultural politics.

> If there is any one word on which we can fix, which will suggest the maximum of what I mean by the term "a classic," it is the word *maturity* . . . A classic can only occur when a civilization is mature, when a language and a literature are mature; and it must be the work of a mature mind.[1]

Eliot refuses to say just what he means by "maturity," rationalizing that mature readers already know the definition, and immature ones are incapable of understanding it. In spite of this evasion, he deigns

---

1. T. S. Eliot, *On Poetry and Poets* (London: Faber and Faber, 1957), 54. Subsequent references will be indicated in the text, abbreviated as *OPP*.

to give a criterion. The measure of maturity is the extent to which it consists of what is common. At bottom, the maturity of Virgil, like the universality of Dante, contains as semantic core the simple idea of commonness.

The Virgil essay, like the Dante essay, features one of Eliot's perennial contrasts, that between what is merely personal and what is shared. It is not Virgil's originality that makes him a classic, but the harmonious marriage of that originality with collective achievement. The common resources that made Virgil's greatness possible were, first of all, linguistic. He inherited a mature language, characterized by "a common standard, a common vocabulary, and a common sentence structure" (*OPP*, 56). Even style, the slippery concept usually related to individual genius, is measured by its inclusion of the common. The development of classic literature, Eliot maintains, "is the development toward a *common* style" (*OPP*, 57). English literature cannot adequately illustrate a common style, especially not the greatest poets, Milton and Shakespeare, because in reading these poets, one is bound to be distracted by individual style.

> In modern European literature, the closest approximations to the idea of a common style, are probably to be found in Dante and Racine; the nearest we have to it in English poetry is Pope, and Pope's is a common style which, in comparison, is of a very narrow range. A common style is one which makes us exclaim not "this is a man of genius using the language," but "this realizes the genius of the language." (*OPP*, 65)

Eliot goes on to suggest that the rise and fall of a civilization can be charted by observing the style of its literature. "The age in which we find a common style, will be an age when society has achieved a moment of order and stability, of equilibrium and harmony; as the age which manifests the greatest extremes of individual style will be an age of immaturity or of senility" (*OPP*, 57). To review more of Eliot's address on Virgil would be to repeat in different words his analysis of the universality of Dante. Eliot concludes that the perfect classic will be popular with the general public because it will have sprung from a community of taste, a community of ideas.

Eliot regularly emphasizes the importance of common ground in his prose writings from 1917 to the early sixties. The argument he makes is less interesting than the fact that he seems compelled to continually make it. His obsession is related to a crisis in history. All of Eliot's essays on the importance of common ground, such as those on Dante and Virgil, are based on an analysis of the relation of art to conditions of history. Consistently, his analyses involve a contrast between the past and the present—not the glorious past and the sordid present, but a past when art was possible and a present when it is impossible. The situation in thirteenth-century Florence or in pre-Christian Rome, then, is only a pretext in those essays. Eliot's real subject is the situation in twentieth-century London, what he refers to in his 1923 review of Joyce's *Ulysses* as "the immense panorama of futility and anarchy which is contemporary history" (*SP*, 177). In describing the common ground connecting Dante to his audience, Eliot is lamenting the absence of common ground between the modern poet and his audience. He is saying how "easy" art was then in order to underscore how difficult it is now. His amazement at "just how *little* each poet had to do" is a form of astonishment at just how *much* he and his contemporaries would have to do. His great predecessors had received the common ground they needed as a gift from history. But for the modern poet, history had no such gratuities. The generous mother, in the language of "Gerontion," had become a parsimonious whore who

> . . . deceives with whispering ambitions,
> Guides us by vanities. Think now
> She gives when our attention is distracted
> And what she gives, gives with such supple confusions
> That the giving famishes the craving. Gives too late
> What's not believed in, or is still believed,
> In memory only, reconsidered passion . . .

This lamentable metamorphosis in the character of history is crucial to understand Eliot and his contemporaries. In their time, the basic assumptions of reality that had supported Western thought for some three hundred years were swept away, producing the epistemological limbo in which the modern mind still lingers.

The enormity of the crisis faced by modern artists can be understood in terms of a concept of historical progression outlined by José Ortega y Gasset in *Man and Crisis*. Ortega suggests that when the world as it is known by one generation is succeeded by a different world, when the way of knowing that world is succeeded by a different way of knowing, the skeleton of the old world usually remains intact, leaving a structure for measuring losses and for interpreting the new world. But occasionally, Ortega argues, a very different type of succession of worlds occurs in which, to extend his metaphor, the backbone of the universe collapses, producing a catastrophe he calls a "historical crisis." Basic long-standing and widely diffused systems of thought that have served as the skeleton of the world are totally fractured, producing an epistemological void and creating a sense of disorientation and panic as one stands on the terra incognita dividing two worlds.[2] The crises associated with the Enlightenment and with the romantic or revolutionary period do not qualify as historical crises. In both epochs, the world retained its epistemological skeleton and could be interpreted in terms established by Newton and Descartes. The distinguishing feature of people in historical crisis is that they are tossed violently into an epistemological vacuum. The only imbroglios of the last two millennia that satisfy Ortega's criteria are the Copernican revolution of the early Renaissance and the Einsteinian of the early twentieth century.

That the early twentieth century was a time of historical crisis is perhaps now a commonplace in the history of ideas. Ortega y Gasset's famous essays on art and culture, e.g., "The Dehumanization of Art," are based to some extent on this notion of crisis.[3] Karl Jaspers's classic of existentialist theology, *Man in the Modern Age,* proceeds from a similar idea of the modern situation.[4] A. O. Lovejoy's *Revolt Against Dualism* shows that the early twentieth-century dethronement of Descartes constituted a historical crisis in philosophy.[5] The analogous crisis in physics, discussed in such books as Jacob Bronowski's *The Common Sense of Science,* was the dethronement of Newton.[6] Even literary critics, for example Nathan Scott, have discussed

2. José Ortega y Gasset, *Man and Crisis,* trans. Mildred Adams (New York: W. W. Norton, 1958).

3. José Ortega y Gasset, *The Dehumanization of Art and Other Essays on Art, Culture and Literature,* 2nd ed, trans. Helene Weyl (Princeton: Princeton University Press, 1968).

4. Karl Jaspers, *Man in the Modern Age,* trans. Cedar and Eden Paul (London: Routledge & Kegan Paul, 1951).

5. Arthur O. Lovejoy, *The Revolt Against Dualism: An Inquiry Concerning the Existence of Ideas* (1929); rpt. La Salle, IL: Open Court, 1955).

6. Jacob Bronowski, *The Common Sense of Science* (Cambridge: Harvard University Press, n.d.).

70

the early part of this century as a time when the progress of knowledge seemed to cancel the possibility of knowing.[7] In *Existence and Being*, Heidegger calls this time of epistemological crisis a great "Between." It is the age of need between the era of the gods who have fled and the gods who are coming, the "No-More" of Newton's God and the "Not-Yet" of his successor.[8] Eliot puts it this way: "The present situation is radically different from any in which poetry has been produced in the past; namely, . . . now there is nothing in which to believe, . . . Belief itself is dead" (*UPUC*, 130).

THE COLLAPSE of common ground in history, then, is behind Eliot's obsession with the idea of common ground. But why is common ground so important for an artist? Why does its presence make Dante a beneficiary of history and its absence make Eliot a victim of history? The answer is not, as may be supposed, that Eliot thought of art as communication. This ancient idea, advocated in the twentieth century by such eminent voices as the antiformalist Tolstoy and the formalist I. A. Richards, has limited importance in Eliot's aesthetic. Eliot required common ground because he thought of art as collaboration and collaboration as contingent upon common ground.

Eliot's definition of collaboration, like his definition of commonness, may be found in the most ordinary dictionary. To collaborate means simply "to labor together" or "to cooperate willingly in a project." Collaboration is the performance of one job by more than one person. Eliot's theory of art centers around two views: first, that the greatest art can only be achieved through collaboration; and, second, that the greatest artists are not necessarily the most brilliant or energetic but are the most willing and able to collaborate.

The greater artists, according to Eliot, realize at least three types of collaboration. Giants such as Dante and Virgil realize all three at once. The first is collaboration with the auditor or reader of the poem. The audience contemporary with Dante, say, joined in creating *The Divine Comedy;* each future audience in turn participates in its creation. The second type of collaboration is philosophic or ideational.

---

7. Nathan Scott, *The Broken Centre: Studies in the Theological Horizon of Modern Literature* (New Haven: Yale University Press, 1966).

8. Martin Heidegger, *Existence and Being,* trans. Douglas Scott (Chicago: Henry Regnery, 1949), 289.

Great artists do not use their own private ideas but collaborate with those who generate ideas that pervade cultures, such as philosophers and theologians. Dante did not think up original material; in building the intellectual structure of his poem, he collaborated with Aquinas and others. The third type of collaboration involves the poet with other artists, both living and dead, in the production of a "really new" work of art. Dryden, for example, did not perfect his particular forms as much through invention as through collaboration with other poets.

The collaboration of an artist with his immediate audience is discussed by Eliot in his 1923 memorial essay on Marie Lloyd. Eliot's admiration of this music hall comedienne, sometimes seen as an affectation, is entirely consistent with his admiration of Virgil and Dante. The superiority of all three derives from the fact that they did not work alone, as mere individual talents, but collaborated with their audiences. "The working man who went to the music-hall and saw Marie Lloyd and joined in the chorus was himself performing part of the act; he was engaged in that collaboration of the audience with the artist which is necessary in all art" (SE, 407). Miss Lloyd's work of art, her act, was not what she did alone on stage, but what she and her audience did together. Like Virgil and Dante, she avoided gestures that would have attracted attention to her individuality. "There was nothing about her of the grotesque; none of her comic appeal was due to exaggeration" (SE, 406). She was a "representative" of the British lower classes, in collaboration with whom she raised both her life and theirs to a kind of art. Like all great dramatic art, her performance was a cunning exploitation of what she and her audience had in common. Her ability to control them, to convert even hostile responses into part of the show, was gained by suspending self in a cooperative enterprise.

The collaboration of an artist with philosophers is discussed in Eliot's 1920 essay on William Blake. Eliot contrasts Blake, "only a poet of genius," to Dante, "a classic." The main difference is that Dante "borrowed" ideas, whereas Blake "fabricated" them.

> His philosophy, like his visions, like his insight, like his technique, was his own. . . . this is what makes him eccentric, and makes him inclined to formlessness. . . . The borrowed philosophy of Dante and Lucretius is perhaps not so interesting, but it injures their form less. (SE, 278)

Blake's poetry illustrates "the crankiness, the eccentricity" of the artist who is unwilling or unable to collaborate. "What his genius required, and what it sadly lacked, was a framework of accepted and traditional ideas which would have prevented him from indulging in a philosophy of his own" (*SE*, 279). Eliot's censure of Blake is softened by the conviction, centrally expressed in the Dante and Virgil essays, that the common ground a poet needs for collaboration must be given by history. "The fault is perhaps not with Blake himself, but with the environment which failed to provide what such a poet needed; perhaps the circumstances compelled him to fabricate" (*SE*, 280). Forced to be philosopher and poet at once, Blake was bound to stumble, in Eliot's view, as philosopher or as poet or as both.

The third type of collaboration, between poets and other artists, Eliot repeatedly attributes to his admiration of poets' "capacity for assimilation" (*SE*, 271). In what must seem like an odd compliment, Eliot says that "Dante had the benefit of years of practice in forms employed and altered by numbers of contemporaries and predecessors, . . . and when he came to the *Commedia*, he knew how to pillage right and left."[9] Eliot is even more explicit in a 1927 essay on the Jacobean dramatist, Thomas Middleton. He praises this rather obscure writer for "collaborating shamelessly" with Dekker, Rowley, and others. Admitting that Middleton is not the equal of Shakespeare or Webster, Eliot insists that in one way he is their superior. "Of all the Elizabethan dramatists, Middleton seems the most impersonal, the most indifferent to personal fame or perpetuity, the readiest, except Rowley, to accept collaboration" (*SE*, 140). The art of Jonson, Chapman, Donne, and Webster is vitiated by intrusion of personality, but the art of Middleton, "who collaborated shamelessly, who is hardly separated from Rowley," is impersonal: "Middleton remains merely a collective name for a number of plays" (*SE*, 140). "His greatness is not that of a peculiar personality, but of a great artist or artisan of the Elizabethan epoch" (*SE*, 141). This is Eliot's criterion for the classic, to be stated again some twenty years later in his address on Virgil.

Crucial to Eliot's view of art as collaboration is his idea that collaboration must not be limited by time. A poet must actively collaborate,

9. T. S. Eliot, *The Sacred Wood: Essays on Poetry and Criticism*, 2nd ed. (London: Metheun and Co., 1928), 63. Subsequent references to this volume will be indicated in the text, abbreviated as *SW*.

not only with present, but also with future audiences. In addition, a poet must collaborate not only with present philosophers and artists, but also with past ones. Extratemporal collaboration is the subject of Eliot's celebrated 1919 essay "Tradition and the Individual Talent." The first, perhaps the fundamental, point is contained in the title. Ordinarily, tradition and individual talents are opposite concepts in criticism. Critics tend to measure value in art either by the extent to which a work is traditional or the extent to which it is original. Eliot says that tradition and individual talent are not opposites, but complements, not two concepts, but two parts of one. He equally deprecates the tendency to praise an artist for conformity to past models and the tendency to praise him for "those aspects of his work in which he least resembles anyone else" (*SE*, 4). In this famous essay, Eliot abrogates a number of other antitheses, all more or less parallel to that between tradition and the individual talent, e.g., mind of Europe versus private mind; timeless versus temporal; past versus present; Ideal order of monuments versus new work; mind of poet versus ordinary mind. Central to his meaning in each instance is a contrast between what is or should be common and what is private or individual. In each case, Eliot replaces the "or" with "and," i.e., he replaces the antithetical relationship with a complementary, interdependent one.

Eliot's insistence on the interdependence of tradition and the individual talent endured throughout his career. In "What Is a Classic?" the 1944 essay referred to earlier, for example, he argues that "literary creativeness in any people . . . consists in the maintenance of an unconscious balance between tradition in the larger sense—the collective personality, so to speak, realized in the literature of the past—and the originality of the living generation" (*OPP*, 58). This statement is entirely consistent with the earlier and more famous formulation in "Tradition and the Individual Talent," in which tradition is associated with the "historical sense." The "historical sense"—the living presence of other artist-collaborators, dead ones included, within an artist—is an internalization, an organic assimilation of the common ground that unites one artist to all others, living and dead.

> The historical sense involves a perception, not only of the pastness of the past, but of its presence; the historical sense compels a man to write not merely with his own generation in his bones, but

> with a feeling that the whole of the literature of Europe from Homer and within it the whole of the literature of his own country has a simultaneous existence and composes a simultaneous order. (*SE*, 4)

Eliot admits that putting Homer, Virgil, Dante, and Shakespeare into one's bones, wherefrom they cannot be removed even by surgery, is possible only through great labor. Nevertheless, this labor is indispensable for individuals because it insures that their work will be achieved in collaboration with the dead artists living in their bones. It protects work against narrowness and eccentricity. To artists who take the pains to acquire this historical sense, collaboration will be "compelled," i.e., unconscious and impersonal. Automatically, the new work will develop and modify the art of predecessors.

Eliot's longing for collaboration with his audience accounts for his lifelong interest in drama. Many of his early essays, for example, "A Dialogue on Dramatic Poetry," argue that the possibilities for collaboration are maximal in the theater. And one of his most striking attempts to bring his audience into his art is found in *Murder in the Cathedral.* In no uncertain way, he forces his audience to take a part in the play. Becket's sermon, for example, is not addressed to any of the characters on the stage, but to the spectators. This transforms Eliot's audience in the theater into Becket's congregation in the cathedral. Again, after the murder, the guilty knights harangue the audience, forcing them to play the role of the judge who has superior perspective. Eliot also works in a temptation of the audience, and he manages to implicate the spectators as accomplices in the murder. Eliot's ability to gain collaboration through form is evident here. He initiates the collaboration by including a role for the audience, a role it cannot possibly refuse. Simply by being members of the audience, the spectators are automatically involved as collaborators. Each new audience encounters *Murder in the Cathedral* only partially written; unconsciously, each new audience completes it. Each new audience encounters a play with players missing from principal roles; seduced by form, each new audience performs its part, making the play a reality.

Eliot's view that great art is based on collaboration has analogues in his views on most subjects. Great religion, for example, is based on collaboration. Eliot especially disliked the performer-spectator ser-

75

vice prevailing in American Protestantism, in which the pulpit is often used to harangue a congregation with eccentric and divisive views. On the other hand, he deeply appreciated the Anglican service in which the priest does not dominate or dictate, but joins in common prayer and Holy Communion with the congregation. Eliot's appreciation of the Mass, "the consummation of the drama, the perfect and ideal drama" (SE, 35), is related to the audience's participation in the drama of the Mass through collaboration. Theology also must be constructed collaboratively.

> No religion can survive the judgment of history unless the best minds of its time have collaborated in its construction; if the Church of Elizabeth is worthy of the age of Shakespeare and Jonson, that is because of the work of Hooker and Andrewes. (SE, 301)

The spirit of Anglicanism, the via media where Puritanism and Catholicism meet on common ground, was attractive to Eliot. The Calvinists and the Jesuits, whose doctrines are crucial to understand Donne, were little more to Eliot than sects. They were eccentric concerning matters of faith; they refused to collaborate. In other areas, too, from public education to political science, Eliot measured value by the presence or absence of collaboration.

Much that has been considered merely iconoclastic about form in Eliot's poetry (and in the modern arts generally) can be explained in terms of the incongruity between a fundamental in art, i.e., that art requires collaboration, and a condition in history, i.e., a dissolution of common ground. He and many others who endured the same deprivation tried to bypass the epistemological crisis by gaining collaboration entirely through form. Many problematic aspects of form in Eliot's poetry (and in the modern arts generally), e.g., allusiveness, juxtaposition, fragmentation, multiperspectivism, deliberately unfinished surfaces, are comprehensible as stratagems for forcing collaboration from a reader. And Eliot's collaborators include, in addition to the reader, artists and philosophers. His collaboration with other artists, such as Dante and Ezra Pound, is undisputed. His collaboration with philosophers, such as Bradley and Russell, is less obvious than that with other artists, but it is just as important.

Eliot's obsession with common ground in culture and his emphasis on the necessity of collaboration in art lend themselves to generaliza-

76

tions regarding one of the great watersheds in the history of aesthetic form. Particularly suggestive is his contrast between the art produced in times of cultural unity and that produced in times of cultural chaos. When the members of a culture share basic beliefs and basic ways of organizing ideas, artists can use these common assumptions not only as reference points in their art, but perhaps of even greater importance, they can use these common ways of ordering experience as a guide to form. Collaboration with contemporaries, especially with an audience, is possible on many levels, e.g., religious, philosophic, nationalistic. Collaboration with artists and with thinkers of other periods is also possible, or at least is unimpeded by any traumatic repudiation of the past. With common ground to endow it, collaboration is spontaneous and unproblematic; it does not become a conscious aim in aesthetics. The art produced in such periods of grace will tend to be an extension of life into art, blurring the boundaries between life and art.

But when the members of a culture share no basic intellectual assumptions and share no framework for interpreting experience, artists must purge art of ideas and construct their own mental frameworks. Collaboration with contemporaries, especially with an audience, seems to be at once required and precluded. Collaboration with earlier thinkers and artists is also forbidden because of a disastrous repudiation of the past. To return to Ortega y Gasset's description of a historical crisis, the backbone of a world collapses, requiring artists to create, if at all, ex nihilo. With no valid reference points in the external world, art becomes ingrown, referring only to itself. And artists, for the same reason, tend to become solipsistic. Collaboration, without common ground to support it, demands conscious attention from the artist. To gain collaborators, one must work by force or by stealth, using techniques that circumvent the epistemological crisis by displacing the grounds of collaboration from life to art itself. In such periods, art and life will be separated by a great gulf. Purified of ideas, out of harm's way, art will be abstract and nonrepresentational.

Eliot once said that Yeats was part of the consciousness of an age that could not be understood without him. This statement, certainly, is true of Eliot himself. He often denied that he intended to express the deprivation of a generation in his poetry. And from one point of view, his poems from "The Love Song of J. Alfred Prufrock" to *The*

Waste Land are just an elegant grouse; but from another, they constitute an invaluable document on a major crisis in the history of aesthetic form and in the history of modern Western civilization. When read with the assumption that Eliot was an elitist, these poems are bound to be misinterpreted. And to misunderstand poems like "Gerontion" and *The Waste Land* is to misunderstand to some extent both our century and ourselves.

The Mind of Europe: Anxiety, Crisis, and Therapy

The Structure of Eliot's "Gerontion"

An Interpretation Based on Bradley's Doctrine of the Systematic Nature of Truth

> One poem like this is enough; it purges the language.
> —*Hugh Kenner*[1]

The notion that a reader must qualify for the experience of reading a poem is repugnant to many literary critics. The greater artists, it is argued, utilize common ground that is universal. One does not need to have read philosophy or to carry a reader's guide in order to appreciate, say, "Ode on Melancholy" or *David Copperfield* or even *King Lear.* The knowledge one must bring to such masterpieces is not acquired in the library of any university, but in the laboratory of human existence.

But is the common person's access to art an acceptable measure of value in art? Many of the best modern writers have insisted that it is not. The major theoretician of the symbolist movement, Stéphane Mallarmé, held in utter contempt the idea that a reader's credentials properly consist of his birth certificate and his ABC reading book. This famous elitist argued that reading a poem requires as much preparation and discipline as writing one. James Joyce assumed that readers of *Ulysses* and *Finnegan's Wake* would, and should, spend years preparing themselves to become partners in the actualization of those difficult novels. T. S. Eliot once remarked that a prospective reader of one of his poems should be willing to put in at least as much preliminary study as a barrister puts in before arguing a case in court. To these and other artists, readers are collaborators in art and should honor this role by preparing assiduously for the task.

One of the poems that has suffered most from readers' refusal to

1. Hugh Kenner, *The Invisible Poet: T. S. Eliot* (New York: Harcourt, Brace & World, 1959), 135.

qualify themselves to be collaborators is Eliot's "Gerontion." To understand "Gerontion," it is not enough simply to exist and to be able to read. To understand "Gerontion" properly, it is important to know something of modern philosophy, particularly of post-Hegelian idealism. The most important philosophy in both England and America at the turn of the century was a form of Absolute idealism, usually called neo-idealism, sometimes called neo-Hegelianism. In England, neo-idealism was associated principally with the ideas of Bernard Bosanquet and Francis Herbert Bradley; in America, with Josiah Royce (Eliot's teacher at Harvard University) and James E. Creighton. Bradley, the most eminent of these thinkers, was in the first quarter of this century revered (even by Bertrand Russell)[2] as probably the finest living philosopher. In 1916, just before writing "Gerontion," Eliot had finished a Ph.D. dissertation for the Harvard University Department of Philosophy on the epistemology of Bradley. A year of general crisis in Western history, 1916 was also one of the most stressful years in Eliot's personal life. His study of Bradley suggested ways to cope with the rubble of his personal life and methods to structure the ruins of history into art. Knowledge of Bradley's ideas is immediately helpful in understanding "Gerontion," the most important poem Eliot wrote between "The Love Song of J. Alfred Prufrock" and *The Waste Land*.

Of the many problems posed by "Gerontion," the most formidable is structure. Like "The Love Song of J. Alfred Prufrock," "Gerontion" is an interior monologue. The earlier poem exhibits loose psychological coherence, but the later poem is radically incoherent. The seven verse paragraphs are heterogeneous in length and content, and contiguous semantic integers are not continuous in logic. Some critics view "Gerontion" as a failed attempt to extend the method used in "The Love Song of J. Alfred Prufrock," i.e., interior monologue, to an older persona. Other critics explain that in modern poetry, juxtaposition has supplanted sequence as a principle of literary structure. Unfortunately, this observation has degenerated into a cliché that, in itself, is not very helpful to the reader. The more astute and fundamental observation is that the essence of such modern poems con-

2. When asked to name the greatest living philosopher, Russell is reputed to have named himself as the greatest and Bradley as second. See T. S. Matthews, *Great Tom: Notes Towards the Definition of T. S. Eliot* (New York: Harper & Row, 1973), 35.

sists not in the fragments strewn on a page, but in some "other-than-they" created by their collision in the minds of readers. But even this principle is likely to leave the reader of "Gerontion" in confusion. Can no other, more specific, explanation of the structure of this baffling poem be offered to the reader? One explanation that makes "Gerontion" more accessible is based on one of Bradley's principal ideas: the systematic nature of truth or reality, if speaking of ontology, or the systematic nature of judgment, if speaking of epistemology. This doctrine is not unique to Bradley. As the doctrine that leads inescapably to the Absolute, to the all-inclusive Idea, to the supramaterial reality outside of which nothing exists, it is common to all Absolute idealists. Bradley has his special version of the doctrine, of course, and it is his version that is described below and, in more detail, later in this book.[3]

Absolute idealists are distinguished from other philosophers by their belief in an all-encompassing Absolute as the ultimate reality. Any discussion of Bradley must begin by defining his particular conception of the Absolute. The most basic point is that Bradley's Absolute is not intellectual or mental, but empirical. In other words, it is of the nature of experience rather than of thought. Bradley's Absolute is to some extent a reaction against Hegel's. Hegel was a rationalist who believed that reality is the actualization of Mind. All reality, he claimed, is both rational and knowable. Bradley, on the other hand, was a radical skeptic who rejected the idea that reality could be mental. "[T]he notion that existence could be the same as understanding strikes as cold and ghost-like as the dreariest materialism." "Our principles may be true," he admits "but they are not reality."[4]

Bradley's Absolute, then, is not mental. It is empirical, and he actually names it "experience." He explains that "Everything is experience, and also experience is one." In another passage, he states: "There is but one Reality, and its being consists in experience. In this one whole all appearances come together."[5] Bradley is using the

---

3. For a fuller discussion of Bradley's conception of the Absolute, see "F. H. Bradley's Doctrine of Experience in T. S. Eliot's *The Waste Land* and *Four Quartets*" in this volume.

4. F. H. Bradley, *Principles of Logic* (1883; rpt. London: Oxford University Press, 1928), 2:590, 591.

5. F. H. Bradley, *Appearance and Reality: A Metaphysical Essay,* 2nd ed. (Oxford: Clarendon Press, 1897), 405, 403.

word "experience" in his own unique way, and some caution is required if we are to follow his argument. As Eliot explains in his dissertation, the important thing is to resist "considering experience as the adjective of a subject."[6] More simply, we must avoid thinking of experience as "my" experience, or as any person's experience. Bradley is not referring to experience as something that is experienced by an experiencer, but as something that simply is, as a complex that encompasses experiencer and experienced. The Absolute is pure experience, and it systematically includes all entities that can be identified as real. Bradley's experience is not an abstraction lying behind the appearances in the external world. "The Absolute *is* its appearances; it really is all and every one of them"[7]—not all totalled together, but all unified.

From this simplified definition of Bradley's Absolute, it is possible to move to his conception of the systematic nature of reality, a doctrine that concerns the structure of the Absolute. Experience, Bradley claims, is all-inclusive; everything that exists is included simply by virtue of being. It follows that every judgment, every perception, every object, every thing in the universe, is a part rather than a whole, a fragment moving within a system; and that system, according to Bradley, is reality or experience. Each fragment of experience is self-transcendent, i.e., each fragment reaches beyond itself and is taken up into successively greater fragments until it reaches reality. In other words, every fragment has a context, which in turn has a context, which in turn again has a context that finally is reality or experience. And experience, Bradley insists, is one. It follows that these fragments do not simply coexist; they are necessarily and systematically related.

Bradley calls the immediately given fragment of experience in any situation the proximate object; from the proximate object, one must move outward in an ever more inclusive circle through many layers of intermediate objects until the true object, reality or experience, is reached. Eliot endorses this doctrine in his dissertation. "No judgment is limited to the matter in hand" (*KE*, 167), and

6. T. S. Eliot, *Knowledge and Experience in the Philosophy of F. H. Bradley*, 1916, (New York: Farrar, Straus and Company, 1964), 15. Subsequent references will be indicated in the text, abbreviated as *KE*.

7. Bradley, *Appearance and Reality*, 431.

> the thing [i.e., the proximate object] is thoroughly relative, . . . it
> exists only in a context of experience, of experience with which it
> is continuous. (*KE*, 165)

Radical skepticism follows—"the only truth is the whole truth" (*KE*,
163). The "whole truth," which includes both knower and known, is
of course unattainable. One can never know how and to what extent
the more inclusive context will modify the immediately given datum.
No judgment, then, has its meaning alone; it exists as part of a timeless system.

An allegory in the first volume of Bradley's *Principles of Logic*
brings together his basic ideas on the systematic nature of the structure of experience. Interestingly, he introduces this allegory by describing the very mistake many critics make in trying to understand
the structure of "Gerontion." "We deceive ourselves grossly," Bradley says, if we break reality into pieces, and then, for the sake of order,
serialize these pieces. For this disastrous way of thinking, he gives an
image of viewing reality as a chain of events, made up of separate,
but regular time links. His image for "knowing the real" which,
though inadequate, "may save us from the worse" is the following.

> Let us fancy ourselves in total darkness hung over a stream and
> looking down on it. The stream has no banks, and its current is
> covered and filled continuously with floating things. Right under
> our faces is a bright illuminated spot on the water, which cease-
> lessly widens and narrows its area, and shows us what passes
> away on the current. And this spot that is light is our now. . . . We
> have not only an illuminated place, and the rest of the stream in
> total darkness. There is a paler light which, both up and down
> stream, is shed on what comes before and after our now. And this
> paler light is the offspring of the present. Behind our heads there
> is something perhaps which reflects the rays from the lit-up now,
> and throws them more dimly upon past and future. Outside this
> reflection is utter darkness; within it is gradual increase of bright-
> ness, until we reach the illumination immediately below us.[8]

The proximate object, the immediately given datum, is in the illuminated spot. This object may appear as one separately defined thing,
but it is continuous with all the other freightage, which in turn is

---

8. Bradley, *Principles of Logic*, 1:54–55.

continuous with the stream, which is continuous with the stream bed, which is continuous with a world that includes the viewer or subject. As far as the viewer is concerned, the whole, reality or experience, is in blackness, but this has nothing to do with its existence. The blackness is related, rather, to the limited reflection of the "now." The knower cannot fit himself into this picture, for he cannot at once be in the whole, a part of it, and outside the whole, a spectator of it. In Eliot's words, "the knower, *qua* knower, is not a part of the world which he knows" (*KE*, 154). Anything the viewer can see is a "mere adjective" of Reality, Bradley's way of saying that it has no meaning in itself. Our "now," without which everything would vanish, does not consist of discrete and resting moments, but of "any portion of that continuous content with which we come into direct relation."[9]

It is not necessary to go to Eliot's dissertation to document his belief in systematic wholes. His poetry, as the discussion of "Gerontion" will show, can be explained partly in terms of this cardinal idea; more apparent, his social, religious, and literary criticism is saturated in Bradleyan idealism. A clear example of his emphasis on the self-transcendence of parts and on the systematic nature of the whole is his celebrated doctrine of tradition and the individual talent. The proximate object of critical judgment is the individual talent; the true object is the tradition.

> No poet, no artist of any art, has his complete meaning alone. His significance, his appreciation is the appreciation of his relation to the dead poets and artists. You cannot value him alone; you must set him . . . among the dead. . . . what happens when a new work of art is created is something that happens simultaneously to all the works of art which preceded it. The existing monuments form an ideal order among themselves, which is modified by the introduction of the new . . . work of art among them. The existing order is complete before the new work arrives; for order to persist after the supervention of novelty, the *whole* existing order must be . . . altered; and so the relations, proportions, values of each work of art toward the whole are readjusted. (*SE*, 4–5)

To Eliot, then, as to Bradley, it is axiomatic that the all-inclusive and ever-developing whole is qualified and altered by its terms. It is not surprising, then, that *The Divine Comedy* is altered by *The Waste Land.*

9. Bradley, *Principles of Logic*, 1:55.

Being parts of one thing, the tradition, they are necessarily and internally connected.

An important part of Bradley's idea of the systematic nature of truth is his doctrine of internal relations. This doctrine, accepted by Eliot in his dissertation (*KE,* 153), is basic in understanding "Gerontion." Roughly stated, it means that all fragments of reality, all appearances, are related to one another simply because they are all part, in the final analysis, of one thing that is the Absolute or experience; and because experience is all-inclusive, all relations are "internal." Relatedness does not have to do with satisfying logical or spatial or temporal or psychological formulae; it has to do, rather, with the fact that all fragments are constituent of one systematic thing. Bradley says that any two terms of maximum incongruity, "two terms which had no more visibly in common than the fact that they exist or are thought . . . somehow are connected in and qualify this unity."[10] The doctrine of internal relations means that

> if you could have a perfect relational knowledge of the world, . . .
> you could start internally from any one character in the Universe,
> and you could from that pass to the rest. You would go in each
> case more or less directly or indirectly, and with unimportant
> characters the amount of indirectedness would be enormous, but
> no passage would be external.[11]

The doctrine of internal relations must be true, Bradley argues, because "logically and really, all relations imply a whole to which the terms contribute and by which the terms are qualified."[12]

Eliot's belief in the self-transcendence of objects is evident in the use he makes of a literary device that some critics consider his trademark—allusiveness. In literature, allusiveness is not peculiar to Eliot; in fact, it is a stock-in-trade of most great writers, including Dante, Shakespeare, Milton, Pope, and Joyce. Nor is allusiveness unique to the literary arts; it is a standard device of musicians and painters, including Mozart and Wagner, Mantegna and Picasso. Nevertheless, Eliot did make allusiveness more structurally prominent than it had ever been before. It is well known that early reviewers of *The Waste Land* were outraged at Eliot's unashamedly conspicuous use of other literature. But the allusions in *The Waste Land* (and in all Eliot's

10. Bradley, *Appearance and Reality,* 519–20.
11. Bradley, *Appearance and Reality,* 520.
12. Bradley, *Appearance and Reality,* 521.

poems, including "Gerontion") are not primarily shock tactics, nor are they primarily a scheme to generate employment for pedants; they are, rather, a fundamental structural dynamic. An allusion is by definition a self-transcendent fragment. In a period of perhaps unparalleled alienation of artists from audiences, Eliot used allusions to force readers to move from object to context to enlarged context. By leading readers from an allusion to its referent and back to its new context in his poem, Old Possum is helping them to discover internal relations necessary to complete the ideal construction that is the poem.

The basic situation of "Gerontion" is clear enough. The poem is an interior monologue spoken by Gerontion, whose name, a transliteration of the Greek word for little old man, is also a description. He is withered, old, and descended from the Greeks. This vestige of Greek civilization is no Achilles, however, and he immediately dissociates himself from usual notions regarding the glory of the Athenians. His opening words, an apology of sorts, reveal that he did not fight in the great battle between the Greeks and Persians at Thermopylae (literally, "hot gates") in 480 B.C. This hollow old man ruminates about a past and a present without meaning and a future without hope. But the dynamic that controls movement from one part to another in "Gerontion" is not flow of an old man's consciousness; it is, rather, expansion and contraction of the contexts of fragments. All of the fragments in the poem are unified by reference to more inclusive contexts. Movement from one part of the poem to another, from fragment to context, requires that readers be constantly shifting their vantage point—backwards, forwards, sideways—in dimensions sometimes temporal or spatial, sometimes logical, sometimes both. Not only are readers required to assume a different vantage point in moving from one part of "Gerontion" to another, but they also must continually make perspectival adjustments within a single verse paragraph; often they must dance upon a word if they are to collaborate with Eliot in the poem's multicontextual technique.

The following analysis of the structure of "Gerontion" is based upon the idealist principles discussed in this essay: the self-transcendence of objects, the necessary and internal relations among objects, and the systematic nature of the whole. Eliot arranges the poem into an almost endless number of superimposed contexts by using the image of a house. The idea of the self-transcendence of objects from fragment to context is shown by placing houses within houses within houses. The objects contained in the houses become less inclusive houses that in turn contain other houses; at the same time, all of the houses are included in more inclusive houses. The house serving as the model for all others is Gerontion's literal house. In the first stanza, this house, its tenants, and its surroundings are described. In the second through the fifth stanzas, other major houses are superimposed. In the sixth stanza, there seems to be an acceptance of the fact that disaster has overtaken the houses; and in the seventh, there are images of annihilation and scattering of fractured atoms whirling through nothingness.

The house image appears at the beginning of the poem, but its function as a structural element is not clear until one has read the entire poem and then returned to the beginning. The coda of the poem is

> Tenants of the house,
> Thoughts of a dry brain in a dry season.

This coda would be superfluous if its purpose were simply to show that the poem is an interior monologue. The first two lines of the poem,

> Here I am, an old man in a dry month,
> Being read to by a boy, waiting for rain,

establish the genre as interior monologue and identify the speaker as a blind old man. The last two lines reveal the structural key by pointing to the principle of superimposed contexts. However, the image in the coda—thoughts in a brain as tenants in a house—does not in itself constitute a structural key. This image becomes a key only when it is in the mind of a reader who is rereading the poem. In the first stanza, Gerontion describes his literal house and its desiccated tenants. Readers who have the final image in their minds—thoughts in a brain as tenants in a house—will immediately perceive that not only is Gerontion a tenant in this old house he is describing; he himself, his body, is an old house with tenants, one of which, his brain, is again a house with tenants, his thoughts. At this point in the rereading, the coda that until now has been just another image will emerge as a structural key: a brain is necessarily self-transcendent: i.e., it can exist only as part of a more inclusive whole. This fundamental clue is placed at the end of the poem to undermine the reader's expectations of linear structure. What Joseph Frank said nearly half a century ago about *The Waste Land* and *Ulysses* is also true of "Gerontion"—it cannot be read; it can only be reread, because the whole, of which the last lines are a part, must be in readers' minds throughout.[13] Linear structure would be a glaring defect in "Gerontion," anyhow, for at the center of the poem is a root-and-branch attack on discursive intelligence.

The first sixteen lines of "Gerontion," marked by Eliot as a verse paragraph, clearly constitute a semantic unit. The paragraph begins as a proper interior monologue should—by identifying the speaker and his present situation; it ends, as thousands of traditional stanzas do, with a return to the opening lines. This return to the beginning has a strong closural effect; it also defines the paragraph as a unit and imparts a certain degree of authority to the structure. Within the paragraph is an obvious psychological coherence.

> Here I am, an old man in a dry month,
> Being read to by a boy, waiting for rain.
> I was neither at the hot gates
> Nor fought in the warm rain
> Nor knee deep in the salt marsh, heaving a cutlass,
> Bitten by flies, fought.
> My house is a decayed house,
> And the jew squats on the window sill, the owner,
> Spawned in some estaminet of Antwerp,
> Blistered in Brussels, patched and peeled in London.
> The goat coughs at night in the field overhead;
> Rocks, moss, stonecrop, iron, merds.
> The woman keeps the kitchen, makes tea,
> Sneezes at evening, poking the peevish gutter.
>   I an old man,
> A dull head among windy spaces.

Gerontion's literal house, carefully described in this stanza, is in one way the most important image in the poem, for most of the other

13. See Joseph Frank, "Spatial Form in Modern Literature," in *The Widening Gyre: Crisis and Mastery in Modern Literature* (Bloomington: Indiana University Press, 1963), 3–62.

houses are replicas of this first one. From this house begins a pro-
liferation of houses in many directions at once; but whereas Gerontion's literal house, its tenants, its yard, and its landlord are clearly
described, the other houses are not. An understanding of the other
houses, then, is contingent upon an understanding of this principal
house.

The principal house is situated on the edge of doom, with absolutely nothing to stay disaster. First, it is a "decayed" house. The use
of the past rather than the present participle carries an implication of
finality—the house is not merely showing signs of decay, nor is it in
the process of decaying; it is decayed already. Moreover, the agent of
its decomposition is on the scene. The reader who has the entire
poem in mind remembers Gerontion musing at the end of the third
stanza that he is "An old man in a draughty house / Under a windy
knob." The decayed house, then, is located under a windy hill, and is
being battered by wind. The windows are already gone, allowing the
wind to blow not only against but through it. The impending destruction by wind is underscored by the dryness. It is a time of
drought, the "dry month," and Gerontion is "waiting for rain." The
dissolution of this dry, brittle house is imminent; at any moment, it
may be "whirled / Beyond the circuit of the shuddering Bear / In
fractured atoms." The house has several rooms, one of which, the
kitchen, is mentioned. Finally, Gerontion's house is a rented house.
He occupies it as tenant, not as owner.

Three occupants of this dilapidated domicile are mentioned—the
woman who keeps the kitchen, the old man who endlessly ruminates, and the boy who reads to him. These individuals—from one
point of view, fragments, and from another, wholes—are closely
identified with the house enclosing them. They too are decayed.
The woman, like Madame Sosostris in *The Waste Land*, has a bad
cold. Gerontion himself is old and weak, desiccated and blind, dull-
headed. His past is described in negative terms—where he was not
and what he did not do. His present is meaningless and cannot be redeemed by reference to a glorious past. The boy, at an earlier stage in
the cycle of decay, will probably become another Gerontion. The only
occupant named is Gerontion, and his name, as has been noted, is a
transliteration of the Greek word for little old man. As the name
of the title character in an English poem, the Greek word suggests

exile, homelessness. Perhaps Gerontion is a displaced person, an old sick Greek in London or New York. In a poem that even on a first reading catalogues the decay of Western culture, Gerontion's name and condition suggest that he is a symbol of Western culture, born in Greece centuries before Christ and dying in the war-torn European capitals—Paris, Berlin, Brussels, London, Rome—of 1919. Gerontion and his companions are not exactly busy; yet they are not idle. The sick woman makes tea and tries to keep a sputtering fire alive; the boy reads to Gerontion; Gerontion waits for rain and thinks. The depiction of Gerontion as a withered thinker is consistent with his Greek origin; his cradle was in the cradle of the Western philosophic tradition; his ancestors include Socrates, Plato, and Aristotle.

The decayed house, then, is occupied by decayed tenants who themselves become, as the reader refocuses, decayed houses containing decayed tenants. In Gerontion's body, the decayed tenant emphasized by Eliot is a dull, dry, brain, that in turn becomes a decayed and windswept house with decayed tenants. The brain, containing the tenants of thought, is in a way the smallest house; but in another way, the brain is far more inclusive than the house of flesh or the house of wood containing it. "The Brain—is wider than the Sky" is the way Emily Dickinson put this elementary paradox of the brain—containing sky and sea, time and space, god and man, it is at the same time imprisoned within a sphere having a diameter of just a few inches. Gerontion's brain, of course, is a very inclusive house, for the poem is an interior monologue, and all of its houses are contained in his mind. These tenants, these houses, have no meaning in themselves; their meaning consists in the whole created by their internal relations with fragments on the same level, and then in the more inclusive contexts of which they in turn become a part. Within the brain, diverse thoughts both remain fragments and are unified; within the body, brain and blood maintain separate identity and function and yet are unified; within the house, the boy, man, and woman—reading, thinking, sneezing—are not blurred but enclosed as systematic parts in a whole. Each of these houses is self-transcendent until the all-embracing Absolute, i.e., reality or experience, is reached.

The immediate context of the house in which Gerontion waits is also given in the first verse paragraph. The house is located in a yard filled with symbols of long-term neglect and decay—rocks, moss, excreta of straying beasts. The yard in turn is situated in a field that, like all of the other houses, contains a sick tenant—a goat who coughs at night, paralleling the woman who sneezes at evening in the principal house. The most interesting detail about the context of the house is that its owner, Gerontion's landlord, "squats on the window sill." The landlord Jew, surrealistically presented as a predator, is a caricature of a modern businessman, just as the tenant Greek is a caricature of a modern philosopher. Both are waiting, the landlord for profit and the tenant for rain. Gerontion, even as he waits, suspects that there is nothing in fact to wait for, but the landlord is unaware that there is no profit to be realized. The blind old Greek will soon vacate the property, to be sure, but the landlord is also decayed and dying, and his house is also crumbling in the dry wind. This Jew, spawned, patched, and peeled, is an obvious symbol of decay whose presence puts Gerontion's house in a world of predatory commercialism and materialism. This dehumanized figure is squatting on the window sills of the great financial and cultural capitals—London, Antwerp, Brussels—and, by extension to the more inclusive house, he is also squatting on the window sill of the decayed house of Europe.

In the first stanza, other houses are superimposed via Eliot's allusions. But these houses are omitted from this discussion in order to clarify the principal house, its tenants, and its surroundings. To summarize: the tenants (or houses, from a different point of view) in the first verse paragraph are Gerontion's thoughts, his brain, his body, his house, his yard, the field, the knob or hill, and Europe. All of the houses are old, brittle, decayed, wind-filled, windswept; all of the tenants, being houses also, are the same. All of the houses are owned by a diseased and depraved predator; all of the occupants are transients. The corruption in each house is emphasized by including correlative occupants. The main house includes not only the blind Greek, but also the sick woman. The yard includes not only the decayed house, but also the retrograde Jew and, all around the house, obvious symbols of time and decay, disease and death. The field includes not only the yard, but also the sick goat. Europe contains not only the Jew's rental property, but also London, Antwerp, Brussels, Athens. These cities are likewise decayed houses owned by degraded Jews; they too are trembling in dry wind, crumbling down upon their diseased tenants.

The psychological coherence of the first verse paragraph, instrumental in clarifying both the main structural principle of superimposed contexts and the main image of the house within the house, is abandoned as Eliot moves to his second stanza. The tenuous psychological connections that critics have pointed to as transitions between these two stanzas are inventions, not discoveries. They are fabrications compelled by a desire for order. The fact is that the second stanza "follows" the first only in its arrangement on the page; logically and psychologically, the second does not follow at all. It does not properly begin, and it does not end; it simply starts, and then, without a period or even a comma, in the middle of a sentence, in the middle of a line, it stops.

> Signs are taken for wonders. "We would see a sign!"
> The word within a word, unable to speak a word,
> Swaddled with darkness. In the juvescence of the year
> Came Christ the tiger

This stanza relocates readers, giving them a far more inclusive vantage point. All of those ruined houses in windy spaces—from Gerontion's withered brain to Europe's war-shattered civilization—are suddenly placed in the context of the rejection of Christ. Although the second stanza lacks the internal coherence of the first, it is unified by the fact that all these fragments are related to the Christian religion and, as will become evident, to a special relation between knowledge and unbelief. As far as the overall structure of the poem is concerned, this stanza takes the most teratical image of the previous stanza—the Jew lying in wait for his prey—and superimposes one of history's greatest houses, the house of David. The principal tenants in this vision of the house of Israel are the Pharisees, Christ, and pulling together nineteen hundred years of history, the landlord squatting on the window sill of Europe. But these sons of David are not the only tenants of this antique house. Joining the natural brothers are many half brothers, audacious upstarts who irreversibly alter Abraham's line. The rejection of Christ by his brothers in blood led to an expansion of the house of Israel. Anyone of any race whatsoever who would accept Christ in faith was adopted into what the Bible calls the new Israel, the Christian Church. The tenants in Jacob's greater house include, then, Christ's adopted brothers and joint heirs, including in this stanza the seventeenth-century preacher, Lancelot Andrewes. The house of Israel, like the house of Gerontion, is decayed, dry, wind-sieged.

Eliot's main allusion in this second verse paragraph is to a sermon preached by Lancelot Andrewes before King James I on Christmas Day, 1618:

> *Verbum infans,* the Word without a word; the eternal
> Word not able to speak a word; a wonder sure and . . .
> swaddled; and that a wonder too. He that takes the sea
> "and rolls it about the swaddled bands of darkness," to
> come thus into clouts, Himself.[14]

This sermon deals with the particular theme of Christmas—the Incarnation. The mystery of the Incarnation, of course, is the mystery of God being immured in a house of flesh. The ancient image of the body as a house, central in the previous stanza of this poem, has a special meaning here. In the case of Jesus of Nazareth, the tenant of the body is a god; the house, therefore, is much more than a house—it is a temple. The Bible frequently describes the body of Christ as a temple. The book of Hebrews, for example, contains a detailed analogy between the Jewish house of God, the tabernacle, and the incarnate Christ, "a greater and more perfect tabernacle, not made with hands" (Hebrews 9:11).[15] And Christ referred to his own body in just these terms in a text alluded to by both Andrewes and Eliot (John 2:18–21). The temple of the Christ, then, is superimposed upon the Jewish temple which it transformed. The greater temple was swaddled in darkness, the darkness of infancy's powerlessness, the darkness of corrupted Judaism, the darkness of history. The body of Christ is a house apart in "Gerontion"; it also stood in a dry and windy land, but instead of decaying in the general aridity, it was arrested in full strength and destroyed. The ruin in all of the houses in the poem is related to the destruction of this temple.

The text for Andrewes's sermon (and for Eliot's poem) is the demand by the Pharisees that Christ give them proof of his divinity— "We would see a sign!" This text focuses attention on another house

---

14. Lancelot Andrewes, *Works* (Oxford: Clarendon Press, 1854), 1:204.
15. All quotations from the Bible are taken from the King James Version (1611).

within the house of Israel. The mind of the Pharisees is this new house, and it is in certain ways analogous to the mind of Gerontion.

> Then certain of the scribes and of the Pharisees answered, saying, Master, we would see a sign from thee. But he answered and said unto them, An evil and adulterous generation seeketh after a sign; and there shall no sign be given to it, but the sign of the prophet Jonas. (Matthew 12:38–39)

This passage is of the essence in "Gerontion," for it identifies the curse that has brought all these houses (Greek, Jewish, Christian) to ruin; this curse is a mentality that isolates intelligence from passion and from belief. Separated from its context, the above passage seems to say that Christ refused to give the Pharisees a sign, demanding that they accept him by faith alone. In context, the passage says almost the opposite. Most of Christ's career was devoted to giving signs to these professors of law and religion; but whenever a sign was given, the proud but unperceiving scholars took it for a wonder and, ironically, resumed their campaign for a sign. In the incident quoted above, Christ gave two signs of his divinity. First, he restored a paralyzed hand, and then he cast out a demon which was making its victim blind. The Pharisees witnessing these signs responded with their usual request, "We would see a sign!" They accepted the authenticity of the miracles, but they refused to accept their validity as signs.[16] They would soon see the supreme sign, but their unbelief, inseparable from their learning, would prevent them from recognizing it.

This rejection by the Pharisees, quoted by Andrewes and by Eliot, was a turning point in the life of Christ and in history, because it led to an expansion of the house of Jacob. In his immediate response to these Pharisees, Christ oversteps the racial definition of Israel by asking "Who is my mother? And who are my brethren?" and by answering "Whosoever shall do the will of my Father, who is in heaven, the same is my brother, and sister, and mother" (Matthew 12:48–50). In the second stanza of "Gerontion," Eliot's use of Andrewes's sermon superimposes this more inclusive house of Israel,

16. Regarding the first miracle, the Pharisees say to Jesus, "Is it lawful to heal on the sabbath days?" (Matthew 12:10). Regarding the second, they respond "This fellow doth not cast out devils, but by Beelzebub, the prince of devils" (Matthew 12:24). Receiving the sign they ask for, they attribute it to devils and demand another sign.

the Christian Church. It may be supposed that Eliot, who became an admirer of Andrewes's theology, is contrasting the rejection of Christ by the Jews to the acceptance of Christ by the Church, or that he is contrasting the Pharisees' blindness to Andrewes's insight. But Eliot's opening fragment, "Signs are taken for wonders," is as applicable to Andrewes as it is to the Pharisees, as applicable to the Christian Church as to Israel. In the specific part of the sermon to which Eliot alludes in his poem, Andrewes repeatedly declares that the Incarnation is a "wonder too," a "wonder sure." The seventeenth-century divines loved to preach about the supreme wonder of infinity incarcerated in a finite prison, of the one who swaddled the sea being swaddled in baby clouts. Seduced by paradox, they were enthralled by the wonder of omnipotence dependent upon a young woman for diaper changes, of omnipresence locked up in infant flesh. By transforming the Incarnation into an abstraction, by treating it as an occasion for rhetorical play, the Church had also taken the sign for a wonder. The Church is another of this poem's decaying, crumbling houses in dry and windy lands. The Church, furthermore, is occupied by desiccated and dying tenants housing dull and shriveled thoughts; the churchyard is parched and, literally as well as figuratively, packed with dry bones, dry stones, dry excreta.

The third stanza, which describes a corrupt eucharist ceremony, elaborates and complicates the houses already introduced in the poem. Attention is focused on the house of the twentieth-century Church as contemporary participants in the Mass are superimposed upon the Pharisees and upon the seventeenth-century Church as accomplices in the ongoing rejection of Christ. The motif of the body as a house is extended in this stanza. In the Church Age, i.e., after Pentecost, the bodies of Christians constitute the house of God. "Ye are the temple of the living god," Paul tells the weak Christians in Corinth (II Corinthians 6:16). Mr. Silvero, Hakagawa, Madame de Tornquist, and Fraulein von Kulp, then, are decayed temples, windswept, wind-sieged, wind-abandoned, wind-destroyed.

The extreme disjunction between the first and second verse paragraphs of "Gerontion" is replaced by extreme conjunction between paragraphs two and three. Eliot breaks stanzas two and three spatially; but at the same time, he shoves them together grammatically. Readers, unless they be blind, must see the gap, but they are not allowed to stop. They are pushed from stanza two by punctuation and pulled to stanza three by squinting adverbial phrases.

> Signs are taken for wonders. "We would see a sign!"
> The word within a word, unable to speak a word,
> Swaddled with darkness. In the juvescence of the year
> Came Christ the tiger

> In depraved May, dogwood and chestnut, flowering judas,
> To be eaten, to be divided, to be drunk
> Among whispers; by Mr. Silvero
> With caressing hands, at Limoges
> Who walked all night in the next room;

> By Hakagawa, bowing among the Titians;
> By Madame de Tornquist, in the dark room
> Shifting the candles; Fraulein von Kulp
> Who turned in the hall, one hand on the door.
>   Vacant shuttles
> Weave the wind. I have no ghosts,
> An old man in a draughty house
> Under a windy knob.

Several important points emerge from attention to Eliot's grammar. The five lines of the third stanza and the first four of the fourth complete, both structurally and semantically, a sentence that began in stanza two—"In the juvescence of the year / Came Christ the tiger." It is a complex sentence, conscientiously punctuated. The nine lines carried over to stanzas three and four consist entirely of adverbial phrases modifying the predicate of the main clause, i.e., "came." The primary modifiers identify the time of the coming ("In depraved May") and the reason or consequence ("To be eaten"); the secondary modifiers tell who is eating ("by Mr. Silvero"), and how ("With caressing hands"), and where ("in the dark room"). Eliot's masterful handling of grammar here has a number of interesting effects. First, enormous weight falls on the line "Came Christ the tiger." It is emphasized by its length, by its incompleteness, by its pivotal position in the stop-continue tension generated between stanzas, by its position as the last line in a stanza already emphasized by being shorter than contiguous stanzas, and by its function as the main clause in this stanza-straddling sentence. The verb "came" is additionally emphasized by syntactic inversion, by alliteration, by position in the line and the stanza, and by being the focus for the following nine lines of modifiers. Eliot achieves a second interesting effect through sentence structure. The structure of this sentence is technically loose, i.e., the main clause with its extraordinary emphasis comes first, and then many roughly parallel modifiers are appended. The rhythm and structure of this long series of modifiers tend to reduce the force of that momentous line "Came Christ the tiger." What began as a striking assertion dwindles in a series of dull and repetitive phrases, providing a sort of grammatical analogue to Western history from the first to the present century.

The weight Eliot forces onto the last line of the second stanza is indicative of the line's overall significance in "Gerontion." The arresting image of Christ as a tiger, at the heart of the poem's meaning, will be discussed later in this essay. At this point, it is enough to notice that the verb "came" collects the coming described by Andrewes—Incarnation, and it superimposes that described by John—Judgment. The language in the third stanza adds two more comings of Christ—one on Good Friday, in the Crucifixion (depraved May, flowering judas); the other repeated innumerable times over nineteen centuries, in the ceremony of the Mass (eaten, divided, drunk). Christ's coming in spring ordinarily suggests resurrection, but in Eliot, the gods appear in spring to be killed. From "Portrait of a Lady" to *The Family Reunion,* spring is associated with death, not with life. April is the cruellest month and May is depraved; "Is the spring not an evil time, that excites us with lying voices?" (*The Family Reunion,* I, ii). April, with her abundant analogies to resurrection, whispers promises she does not keep. She is the forerunner of "depraved May," of the blooming judas tree, deception, betrayal, and death.

In the ceremony of the Mass, April's lie has been taken up and made the central sacrament in the Christian Church. The Mass, of course, reenacts the death and resurrection of Christ. His body as bread is broken and his blood as wine is spilt; these fractured elements are then taken into the several bodies of Christians, theoretically transforming these several persons into one new person in a symbolic resurrection. But in "Gerontion," May is the season of the non-Resurrection, and the shadowy figures in this ceremony—Mr. Silvero, Hakagawa, Madame de Tornquist, and Fraulein von Kulp—

eat, divide, and drink, without achieving unity. This depraved ceremony takes place in the dark rooms and hallways of the modern
Church. Mr. Silvero's presence in Limoges and Mr. Hakagawa's
seeming presence in Venice suggest that the "next room" is Italy and
that the decayed house is not only the Christian Church but Europe.
By both superimposing and problematizing the Incarnation, Crucifixion, Resurrection, Mass, and Judgment; by superimposing the
Pharisees who rejected, the Judas who betrayed, the preachers who
wondered, and the phantoms who participate in the cosmopolitan
mass, Eliot is forcing a reevaluation of the relations connecting all of
these events in the crumbling house of Western history.

The account of the Mass is followed by a summary image—"Va-
cant shuttles / Weave the Wind." This image of nothingness at work
summarizes the activities in all of Gerontion's houses. In philosophy,
beginning with Plato; in Judaism, beginning with the Pharisees; in
the institutional Church, beginning with figures such as Origen,
shuttles without thread have woven the wind into some of its most
elaborate patterns. The wind that blows through all of these superimposed houses, from Gerontion's brain to history's womb, is a complex image. On the literal level, wind in this poem functions as an
agent of ultimate decomposition and destruction and scattering of
fragments. In one way, of course, wind is nothing at all, mere absence. But paradoxically, as the absence of God, it is a dynamic absence with enormous power to corrupt and destroy. Yet simultaneously, wind is the presence of God (God the Holy Spirit) and perhaps
a demon (Dante's Black Wind in *Inferno* V). If God is a real presence in
or behind history, then this *Deus absconditus*, this God who hides himself, must be seen as the final cause of the destruction wrought in all
these houses by his absence. And, of course, wind is a pun in such
lines as "I an old man, / A dull head among windy spaces," suggesting the labyrinthine passageways of these decayed old houses.
The final lines of the fourth stanza return to the principal house,
draughty, with its little old man, ghostless, waiting under his windy
knob.

The principal house in the fifth verse paragraph is the house of
history. Three other houses, inextricable from the house of history,
are superimposed—the whore's womb, memory or mind, and hell.
From one point of view, history contains memory and hell; from

another, the mind contains history and hell; from another, hell swallows up all of the houses. Or history may be seen as moving through the other houses—proceeding from the whore's womb, existing in memory, progressing toward an all-inclusive hell. Not only does history contain the whore and proceed from the whore's womb, but also, in the imagery of this stanza, history is herself the great harlot.

> After such knowledge, what forgiveness? Think now
> History has many cunning passages, contrived corridors
> And issues, deceives with whispering ambitions,
> Guides us by vanities. Think now
> She gives when our attention is distracted
> And what she gives, gives with such supple confusions
> That the giving famishes the craving. Gives too late
> What's not believed in, or is still believed,
> In memory only, reconsidered passion. Gives too soon
> Into weak hands, what's thought can be dispensed with
> Till the refusal propagates a fear. Think
> Neither fear nor courage saves us. Unnatural vices
> Are fathered by our heroism. Virtues
> Are forced upon us by our impudent crimes.
> These tears are shaken from the wrath-bearing tree.

The general grimness in "Gerontion," often attributed to Eliot's philosophic negativism, is more directly related to a despondency regarding the history of Western civilization, a despondency shared by the most intelligent and sensitive people of his generation. This historical pessimism pervades not only "Gerontion" and *The Waste Land,* but much of the greatest art of the early part of this century. Joyce called history a nightmare from which we are trying to awake; and Eliot, in his 1923 review of Joyce's *Ulysses,* called contemporary history an immense panorama of futility and anarchy. The unprecedented catastrophe that led to Versailles had destroyed not only the people and the land, but the culture and institutions of Europe. Most of the once great and ancient houses of European royalty were dissolved and scattered in the wind. The context of this calamity must include the scientific, philosophic, and religious revolutions that were collapsing the intellectual structures that had undergirded the Western mind for centuries. The desolation, too well known to be discussed in detail, received consummate expression in *The Waste*

Land, that great poem Eliot was to publish a couple of years after he published "Gerontion."

The fifth stanza of "Gerontion" begins with an image of history as a house with cunning corridors and blind passageways, thus pulling in all the characteristics of decay and ruin clustering around the house image. But immediately and almost imperceptively, the house image merges into that of a woman—not a virtuous woman, but a Brobdingnagian harlot bent on deceiving, seducing, and destroying her partners. Taking advantage of her partner's vanity, she feeds him false ambitions and cunningly (a sexual pun) works him into a frenzy of desire. Then she gives "with such supple confusions" that his craving is famished rather than satisfied. Her gifts are all timed for minimum satisfaction, maximum disorientation—she gives them "too late," "too soon," "when our attention is distracted." We can never hope to understand history, never expect to be undeceived, because we are always intimately involved with her and, therefore, unable to be objective about this great whore. Generative images point to the offspring of our affair with history. Our heroism fathers unnatural vices; our refusal propagates fear. And there is an image of rape—"Virtues / Are forced upon us by our impudent crimes"—of rape upon rape, since virtue is also a victim of force.

Much in this stanza emphasizes the house of the coda—the brain with its tenants of thought. The repeated injunction—"Think now"— underscores the suggestion that Gerontion is a latter-day Socrates. The emphasis on reason, of course, is not limited to the Greeks; it is at the heart of the synthesis of Greek, Jewish, and Christian philosophy that constitutes the Western tradition. That tradition culminated in the great nineteenth-century thinkers—Hegel, Marx, Darwin, Nietzsche, Freud, and others—who precipitated what Eliot feared might be the death throes of Western civilization. Eliot's focus on the role of thought in the decay of the house of history is revealing. The mind not only contains history in memory, but to reverse the generative image, the mind gives birth to history, is the great maternal womb from which disasters issue. Contemporary calamity is inseparable from discursive thought and from memory. It is the brain that reconsiders passion and nullifies belief; it is the brain that transforms immediate experience into abstractions. This deep suspicion of discursive intelligence is common to Eliot and Bradley, but Eliot goes beyond Bradley by making discursive intelligence the main cause of the devastation of the early twentieth century. Eliot's most profound exploration of the theme is in *The Waste Land,* where knowledge divorced from value is largely responsible for the curse that has settled in upon the modern world.

The relation of knowledge to catastrophe leads to the final house of this stanza, i.e., hell. The opening line—"After such knowledge, what forgiveness?"—associates knowledge with damnation. This is an allusion to the exact passage in Matthew used by Andrewes as sermon text—"We would see a sign!"—and quoted by Eliot in stanza two. When the Pharisees persist in denying that Christ's power of healing is a sign from God, Christ responds by referring to an unpardonable sin. "All manner of sin and blasphemy shall be forgiven men; but the blasphemy against the Holy Ghost shall not be forgiven men" (Matthew 12:31). Christ does not precisely identify this sin of sins, and in nineteen hundred years, theologians have been unable to agree on one candidate. One formulation that is consistent with Matthew's account of Christ's confrontation with the Pharisees, with Andrewes's sermon, and with Eliot's poem is that the unforgivable sin is not any specific act, but is any state of mind that permanently precludes affirmation or belief. The Pharisees had this sort of mentality, Gerontion has it, and twentieth-century intellectuals receive it as a birthright. In the early twentieth century, only negatives could be affirmed. Particularly in the physical and biological sciences, knowledge cancelled the possibility of affirming any position. This crisis in epistemology precluded forgiveness because it precluded belief. Eliot once said that this period in history was different from all previous periods in that belief was no longer a possibility. "Belief itself is dead" (*UPUC,* 130). The murderer of possibility, of belief, the guarantor of damnation, is knowledge.

The last line in the fifth stanza—"These tears are shaken from the wrath-bearing tree"—also associates knowledge with damnation. The image of the wrath-bearing tree telescopes all history by superimposing the Garden of Eden, Golgotha, and the White-Throne Judgment. In Eden, the tree was the Tree of the Knowledge of Good and Evil. God told Eve that she would be doomed if she should eat of the fruit of this tree; the serpent said, on the contrary, that she would not be doomed, but would "know" good and evil, and that this knowl-

103

edge would make her as gods. The mortal taste of that forbidden fruit brought knowledge aplenty, but it also brought loss of Eden and all our woe. All tears—Eve's, Mary's, Gerontion's—are shaken from that wrath-bearing tree. But there is another wrath-bearing tree: the cross on which Christ was crucified. In the Crucifixion, Christ bore God's wrath for sin. Again, it was knowledge, that of the Pharisees, but also that of Eve and that of ourselves, that led to Christ's rejection and murder. Contemporary tears are shaken also from that God-forsaken tree. The ultimate showering of wrath, final Judgment, is also associated with knowledge.

If "Gerontion" were structured according to some linear principle, one could say that the opening of the sixth verse paragraph is a climax or turning point. There is actually no "turning point," but there is a structural cynosure. In the first five stanzas, Eliot describes the decayed houses. The image at the beginning of stanza six brings all of the houses, already united in decay, together in a common disaster. The remainder of stanza six and all of stanza seven descend from an understanding of this disaster.

> The tiger springs in the new year. Us he devours. Think at last
> We have not reached conclusion, when I
> Stiffen in a rented house. Think at last
> I have not made this show purposelessly
> And it is not by any concitation
> Of the backward devils.
> I would meet you upon this honestly.
> I that was near your heart was removed therefrom
> To lose beauty in terror, terror in inquisition.
> I have lost my passion: why should I need to keep it
> Since what is kept must be adulterated?
> I have lost my sight, smell, hearing, taste and touch:
> How should I use them for your closer contact?

The image of the tiger is one of the most important in the entire poem. It was introduced in the second stanza in the context of Incarnation. "Came Christ the tiger," however, is extremely startling as a reference to Incarnation. The third stanza suggests that Christ the tiger came in his Crucifixion. The suggestion is also startling, for the Crucifixion transformed him not into a tiger, but into a lamb. Eliot is capitalizing on the biblical teaching that whereas Christ came first in

104

meekness as the Lamb of God, submitting to his enemies without a whimper, he will come again in power as the Lion of Judah, slaying his enemies with the breath (wind) of his mouth. But Eliot's tiger is no eschatological beast; Eliot's tiger has already come. Later in the third stanza comes the remarkable image of a mass in which the unholy cosmopolitan participants eat and drink the body and blood of a broken tiger. The tiger image culminates in the opening lines of stanza six—"The tiger springs in the new year. Us he devours." This arresting line reverses the situation of stanza three. Instead of the tiger being eaten among caresses and whispers, he springs and devours those who are devouring him. Who or what is this tiger? An understanding of the poem hinges on an interpretation of this beast.

The image of the tiger links Christ to the figure on Gerontion's window sill. Both are Jews; both are described in animal imagery as predators. Christ and his depraved kinsman are further linked by the fact that the landlord was "spawned in some estaminet of Antwerp." An "estaminet" is a cafe, of course, but it derives from a French dialect word, "stamine," which means cow house or manger. And in the first lines of stanza six,

> The tiger springs in the new year. Us he devours. Think at last
> We have not reached conclusion, when I
> Stiffen in a rented house.

the reader cannot avoid thinking of Christ; but Gerontion seems to have in mind the expiration of his lease from a voracious Jewish landlord. The fact that the house is Jew-owned is particularly important, for all of history is implicated in the house image and Christ in the Jew image. The slum landlord and the god landlord are also brought together in the lines "We have not reached conclusion, when I / Stiffen in a rented house." The primary application, of course, is to Gerontion—it points to his house, first, but also to his whore's womb and to his tomb. All of Gerontion's draughty, decaying houses, from his brain to his broad, from his shanty to his sepulchre, are owned by a Jewish predator. But the lines also refer to Christ, who stiffened in a rented house, the tomb of Joseph of Arimethea. In this context, "We have not reached conclusion" points to the Resurrection, probably, and to the Judgment, certainly.

Two predators, then, crouch on the window sill of the decayed house of Western civilization—one, whore-spawned in an estaminet in Antwerp; the other, virgin-born in a barn in Bethlehem. The first is relatively easy to identify. As other critics have said, the slum land-lord can be associated with the materialistic values of Western cul-ture. As Gerontion is to Socrates, so this landlord is to King David, a shrunken shadow of ancient splendor, a vestige shaped by millennia of history and, in the latter case, by millennia of marginalization and exile. The second beast is more difficult to identify. In the poem, Christ the tiger is associated with flagrant rejections of Christ the god. First, the Pharisees rejected all the signs, from Incarnation to the great miracles, of his divinity. Their rejection issued in Calvary. Sec-ond, the preachers and theologians of the Christian Church have rejected Christ by recreating him an abstraction, an idea. Contempo-rary participants in the Mass reject him too. Their rejection is the most damnable, for these automatons blaspheme the body and blood of Christ by eating and drinking without belief. Christ the tiger, in my reading, is Christ demoted to a non-god by people who are learned but blind, e.g., Pharisees, Christian theologians, philoso-phers, Gerontion. Eliot uses the image of a ferocious, powerful, de-vouring presence as an extraordinary conceit for absence—the ab-sence of god, of belief, in the modern world. The absence of god is not a simple absence, but an absence with claws and teeth. Nothingness, in Eliot's view, is an overwhelming and terrifying beast devouring the inhabitants of the contemporary wasteland. The idea of absence, or Nothingness, as a perilous presence is not unique to Eliot; it has figured prominently in the thought of modern existentialist theolo-gians. Some ten years after "Gerontion" was published, Karl Jaspers expressed the same idea in his classic *Man in the Modern Age.* And Heidegger, though not strictly a Christian theologian, saw the mod-ern age as characterized by an absence of involvement with Being, a "significant" absence with venomous consequences in contemporary history.

The brilliant image of the tiger is followed by a dismal inventory in which Gerontion counts his losses. His remarks are addressed di-rectly to someone he once loved. "I that was near your heart was removed therefrom / To lose beauty in terror, terror in inquisition. / I have lost my passion." Inquisition, the seeking after abstract knowl-edge, is the culprit in Gerontion's removal from his beloved, a removal involving incalculable losses—beauty, passion, and all of his senses. The pun on "passion" makes it clear that the beloved encompasses not only a woman, but Christ. There is at least a hint of sour grapes as the blind and dumb, deaf and numb old man tries to be philosophic. It is just as well, he figures, to have lost everything, "Since what is kept must be adulterated."

The seventh stanza of "Gerontion" shows again that the decayed house, emptied of passion and sense, is still occupied by knowledge.

> These with a thousand small deliberations
> Protract the profit of their chilled delirium,
> Excite the membrane, when the sense has cooled,
> With pungent sauces, multiply variety
> In a wilderness of mirrors. What will the spider do,
> Suspend its operations, will the weevil
> Delay? De Bailhache, Fresca, Mrs. Cammel, whirled
> Beyond the circuit of the shuddering Bear
> In fractured atoms. Gull against the wind, in the windy straits
> Of Belle Isle, or running on the Horn,
> White feathers in the snow, the Gulf claims,
> And an old man driven by the Trades
> To a sleepy corner.

The thousand small deliberations, being all that is left to Gerontion, are used as aphrodisiacs for decayed flesh, but they are ineffective. The tenants in all of the dilapidated houses are beyond revival. As De Bailhache, Fresca, and Mrs. Cammel are "whirled / Beyond the circuit of the shuddering Bear / In fractured atoms," new tenants—spiders and weevils—make new houses. Against the wind (both the presence and the absence of god), Gerontion and all the other gulls are reduced to white feathers in snow. This image of white-on-white is another metaphor for blankness, the nothingness to which nothingness (or wind) delivers these houses. The coda of "Gerontion" returns readers to the dull brain of the little old man whose memories, thoughts, and deliberations furnished Eliot with a perfect metaphor for a ruined and dying civilization.

Many critics have defended the structure of "Gerontion" by arguing that the poem only appears to consist of fragments. The truth is that "Gerontion" does literally consist of fragments and is fully realized only by accepting these fragments. Every fragment in "Gerontion," like every judgment in philosophy, moves within a system. Every fragment is self-transcendent, i.e., it reaches beyond itself to a more inclusive context that in turn is contiguous with a more inclusive context that finally becomes a single unified reality. All parts are essentially connected within the system. The right approach to the meaning is an attempt to see the relations that connect the terms into a whole. The poem, an ideal formed by the united fragments and their relations emerges through the juxtaposition of terms given in the poem, alluded to in the poem, and magnetically drawn into the poem.

The tendency of critics to explain away the fragments in "Gerontion" is based on the premise that a poem exists primarily on a printed page. A poem exists, however, not on paper, but in the minds of readers. It is essentially an ideal construction, consisting of fragments, not blended, but unified; further, the poem *is* its fragments; still further, the whole poem becomes a fragment in a more inclusive context. Self-transcendence means that no fragment has meaning alone, but it also means that every fragment has meaning. The pieces must retain integrity; the whole is inconceivable without them. In his dissertation, Eliot deals with this problem in regard to error.

> In the "transcendence" of error, I insist, the error, as a real object, is not got rid of. An object is not transcended, though a point of view is. . . . The alteration from error to truth is not a change in the object, but a change in the whole situation. (*KE*, 119)

At the heart of all idealism is the idea of the concrete universal that comprehends many-in-one and is arrived at by including differences. The unity of an abstract universal, in contrast, comprehends one-in-many, and is arrived at by excluding differences and emphasizing commonness. The many fragments in "Gerontion" are not dissolved into a unity; they are comprehended as objects in a unified situation that finally includes readers.

It is ironic that discursive knowledge is the destroyer in "Gerontion." Next to Milton, Eliot is probably our most learned poet. Poems like "Gerontion," *The Waste Land,* and *Four Quartets* are soaked in history, philosophy, science, anthropology, and theology. Moreover, Eliot's poems pull in much, if not most, of great literature from Homer to Conrad and Hardy. And a basic argument in this essay is that even Eliot's readers must be exceptionally knowledgeable. The conflict is not as great as it first appears to be. It takes an intelligent and learned person to perceive that abstract knowledge is a malignancy consuming Western culture. The sort of refined anti-intellectualism characterizing not only Eliot but his mentor Bradley derives from the most assiduous intellectual activity.

The Case of the Missing Abstraction

Eliot, Frazer, and Modernism

It [the mythical method] is simply a way of controlling, of ordering, of giving a shape and a significance to the immense panorama of futility and anarchy which is contemporary history.—*T. S. Eliot* (*SP*, 177)

The "material of art", T. S. Eliot wrote in an early essay, "is always actual life" (*SE*, 93). Early in 1916, Eliot confided to Conrad Aiken: "I have *lived* through material for a score of long poems in the last six months."[1] This material included the illness of his wife, the death of one of his best friends, financial problems, and overwork. For Eliot, as for all artists, the material, the horror and ecstasy of everyday existence, is given; the method of transforming the chaos of life into the pattern of art, however, is not given; the method must be found.

Eliot frequently referred in reviews and essays to the need for a method that would enable modern artists to deal with their material. His obsession with method is an obsession with form, and it is at the center of the modernist crisis. He and many others early in this century felt that they had no method for shaping their material, the chaos of their own lives, the chaos of contemporary history, into art. Faced with the disappearance in many fields at once of shared assumptions about the nature of the universe, they were forced to work in a mythic vacuum. And this mythic vacuum, Auden claims in an essay on Yeats, is *the* modern problem. He defines it as "living in a society in which men are no longer supported by tradition without being aware of it."[2] Lacking that broadly shared and largely uncon-

---

1. T. S. Eliot, *The Waste Land: A Facsimile and Transcript of the Original Drafts Including the Annotations of Ezra Pound*, ed. Valerie Eliot (New York: Harcourt Brace Jovanovich, 1971), x.

2. W. H. Auden, "Yeats as an Example," *Kenyon Review* 10, no. 2 (1948): 191.

scious framework that artists have traditionally used as a means of organizing their material, many came to doubt the possibility of art. Eliot usually discusses the modernist crisis in terms of an absence in contemporary life. Sometimes he calls the missing factor belief, sometimes myth, sometimes tradition. In a 1924 preface for a projected book, he describes the problem as the case of the missing abstraction. He argues that great art is never simply an imitation of life. "On the one hand, actual life is always the material, and on the other hand, an abstraction from actual life is the necessary condition to the creation of a work of art" (*SE*, 93).

Eliot's most famous discussion of the method devised to crack the case of the missing abstraction is his review of *Ulysses*. In "*Ulysses*, Order and Myth," published in the November 1923 issue of *Dial*, he announces that at last the "method" has been discovered, and that, as used by Joyce in *Ulysses*, it is virtually an "Open Sesame" to modernist art. Joyce's method, to quote Eliot, is "the parallel to the *Odyssey*, and the use of appropriate styles and symbols to each division." More generally, the method is "using a myth, . . . manipulating a continuous parallel between contemporaneity and antiquity." Eliot goes on to claim that this breakthrough cannot be understood in a purely literary context:

> Psychology . . . , ethnology, and *The Golden Bough* have concurred to make possible what was impossible even a few years ago. Instead of the narrative method, we may now use the mythical method. It is, I seriously believe, a step toward making the modern world possible for art. (*SP*, 177)

Eliot had already acknowledged his own indebtedness to the anthropologists. In the headnote to *The Waste Land*, he says that his "plan" and some of his symbols had been suggested by Jessie Weston's *From Ritual to Romance*, and he acknowledges his profound debt to Sir James Frazer's *The Golden Bough*, a work that influenced his entire generation.

Eliot's discussion of the mythical method is part of most interpretations of modernism, although it is more often applied to *The Waste Land* than to *Ulysses*. The common interpretations fit into one of four categories. The simplest is that *The Waste Land*, like *Ulysses*, is based on a background myth, that this myth provides a shadow plot and shadow hero. Analogous to the quest for home and bed as main action, we have a quest for salvation. Analagous to the crafty adventurer Odysseus as hero, we have the blind prophet Tiresias. The canonical version of this interpretation, articulated decades ago by Grover Smith,[3] remains pervasive in Eliot criticism. This interpretation ignores not only Eliot's distinction between material and method, but also his contrast between narrative and mythical. Myth and epic, of course, are normally narrative, taking temporal sequence as a formal principle. But modernist art takes atemporal, alogical juxtaposition as a formal principle, and Eliot calls this method "mythical." Smith's attempt to fill in the missing links in his hero's quest for the Holy Grail underpins a conspicuously discontinuous work with narrative structure. But the new mythical method is announced not as a means of holding on to narrative, but as a means of avoiding it.

Another interpretation, respecting the enormous differences between Joyce's situation and Eliot's, between Joyce's novel and Eliot's poem, dispenses with the parallel plot and hero, claiming simply that Eliot and Joyce are dealing with mythic material. For example, Elizabeth Drew, drawing heavily on Jung, finds that the underlying themes and patterns in Eliot's poem and in his work as a whole are mythic and archetypal, and she suggests that this reliance on archetypes is the mythical method.[4] Much of Eliot's power, admittedly, comes from an intelligent use of archetypes, but this use is not what he calls the mythical method. Like many other interpreters, Drew blurs the distinction between material and method. Eliot clearly states that the modern problem is not what, but how.

> In creation you are responsible for what you can do with material which you must simply accept. And in this material I include the emotions and feelings of the writer himself, which, for that writer, are simply material which he must accept. . . . The question, then, about Mr. Joyce, is: how much living material does he deal with, and how does he deal with it? (SP, 177)

Joyce's material is the odyssey of James Joyce, not the odyssey of Odysseus. His material is "actual life." The way he deals with actual

3. Grover Smith, T. S. Eliot's Poetry and Plays (Chicago: University of Chicago Press, 1974), 72–98.
4. Elizabeth Drew, T. S. Eliot: The Design of His Poetry (London: Eyre and Spottiswoode, 1950), 19–51.

112

life, as the argument of this paper will show, is mythical. A failure to grasp the essential distinction between material and method has sent many critics on a wild goose chase after the Holy Grail. Eliot referred to this in his 1956 lecture at the University of Minnesota. Expressing mixed feelings about the notes to *The Waste Land,* he said: "It was just, no doubt, that I should pay my tribute to the work of Miss Jessie Weston; but I regret having sent so many enquirers off on a wild goose chase after Tarot cards and the Holy Grail" (*OPP,* 122). This passage is often triumphantly quoted by those who prefer to dismiss the importance of the work of Miss Weston as a factor in *The Waste Land.* Eliot's statement, however, underscores the importance of Miss Weston's work. Those on the wild goose chase are not those trying to understand her method, but those in pursuit of her subject matter, the romance of the Holy Grail.

A third way of reading Eliot's review, illustrated by innumerable critics, is that he is merely pointing to the fact that, like Joyce, he uses complex and systematic literary allusion. This interpretation ignores Eliot's claim that the mythical method was "impossible even a few years ago." Systematic allusion not only has been possible for a very long time; it is, as demonstrated by such masterpieces as *Paradise Lost* and *The Dunciad,* a stock-in-trade of much seventeenth and eighteenth-century art.

A fourth response to Eliot's review, epitomized by Ivor Winters, is that the mythical method either has nothing to do with anthropology or is a deliberate hoax. But Eliot insists that the mythical method comes from the social sciences, that "Psychology . . . , ethnology, and *The Golden Bough*" have made "possible what was impossible even a few years ago" (*SP,* 178). Professor Walton Litz nevertheless argues that "the surest guide" to *The Waste Land* "lies not in Miss Jessie Weston's *From Ritual to Romance,* but in Henry James's 'The Beast in the Jungle' and *The Sacred Fount;*"[5] and Hugh Kenner says that Weston's book on the grail legend and Frazer's on the golden bough are not pertinent to the plan of Eliot's poem.[6] Litz and Kenner are right to lament that generations of readers have been sidetracked

5. A. Walton Litz, "*The Waste Land* Fifty Years After," in *Eliot in His Time: Essays on the Fiftieth Anniversary of* The Waste Land, ed. A. Walton Litz (Princeton: Princeton University Press, 1973), 22.

6. Hugh Kenner, "The Urban Apocalypse," in *Eliot in His Time,* 43.

by a spurious plot and a nonexistent hero, but they are wrong to dismiss Frazer and his fellows.

Most interpretations of the mythical method also ignore the fact that Eliot makes revolutionary claims for it. He argues that it makes the modern world possible for art, that it is a way for an artist in a mythic vacuum to shape his material and to give it significance. In his own words, the mythical method "is a way of controlling, of ordering, of giving a shape and a significance to the immense panorama of futility and anarchy which is contemporary history" (*SP*, 177). None of the usual interpretations show how the mythical method "makes the modern world possible for art."

In the interest of fairness, it must be admitted that many interpreters have been misled by Eliot's choice of the word "mythical." Frazer's *material* in fact is "mythical;" that is, his subject is myth. His *method*, on the other hand, is not mythical, but scientific. He used the inductive method; that is, he collected samples and then generalized from them; he then used the generalizations as a means of understanding the samples with which he had begun. Eliot's use of the term "mythical" led most reviewers to assume that he was referring to material. But a careful reading of the *Ulysses* review shows that he really was referring to method, and that he was using "mythical" in his own way, as a near-synonym for "scientific" or "comparative" or "inductive"; or more precisely, as a term for the scientific method as transformed by its application in the arts. Well-informed about contemporary developments in science and philosophy, Eliot habitually uses scientific metaphors in discussions of the modernist crisis, and often he indicates that possibility in art can be redeemed only by an achievement roughly analogous to the breakthroughs in modern science. In the *Ulysses* review, for example, he insists that Joyce's method

> has the importance of a scientific discovery. . . . Mr. Joyce is pursuing a method which others must pursue after him. They will not be imitators, any more than the scientist who uses the discoveries of an Einstein in pursuing his own, independent, further investigations. (*SP*, 177)

Eliot's distinctions and ostensibly extravagant claims are perfectly intelligible in light of Frazer's method. The necessary context for understanding Frazer's achievement is the development of the modern social sciences, for the term "mythical method," as Eliot uses it, is approximately the method used in those disciplines. Sir James George Frazer began his work in comparative religion and anthropology in the first half-century after Darwin. He was one of those scientists who extended Darwin's thesis (evolution) and Darwin's method (comparative study of fragments) into the social sciences. As Darwin had attempted to discover the origin of the species and chart the descent of man, Frazer and his contemporaries tried to discover the origin of religion and chart the descent of the gods. They wished to demonstrate a single evolutionary sequence in the development of religion from primitive to modern, and as Darwin had postulated a common ancestor for humankind, they postulated a common ancestor for all religions. They believed in the original unity of human consciousness and in the continuous evolution of that consciousness from prehistory to the present. And they believed that although the common ancient myth had broken up in prehistoric times, it could be reconstructed through a comparison of its remaining fragments.

Frazer's fascination with religion began early, in Glasgow, where as a child he listened every night to his Calvinist father read the Bible out loud. Later, at Cambridge, Frazer majored in classics and became interested in the history of Greek and Roman religion. His interest culminated, after many years, in *The Golden Bough*. This famous encyclopedia of myths and customs from all parts of the world and all periods of history had a rather humble beginning. Frazer was trying to figure out the meaning of one myth, and he was led on from that single myth to a twelve-volume work that took him a quarter of a century to write.

Frazer's field of enquiry, his subject, and his method were clearly explained in an 1889 letter to George Macmillan.

> I shall soon have completed a study in the history of primitive religion which I propose to offer to you for publication. The book is an explanation of the legend of the Golden Bough, as that legend is given by Servius in his commentary on Virgil. According to Servius the Golden Bough grew on a certain tree in the sacred grove of Diana at Aricia, and the priesthood of the grove was held by the man who succeeded in breaking off the Golden Bough and then slaying the priest in single combat. By an application of the comparative method I believe I can make it probable that the priest represented in his person the god of the grove . . . , and

that his slaughter was regarded as the death of the god. This raises the question of the meaning of a widespread custom of killing men and animals regarded as divine. I have collected many examples of this custom and propose a new explanation of it.[7]

Frazer's field is primitive religion, and his special subject is the legend of the golden bough. This legend of death and life in Diana's sacred wood is evocatively narrated in the very first paragraph of *The Golden Bough,* and through twelve volumes of data it never passes from Frazer's remarkably one-track mind. His work may seem to be a bizarre collection of primitive customs, but in fact it is a thoroughly systematic attempt to explain this single myth. From beginning to end, everything is related to two questions. The first is, why did becoming king of the wood necessitate killing one's predecessor? The second is, why, before doing so, did the killer have to pluck the golden bough?

Frazer's method is the comparative method. His way of figuring out the myth of the ritualistic murder in Diana's grove was to collect seemingly innumerable analogies and then to carefully compare them. Most of his data, what he calls in one of his prefaces his "entirely independent and well-authenticated facts,"[8] came from questionnaires sent to missionaries living among primitive peoples or from world travellers. He found no exact analogies, and no analogies to the myth as a whole, but he did find many analogies to parts of his myth. So he dissected the myth into small pieces and found analogies to each part. Through constant comparison and analysis of thousands upon thousands of bits and pieces of myths and customs, he was able to construct ever more comprehensive myths, parent myths, and so move backward toward primitive unity. After constructing these more comprehensive myths by comparing fragments, he would then use his rationally constructed abstractions as keys to understand and even to judge the fragments with which he had begun. Each group of stories in *The Golden Bough* is included because it follows one of the branches from Diana's grove. And to Diana's grove for judgment and analysis each abstraction is returned.

7. Sir James George Frazer, *The Illustrated Golden Bough*, ed. Sabine MacCormack (Garden City, NY: Doubleday, 1978), 251.
8. Frazer, *The Illustrated Golden Bough*, 17.

116

Frazer's conclusions, of course, go far beyond his favorite myth, but they are consistent throughout with his Darwinian beginnings. He concludes, first, "that all [myths and the fragments of myth] may be regarded . . . as the shattered remnants of a uniform zone of religion and society which at a remote era belted the Old World from the Mediterranean to the Pacific."[9] More simply, he concludes that all myths derive from a single myth, a monomyth. This parent myth is not identical with Frazer's favorite myth, but in its comprehensiveness, it contains and clarifies not only the legend of the golden bough, but all legends. In the parent myth—the abstraction he generated through a comparison of fragments—the vitality of the land and of the people is intertwined with that of the king. When the king is healthy, the land is prosperous; when he is sick, the land is blighted, becoming a wasteland. The greatest misfortune would be sexual weakness or impotence in the king for in the primitive agricultural economy, the king's reproductive abilities are inseparable from those of his people. To preclude the certain disaster that would accompany his physical decline, he has to be killed and replaced before his vitality wanes. In order to insure the transmission of the king's vitality, his successor must pluck the golden bough, for the life force was associated with the energy of the sun and was thought to be contained in the golden bough of an oak tree. After the possessor of the sacred branch kills the present king, he then takes over and reigns until his own successor appears with the branch in his hand and murder in his eye.[10]

Frazer's consistent focus on a single myth is central to his method. The myth of the golden bough serves him as a necessary reference point. It is the presence of this myth in his mind that enables him to continuously manipulate comparisons between contemporaneity and antiquity, and it is this continuous comparison that generates the parent myths capable of comprehending both the reference point myth and the assembled fragments. Without the legend of the golden bough, or some other reference point, Frazer could not have shaped and controlled his materials, the immense panorama of futility and superstition that is human history.

Frazer also concluded, again consistent with his Darwinian as-

9. Frazer, *The Illustrated Golden Bough*, 202.
10. Frazer, *The Illustrated Golden Bough*, 204.

sumption of continuity and of evolution, that the human mind has developed through three main stages. The first is magic, in which people tried to control external events through ritual; the second, religion, in which they tried to control events through petition to deities; and the third, science, in which people are trying to control events by understanding the laws of nature. Since the transition from magic to religion to science is treated as a function of adaptation, it is closely related to the Darwinian idea of natural selection. When primitive peoples learned through experience that causality was unrelated to magic, they adapted by throwing themselves on the mercy of a deity. And when they discovered that causality is related more to material forces than to prayer, they adapted by embracing science. To Frazer, a shameless celebrant of progress and modernity, the triumph of science is another version of the survival of the fittest.

Frazer's method, then, more or less duplicates Darwin's. And just as the common parent of the human species exists only as an abstraction, only as an intellectual construction built up from surviving fragments changed in the process of evolution, the common parent myth exists only as an abstraction. If one should find widely scattered fragments of pottery, and should be able to reconstruct half of a once-beautiful vase, he would be led to realize the whole, the original, as an abstraction. And in the construction of this ideal vase, he would be using the mythical method. Or if one should visit a museum of natural history and see an exhibit on the evolution of the horse, he would not see the skeleton of the original, for that does not exist. What he would see is a construction made up from available fragments, themselves changed by evolution, and from missing links shaped by a scientist. Frazer's method is roughly analogous to the method of the scientist who constructed the imaginary ancestor of the horse, and Frazer's monomyth somewhat analogous to the ideal horse on display.

Other scientists were quick to use Frazer's method of generating abstractions through the comparative study of fragments. Jessie Weston, for example, used it in *From Ritual to Romance* to generate (construct) a parent myth behind the Grail legends. By acknowledging his debts to Frazer and to Weston, Eliot directs his readers to the great mythmakers of his day and calls attention to their method.

The Golden Bough was published over a couple of decades in the years around the turn of the twentieth century. These were critical years for the arts, with many artists claiming that great art was no longer possible. Eliot, for example, claimed that to be true to history, art must reflect the world in which it is produced; and to be true to itself, art must be unified. To meet both of these conditions, art would have to be at once chaotic and unified, and thus art seems to be impossible.

Traditionally, art has derived its unity in large part from the fact that it could be related to a broadly shared, often unconsciously shared, cultural abstraction. For most of the past two thousand years, that abstraction has been the Christian religion. And traditionally, this relation to an abstraction existing outside itself has been undergirded by a system of internal relations based on either logical or temporal sequence. In the early twentieth century, relating an art work to a shared cultural abstraction would have been a hoax, for as works like *The Waste Land* and "The Second Coming" make clear, there was no shared abstraction capable of holding Western civilization together. And relating parts sequentially, because they follow each other either temporally or logically, would have been untrue to conditions of history and the latest findings of science.

In his review of *Ulysses*, Eliot argues that Joyce's use of the mythical method shows art to be possible in the contemporary world. The mythical method solves the chaos-unity dilemma by allowing the coexistence of surface chaos and subsurface unity. Such unity derives neither from sequence nor from abstractions shared by a culture, but from an abstraction selected by an artist and constructed collaboratively with individual readers. The unity of *The Golden Bough* does not depend on the chronological or logical arrangement of Frazer's fragments. Frazer merely collects and preserves fragments as he finds them in the present—broken, distorted, changed by history and evolution. With minimal or no damage to his thesis, he could rearrange them, or he could throw some out and / or add others. And Frazer does not assume the existence of a culturally shared myth or abstraction. He brings his own myth and takes special care to keep it always in his reader's mind. First, he names his work—all twelve volumes—*The Golden Bough*, and in the first few paragraphs of his first volume, he explains the myth and tells what he wants to discover about it. He unifies his fragments by relating them all back to

119

the myth of the golden bough. He arrives at his thesis by constantly comparing and contrasting his fragments with each other and with his reference point myth, and by constructing abstractions suggested by this process.

In *The Waste Land* and *Ulysses*, the mythical method includes the following essential points:

1. Unity does not derive from the sequential relation of part to part, either chronologically or logically.

2. Unity does not derive from the reference of the work to an abstraction preexistent in culture and shared by the artist and his audience (such as the Christian religion), but from the reference to an abstraction chosen by the artist and brought to his work (such as the legend of Ulysses or of the dying and reviving king).

3. Unity does not exist on the surface of the work, which to be true to history and to science must consist of juxtaposed fragments— fragments of contemporary life, fragments of past life, fragments of myth. The historical and mythic fragments are given as they exist in 1922, changed by history and the evolution of human consciousness. For example, in *The Waste Land*, fragments of contemporary life are juxtaposed with fragments of *Hamlet*. The fragments of contemporary life are remnants of a primitive religious consciousness, changed by history and by the evolution of the human mind. The fragments of *Hamlet* are not fragments of Shakespeare's *Hamlet*, for that is unavailable, but are fragments of *Hamlet* as it has evolved through centuries of materialism and secularism, as it has been changed by the mediation of such figures as S. T. Coleridge, Sigmund Freud, and A. C. Bradley.

4. In the narrative method, unity exists on the surface and disunity beyond the surface. Allusions embellish and enhance, but they do not support and unify the work. In the mythical method, the opposite is true. Disunity exists on the surface and unity beneath the surface. Allusions work to help generate the framework which supports and unifies the surface. Unity derives finally from the relation of the fragments to the comprehensive abstraction generated as the reader compares them to each other and to abstractions that emerge in the process of reading.

5. As Frazer brought a reference point myth to his work, so must the artist bring one. The reference point myth chosen by the artist

(scientist) is kept in the reader's mind throughout the work. In *Ulysses*, the myth is suggested by the title; and it is kept in the reader's mind by roughly analogous episodes and by the presence of characters who loosely parallel characters in the myth. Because the parallels are codified in commentaries authorized by Joyce himself, they cannot be missed or evaded. In *The Waste Land*, as in *Ulysses*, the reference point myth is announced in the title; it is further authorized by the poet's notes and is richly reinforced by fragments of the myth within the poem.

6. The reference point myth exists as an abstraction. It is not contained in the text, but in the mind of the artist and a reader. Artists do not bring the myth in its entirety; they bring, rather, the information needed to construct the myth. In *Ulysses*, the myth is actually a literary work that exists as a whole and that may be recovered by reading the *Odyssey* in a good translation. Readers with the *Odyssey* in mind, even without the aid of Stuart Gilbert's notes, can comprehend the shadow plot (the quest for home and bed) and the shadow characters. By manipulating a continuous comparison between Joyce's text and Homer's, readers construct abstractions that provide the framework of the novel. In *The Waste Land*, the background myth is more elusive. The monomyths of Weston and of Frazer, in their entirety, exist only as re-constructions generated by using the comparative method. But Eliot's background myth is only loosely Frazer's monomyth. The poet assumes readers who are willing to take the fragments on the surface of his poem and re-collect them (both remember where they came from and gather them up again). Each reader of *The Waste Land* will construct a variant of Frazer's monomyth, a variant that will be refined and changed with each reading. In this process of re-collection and re-construction, the reader becomes Eliot's copoet, and with Eliot, will say, "These fragments have I shored against my ruins" (*The Waste Land*, V).[11]

The mythical method, understood as Eliot outlines it in the *Ulysses* review, is all that he claimed it to be; it does make the modern world possible for art. The mythical method enables artists and readers to begin with fragments and generate comprehensive abstractions, to

11. For a pedagogic application of the materials explained in this essay, see " 'The Second Coming' and *The Waste Land* as Capstone Texts in the Western Civilization Course" in this volume.

begin in isolation and end in community. And for this solution to the case of the missing abstraction, modern artists are profoundly indebted to Sir James George Frazer. He taught them how to take a heap of broken images, ruins on the horizon of history, and erect structures beautifully symmetrical, perfectly unified. His own construction (or, as he would admit, re-construction) of vanished myths, his projection of increasingly comprehensive abstractions of universal significance, is a triumph in intellectual history. He took fragments and gave back unified ideal edifices; he took chaos and gave back order; he took nonsense and gave back meaning. No wonder he has enthralled our imagination and that of our artists.

Substitutes for Religion in the Early Poetry of T. S. Eliot

"Thou shalt worship no other god, for the Lord, whose name
is Jealous, is a jealous God."—*Exodus 34:14*

In late June of 1927, in a small church in Oxfordshire, T. S. Eliot was baptized into the Anglican Church. He had a hard time coming to this death, this birth, and he awoke to find himself uneasy in the old dispensation with an alien people clutching their gods. Knowing he had lately clutched the same gods, he was highly conscious of the need to call them up, Baal and his fellows, and formally dismiss them. He was compelled to this housecleaning by the very first commandment of his new God: "Thou shalt have no other gods before me. . . . for I, the Lord thy God, am a jealous God" (Exodus 20:3–5). The seriousness of Eliot's commitment to Christianity can be gauged from how repeatedly he discussed in print during the year of his conversion and for about five years thereafter, the problem of religion and its substitutes. One by one, like an inventory examiner, he inspected Bergsonianism, humanism, aestheticism, and other early twentieth-century "isms"; and in the light of Christianity, he rejected them as inadequate.

Eliot's interest in religion (literally, a retying or rebinding, an attempt to reconnect fragments into a whole) did not appear suddenly in his thirty-ninth year. His awareness of fragmentation, his dissatisfaction with brokenness, had been evident in his earliest work. The Harvard masterpieces—"Portrait," "Preludes," "Prufrock," "Rhapsody"—all exhibit a consciousness of broken connections. People are cut off from friends, from lovers, from any community, from God. The great human problem behind *The Waste Land* is "I can connect / Nothing with nothing" (ll. 301–2). This inability to connect, in fact, is

123

precisely what guarantees the barrenness of the wasteland. Without connection, there can be no birth; without reconnection, no rebirth.

Eliot's early references to religion, found principally in book reviews, indicate that he thought of religion not in terms of a god, or even a primary allegiance, but in terms of a scheme, a system of ideas. The object of such a scheme or system is, first, to enable one to make sense out of experience, and second, to enable one to live and to act. In a 1916 review of Clement Webb's *Group Theories of Religion and the Religion of the Individual,* Eliot argued that "both religion and science [are] pragmatic" and must be evaluated on the extent to which they do or do not work.[1] This pragmatic bias is important. In seriously entertaining the Buddhist option, for example, Eliot was attracted not by a god, but by a scheme. In becoming a Christian, he accepted primarily a scheme, one that includes a god, but first of all, a scheme. In a 1931 discussion of Pascal's religious experience, Eliot underscored his belief in the pragmatic nature of commitment by pointing to the process through which a rational person progresses toward Christianity:

> [One] finds the world to be so and so; he finds its character inexplicable by any non-religious theory; among religions he finds Christianity . . . to account most satisfactorily for the world and especially for the moral world within; and thus he finds himself inexorably committed.[2]

A year later, Eliot explained his own conversion in similar terms:

> the Christian scheme seemed to me the only one which would work . . . the only possible scheme which found a place for values which I must maintain or perish.[3]

Religion is seen, again, as a scheme, a system of ideas, an abstraction, which allows one to make sense of the universe and to maintain values.

The need for religion, then, is universal and timeless. The need for

---

1. T. S. Eliot, Rev. of *Group Theories of Religion and the Religion of the Individual,* by Clement C. J. Webb, *International Journal of Ethics* 27, no. 1 (October 1916): 117.

2. T. S. Eliot, "Introduction," in *Pascal's Pensées,* trans. W. F. Trotter (New York: E. P. Dutton, 1931), xii.

3. T. S. Eliot, "Christianity and Communism," *Listener* 7, no. 166 (16 March 1932): 382–83.

religious substitutes, however, is related to special circumstances, usually to paradigmatic epistemological shifts, which disorient people about matters ordinarily taken for granted. The early twentieth century was a period of such disorientation. José Ortega y Gasset discusses this period as a time in which the epistemological skeleton of the culture collapsed, a time with no broadly shared or shareable religion, no common philosophy, no framework for thought.[4] "When there is distress of nations and perplexity," Eliot says in part V of "The Dry Salvages," people without religion usually fashion substitutes.

> To communicate with Mars, converse with spirits,
> To report the behaviour of the sea monster,
> Describe the horoscope, haruspicate or scry,
> Observe disease in signatures, evoke
> Biography from the wrinkles of the palm
> And tragedy from fingers; release omens
> By sortilege, or tea leaves, riddle the inevitable
> With playing cards, fiddle with pentagrams
> Or barbituric acids, or dissect
> The recurrent image into pre-conscious terrors—
> To explore the womb, or tomb, or dreams.[5]

W. H. Auden once described the problem of religion and its substitutes as *the* modern problem:

> Yeats, like us, was faced with the modern problem, *i.e.,* of living in a society in which men are no longer supported by tradition without being aware of it, and in which, therefore, every individual who wishes to bring order and coherence into the stream of sensations, emotions, and ideas entering his consciousness . . . is forced to do deliberately for himself what in previous ages had been done for him by family, custom, church, and state, namely [to choose] the principles and presuppositions in terms of which he can make sense of his experience.[6]

4. José Ortega y Gasset, *Man and Crisis*, trans. Mildred Adams (New York: W. W. Norton, 1958), 85 ff.

5. All quotations from "The Dry Salvages" and "Burnt Norton" are taken from *Four Quartets* (New York: Harcourt Brace Jovanovich, 1971).

6. W. H. Auden, "Yeats as an Example," *Kenyon Review* 10, no. 2 (1948): 191–92.

For millions of people, the mythic vacuum was filled by political theories, especially when a prophet or saviour figure like Mussolini, Stalin, or Hitler did the preaching. In one of several discussions of this phenomenon, Eliot says in a 1928 essay on "The Literature of Fascism" that "many political beliefs are substitutes for religious beliefs."[7] In most discussions of such matters, however, he focuses on the relation between the decay of religion and modernist imperatives in art. "The ideal condition," he explains in a 1920 review of a play by John Middleton Murry, is that under which a *"framework* is provided . . . as the condition of [one's] time." The modern writer's position "may seriously [be] call[ed] Promethean. He has to supply his own framework, his own myth."[8] There can be no doubt that Eliot was commenting on his own situation as an artist. In 1932, he referred approvingly to I. A. Richards's reading of *The Waste Land* as a work by a poet in a new situation.

> [T]he present situation is radically different from any in which poetry has been produced in the past: namely, . . . now there is nothing in which to believe, . . . Belief itself is dead; and . . . therefore my poem is the first to respond properly to the modern situation and not call upon Make-Believe. (*UPUC,* 130)

"Make-Believe" is surely a pun, indicating the obvious option when no Belief is given. The master of "Make-Believe," of course, is Yeats, who boldly formulated his own personal religion and then presented it to his readers in a handbook.

For many years, Eliot thought he was above "Make-Believe," that he was simply doing without. "My own view," he insists in one of his 1932 Harvard lectures, is that

> nothing in this world or the next is a substitute for anything else; and if you find that you must do without something, such as religious faith or philosophic belief, then you must just do without it. (*UPUC,* 113)

Eliot had come to this straightforward, no-nonsense, no-substitutes view as part of accepting traditional Anglo-Catholic Christianity. But actually, in the twenty years before his conversion, the years dur-

---

7. T. S. Eliot, "The Literature of Fascism," *Criterion* 8, no. 31 (December 1928): 282.

8. T. S. Eliot, "The Poetic Drama," Rev. of *Cinnamon and Angelica: A Play,* by John Middleton Murry, *Athenaeum* 4698 (14 May 1920): 635.

ing which he had struggled to do without religion, he had been moving from one substitute to another. And although his substitutes are more respectable than Yeats's, they are "Make-Believe" just the same.

Eliot's substitutes for religion can be roughly classified as erotic, religious, aesthetic, and philosophical. In a 1918 review, Eliot noted the important "role which the sexual instinct plays in the religion and mythology of primitive peoples [and] (indeed in all religion)."[9] He early associated his own experience of fragmentation and his longing for the Absolute, both of which are by definition religious, with sexual transcendence. From "The Love Song of J. Alfred Prufrock" through "Sweeney Erect," sexual adventure, whether desired or dreaded, hovers, full of possibility. An interrelated failure of sex and religion, moreover, is of the essence in *The Waste Land*. Some critics have claimed that the quality of Eliot's concern with sex makes him especially representative of his generation. I. A. Richards, for example, suggests that Eliot's fascination with Canto XXVI of the *Purgatorio* illustrates his "persistent concern with sex, the problem of our generation, as religion was the problem of the last."[10] This striking insight provoked Eliot to retort that "in his contrast of sex and religion [Richards] makes a distinction which is too subtle for me to grasp. One might think that sex and religion were 'problems' like Free Trade and Imperial Preference" (*UPUC*, 127). The clever evasiveness of Eliot's response suggests that Richards had struck home.

Sexual love has been associated since antiquity with religious rituals, and it includes by definition at least temporary transcendence of physical separateness; it also promises more complex unities. Sex is one way of overcoming brokenness, of retying or rebinding fragments into a whole. Eliot is not unique in seeing sex as a substitute for religion. At times, even Matthew Arnold presents sexual love as the only option left in a world no longer supported by the bright girdle of Christianity, a world he describes in "Dover Beach" as a darkling plain on which lovers are surrounded by ignorant armies clashing by night.

Eliot's sexual needs as a young man and his sensitivity to the

9. T. S. Eliot, Rev. of *Elements of Folk Psychology: Outlines of a Psychological History of the Development of Mankind*, by Wilhelm Wundt, *Monist* 28 (January 1918): 160.

10. I. A. Richards, *Principles of Literary Criticism* (New York: Harcourt Brace, 1925), 292.

symbolism of love as a binder or a rebinder explain in part his quick and disastrous marriage. This marriage precipitated a reevaluation of Eros, and indeed, of all human satisfactions. In a 1919 review, Eliot praised the great French and Russian novelists for having under-stood "the awful separation between potential passion and any actu-alization possible in life" as well as for "indicat[ing] . . . the inde-structible barriers between one human being and another."[11] Such awful knowledge, coming just a few years after his marriage, may represent the death of hope, but unfortunately, not the death of de-sire. Almost a decade later, with his wife incurably ill, his marriage irreparably broken, Eliot confided to close friends in the church that he was struggling with the problem of celibacy.[12] In prospect, then, Eros is kind, promising to heal the brokenness of the human heart; in retrospect, though, Eros is cruel, promising to do what no human lover can. Eliot's marital bond came to reinforce rather than allevi-ate his isolation, to reinforce rather than alleviate his need for tran-scendence.

Eros, then, offers a scheme that does not work. But is an institu-tional religion any better? In "A Dialogue on Dramatic Poetry," writ-ten the year after his baptism, Eliot quipped, "Our literature is a substitute for religion, and so is our religion" (*SE*, 32). The religion he had come to consider as a substitute for religion was Unitarianism. Born into a prominent family in American Unitarianism, Eliot at-tended church regularly throughout his early youth. And yet, after his conversion, when William Force Stead remarked in Trinity Col-lege's magazine that Eliot had returned to the church, the poet wrote in the margin, "Return? I was never there!"[13] His response is in-separable from his conviction that Unitarianism leads to skepticism rather than faith. Years before his conversion, in a discussion about the mind of his cousin Henry Adams, Eliot had associated Unitari-anism with a quality he called the "Boston Doubt":

11. T. S. Eliot, "Beyle and Balzac," Rev. of *A History of the French Novel, to the Close of the Nineteenth Century*, vol. 2, by George Saintsbury, *Athenaeum* 4648 (30 May 1919): 393.

12. T. S. Eliot, Letter to William Force Stead, 2 December 1930, Osborn Collection, Beinecke Library, Yale University.

13. William Force Stead, "Mr. Stead Presents an Old Friend," *Alumnae Magazine of Trinity College* 38, no. 2 (Winter 1965): 66. The copy with the marginal note is in the Hayward Collection, King's College, Cambridge.

> a scepticism which is difficult to explain to those who are not born
> to it. This scepticism is a product, or a cause, or a concomitant,
> of Unitarianism; it is not destructive, but it is dissolvent. . . .
> [Adams] could believe in nothing.[14]

Eliot, like Adams, was born to the Boston Doubt, but he early concluded that liberal Protestant theology could not provide a scheme
for organizing life or a framework for writing poetry.

The inadequacy of liberal Protestant theology led Eliot away from
the institutional church. As artists have done before in times of religious crisis, he and others of his generation turned to art itself as a
means to structure their lives and their work. In the five years after
his conversion, Eliot wrote repeatedly about art as a substitute for
religion. His aestheticism may be divided into two stages. From 1909
to 1911, he was influenced primarily by Matthew Arnold, Walter
Pater, and the French symbolists, especially Stéphane Mallarmé. In
this stage, he used Christian ritual as a framework to support his
poetry, somewhat in the way that Mallarmé used it. After the great
poems of 1909–11, he more or less dropped poetry for five or six
years and applied himself seriously to the study of philosophy. From
1917 through 1922, he returned to aestheticism, but having assimilated much modern science and philosophy, he had transformed the
earlier variety. In this stage, he used the mythical method to force art
to generate its own framework.

Eliot focuses, in his postconversion diagnosis of art as a failed
religion, on a central figure in his own heritage, Matthew Arnold. In
"Cousin Nancy," Eliot's early satire on Boston and family, Arnold the
humanist joins Emerson the Unitarian on respectable bookshelves,
and these guardians of the faith keep watch over Boston. Arnold had
argued, in the nineteenth-century reassessment of Christianity, that
religion was at once unbelievable and indispensable. In order to
maintain religion without belief, he set up Culture, or literature, in its
place. Eliot claims that Arnold was too intelligent and too temperate

> to maintain . . . that religious instruction is best conveyed by po-
> etry, . . . but he discovered a new formula: poetry is not religion,

14. T. S. Eliot, "A Sceptical Patrician," Rev. of *The Education of Henry Adams: An
Autobiography, Athenaeum* 4647 (23 May 1919): 361.

129

> but it is a capital substitute for religion—not invalid port, . . . but
> coffee without caffeine. (*UPUC*, 26)

In the world of art, Arnold's Culture led directly to Pater's aestheticism. As Eliot explains in a 1930 essay, "The gospel of Pater follow[ed] naturally upon the prophecy of Arnold." As quoted by Eliot, Pater's doctrine is

> the love of art for art's sake . . . ; for art comes to you professing
> frankly to give nothing but the highest quality to your moments
> as they pass, and simply for those moments' sake. (*SE*, 390)

This creed, Eliot claims, was a "hopeless admission of irresponsibility." But to the Eliot of 1908, art for art's sake was not an admission of irresponsibility, but a means of self-realization as an artist. Pater's creed, preached by Arthur Symons, gave Eliot the recipe he needed to make an entirely new liquor from Emerson's watered port and Arnold's decaffeinated coffee. For Symons led Eliot to the symbolists, particularly to the high priest of aestheticism, Mallarmé. The symbolist merger of art and religion proved invaluable in writing the great poems of 1909–11.

Mallarmé's aesthetic consists of a reformulation in which the forms and rituals of Catholicism are emptied of Christian content and then appropriated for a new religion of art. Underlying his work is an analogy between art and Catholicism in which the creative act by an artist is analogous to the Passion of Christ, and the re-creative act by a reader is analogous to the Christian Mass.[15] Following Mallarmé, Eliot used Christian ritual as an underlying structural metaphor in "The Love Song of J. Alfred Prufrock" and other early poems. But in his postconversion reevaluation of aestheticism, he argues that one has no business using Christian ritual unless one is a Christian.

In 1928, just after his conversion, Eliot published "A Dialogue on Dramatic Poetry," a fictional debate on the relation between religion and art. Two of the characters in this discussion, dubbed *E* and *B*, closely resemble Eliot himself in two stages of his religious and aesthetic development. *E* sounds like Tom Eliot, twenty-two years old, an American graduate student spending a year in Paris, a Bergso-

---

15. For a detailed discussion of Mallarmé's aesthetic, see "The Dispensations of Art: Mallarmé and the Fallen Reader" in this volume.

nian, in the process of writing "The Love Song of J. Alfred Prufrock" and a few other poems. *B* sounds like T. S. Eliot, thirty-nine years old, in the second decade of his marriage, a British businessman, a literary critic, author of "Gerontion" and *The Waste Land*, a new convert to the Anglican Church. Eliot number one, *E* in the "Dialogue," argues:

> the consummation of the drama, the perfect and ideal drama, is to be found in the ceremony of the Mass. . . . drama springs from religious liturgy, and . . . cannot afford to depart far from religious liturgy. . . . the only dramatic satisfaction that I find now is in a High Mass well performed. (*SE*, 35)

This is a perfect setup for Eliot number two, *B* in the "Dialogue," to comment on aestheticism in his own work. He does this by saying he once knew someone who held such a view, and by attributing to this friend of long ago his own earlier opinions.

> Are we to say that our cravings for drama are fulfilled by the Mass? . . . No. For I once knew a man who held the same views that you appear to hold, E. He went to High Mass every Sunday, and was particular to find a church where he considered the Mass efficiently performed. . . . The Mass gave him extreme . . . satisfaction. It was almost orgiastic. But when I came to consider his conduct, I realised he was guilty of a *confusion des genres*. His attention was not on the meaning of the Mass, for he was not a believer but a Bergsonian; it was on the Art of the Mass. His dramatic desires were satisfied by the Mass, precisely because he was not interested in the Mass, but in the drama of it. Now what I maintain is, that you have no business to care about the Mass unless you are a believer. . . . Literature can be no substitute for religion, not merely because we need religion, but because we need literature as well . . . religion is no more a substitute for drama than drama is a substitute for religion. . . . For there is a difference in attention. If we are religious then we shall only be aware of the Mass as art, in so far as it is badly done and interferes with our devotion. (*SE*, 35–36)

Like *B*, the Eliot of 1927 rejected aestheticism and insisted on a "no substitutes" view. Like *E*, and also like *B*'s old friend, the Eliot of 1910 was a Bergsonian, living in Paris, using the ritualistic aesthetics of Mallarmé in his poetry. The extent to which Eliot, in his 1928 di-

131

alogue, is cleaning his own house can easily be seen by focusing on "The Love Song of J. Alfred Prufrock." On one level, "Prufrock" is an unanswerable judgment on Arnold's religion of Culture. The poem describes a mass in Arnold's post-Christian sanctuary, the drawing room of the intelligensia in Cambridge, Massachusetts, in the shadow of Harvard Square. Mr. Prufrock, in whose mind the drawing room exists, tries to talk himself into going to a communion service in which he and some ladies will share toast and tea and culture with a capital C. A central problem in Prufrock's vision is that Culture can only be shared by using language. He will be forced to use words with these Arnoldian priestesses, and he knows that in a world where belief is impossible, a world without common ground, language will fail as a connector or binder. By mixing gustatory and rhetorical images, Eliot manipulates a parallel between eating together and talking together. In this communion service, the Word, capital W, is replaced by words; in this social sanctuary, questions, after macaroons, are lifted and dropped onto plates; and here, in this modern eucharist, the table scraps include not only crumbs, but also words. "After the cups, the marmalade, the tea, / Among the porcelain, among some talk of you and me. . . ."

In Eliot's communion service, as in Mallarmé's, words are substituted for bread and wine; in Eliot's, as in Mallarmé's, a poet or singer stands in for the priest. But though Eliot may have begun with Mallarmé's service, he ends by transforming it. Mallarmé had predicted that artists would liberate ritual from the bloody and barbarous meal celebrated within the Church by replacing it with a far more civilized celebration of the death and rebirth of nature. But cleaning up the communion ritual was one thing for Mallarmé and quite another for Eliot. "Prufrock" is in part a poem about the disease of solipsism. This is a poem in which the landscape has been emptied of all objects beyond the self, a world where every object is an extension of some thinking subject, where everything finally is an extension of the speaker or thinker. A true brother of Henry Adams, Prufrock can believe in nothing. And believing in nothing, radical skepticism, leads inevitably to solipsism. Mallarmé had predicted that removing Christ from the altar, the body and blood from the table, would purge Christian ritual and enable it to survive as a framework for a higher religion based on art. But in a solipsistic world, an attempt to dispose of Christian dogma while retaining Christian ritual ends by placing the self, the only sure reality, at the center of the ritual. In the modern mass described in "The Love Song of J. Alfred Prufrock," the god to be divided, to be eaten, to be drunk among whispers, the material substance on the platter, is none other than Prufrock himself. This is the horror at the core of the poem, and it can be seen by looking at any one of several passages. For example:

> Should I, after tea and cakes and ices,
> Have the strength to force the moment to its crisis?
> But though I have wept and fasted, wept and prayed,
> Though I have seen my head [grown slightly bald] brought in
>   upon a platter,
> I am no prophet—and here's no great matter.

Prufrock sees himself here as Christ in Gethsemane—"though I have wept and fasted, wept and prayed"—preparing for the sacrifice of his own body. And he sees himself as John the Baptist, a prophet slain, decapitated, and served on a platter. No wonder Prufrock approaches the drawing room with terror. No wonder he shudders in imagining his own head, grown slightly bald, served up by these priestesses of Arnold. No wonder he moans when reflecting that his life—the life is in the blood—has been measured out in coffee spoons.

But the greatest shudder comes not from seeing what is upon the platter, but from biting it. In language suggesting both asking questions and eating, Prufrock asks himself:

> Would it have been worth while,
> To have bitten off the matter with a smile,
> To have squeezed the universe into a ball
> To roll it towards some overwhelming question

"Matter" here is a troublesome topic, an overwhelming question, and biting it off is bringing it up. But "matter" is also any physical substance that occupies space and can be served on a platter, something like toast or a communion wafer or the head of John the Baptist—or the head of Prufrock. And "matter" is "mater" or mother, the great Ur-Womb, the original that both generated and is the universe. When one remembers that the central problem of the poem is that the persona's subjectivity has swallowed up the universe, these and other meanings come together to confirm Prufrock himself as the

THE MIND OF EUROPE

universe that must be squeezed and shaped into a ball and dropped onto the plate. He himself is the "mater" and the matter—the universe, the problem, the question, the physical substance to be distributed among the ladies in the drawing room. In this service devoted to Culture, watched over by Emerson and Arnold, Prufrock plays all parts. He is the bread, he is the priest, and he is the communicant who must partake of himself, must swallow these vitiated elements. Confused and nauseated, he wonders, "how should I begin / To spit out all the butt-ends of my days and ways?" The repeated association of matter with both the universe and Prufrock's head (his physical head, his mind, and perhaps his genitals) emphasizes that through his subjectivity, he has become the universe. This is one meaning of the famous conceit that opens the poem. Prufrock, not the evening, is etherized upon a table. Like everything else in the poem, the tired, sleepy evening is an aspect of Prufrock's mind. The table upon which he projects his etherized head turns out on careful reading to be not only a surgery table, but also a tea table. And the tea table with crumbs of mind beneath is Arnold's communion table.

Eliot's experiments with religious ritual in "Prufrock," and the other poems of 1909–11 led him to reflect on the drastic situation in which a poet is forced to separate belief in a scheme from use of that scheme. In using Christian ritual without taking seriously the beliefs that had generated it, he came face to face with a special horror, the horror of lifting the veil and finding nothing behind it, or perhaps of finding only a mirror behind it. In going beyond the surface, Laforgue and Mallarmé had discovered the Absolute, but Eliot found an emptiness that sent him scampering back to the surface. As poems, these early works are extremely successful in that they lead to frontiers of consciousness where words fail but meanings persist. As raids on the Absolute, they are failures. Like Mallarmé and the romantics, Eliot organizes the campaign and makes the trip, but unlike them, he finds the Absolute to be either a reflection of himself or an absence.

The early experiments with aestheticism sent Eliot back to philosophy in search of some scheme that would enable him to bind up his fragments and unify his life and art. For the next few years, he applied himself diligently to studies preparatory to a career in philosophy. Between 1911 and 1915, at Harvard and at Oxford, he completed all of the course work for a Ph.D., and in 1916 he completed a dissertation on the epistemology of F. H. Bradley.

Eliot found in Bradley a doctrine that, at least on the intellectual level, explains away the fragmentation and chaos that seem to characterize contemporary culture. The relevant Bradleyan principle, common to all absolute idealists and endorsed in Eliot's thesis, is outlined in my chapter on "Gerontion." Behind all of Bradley's work is the assumption that reality consists of parts that are all interconnected in a single system. Everything that exists, simply by virtue of existing, is included in the Absolute, which is an overarching, all-inclusive whole. From the fact that the Absolute is all-inclusive, it follows that every perception, every object, every thing in the universe, is a part rather than a whole. Any fragment, no matter how isolated it may appear, is connected to other fragments; every fragment is self-transcendent, i.e., it reaches beyond itself and participates in successively greater fragments until it reaches the all-inclusive whole. Put more simply, every fragment has a context, which also has a context, which in turn has a context that eventually is the Absolute. Because these fragments are all part of one single thing, they are necessarily and systematically related. No fragment has its meaning alone; it exists as part of a unitary and timeless system.[16] This Bradleyan doctrine, with its primary emphasis on rebinding fragments into a whole, is radically religious. Most of Eliot's criticism, including the famous notion of "tradition," is rooted in it, and many of his poems, conspicuously "Gerontion," take it as a structural principle.[17]

"Gerontion" is one of the most difficult poems in modern literature. It consists of fragments, which may appear to be randomly juxtaposed but which are actually carefully arranged according to the principle described in the preceding paragraph. Eliot arranges the poem into an almost endless number of superimposed contexts by using the image of a house. The idea that every fragment is part of a context that itself is part of a larger context is shown by placing houses within houses within houses. The objects contained within the houses become less inclusive houses that in turn contain other

16. See Bradley, *Appearance and Reality*, 519–20.

17. For a more detailed exposition of this Bradleyan principle and a fuller version of the following explication of "Gerontion," see "The Structure of Eliot's 'Gerontion': An Interpretation Based on Bradley's Doctrine of the Systematic Nature of Truth" in this volume.

houses; at the same time, all of the houses are included in more inclusive houses.

The house in which Gerontion lives is old, decayed, draughty; it is located in a yard littered with debris. The tenants, a Greek intellectual who is old and blind and a woman who has a bad cold, are transients. The collapse of this house is imminent, for it is being buffeted by wind. From Gerontion's house, other houses proliferate in many directions, and all of them are replicas of the first one. All of the houses are, from a larger point of view, tenants; all of the tenants, from a smaller point of view, are houses. In the first stanza alone, there is a series of houses (tenants): Gerontion's thoughts, his brain, his body, his house, the yard, the field, and Europe. All of these tenants are dying transients in rented houses. In subsequent stanzas, other houses are superimposed. An important cluster of houses is related to culture: superimposed on Gerontion's Greek house is the house of Judaism and on that the house of Christianity. All of these houses are crumbling; the ruin in each case is related to a decay of faith and an expansion of knowledge. The coda of the poem returns the reader to the house that, small as it is, includes all of the others, i.e., the arid brain of the withered Socrates whose memories and thoughts, visions and revisions, furnished Eliot with a perfect metaphor for his vision of a godless and dying civilization.

On a purely intellectual level, Bradley's idealism is a scheme that works, a scheme that in fundamental ways is consistent with the religious scheme Eliot accepted in 1927. The religious impulse, as previously stated, is the impulse to rebind, to transcend fragments, to reunify. To be religious is, first, to be aware of fragmentation, of brokenness; and second, since RE-binding suggests a previous unity, to be religious is to be aware on some level that one lives in a post-lapsarian world, that the condition of brokenness and loneliness is not part of one's first world. To be religious, finally, is to be discontent with brokenness and to imagine that it can be transcended. The RE in religion is crucial, for in postulating previous unity, it promises future unity, or at least establishes the possibility of transcendence. Bradley's doctrine of the Absolute assumes previous unity, acknowledges a falling away into fragments, and posits an intellectual scheme for transcendence. Still, in 1927, when Eliot came to reevaluate his old mentor, he found Bradley's philosophy less than adequate. In "Gerontion," all fragments are unified by reference to a larger context. But in the end, Gerontion's ruined houses, even if seen as included in a larger unity, are still ruined. That all the fragments may be unified in some heaven of the mind may be great comfort for the philosopher, but it is little comfort for the individual who must live and work among the ruins.

By the time Eliot finished "Gerontion," he had become disillusioned with most religious substitutes. He had discovered that Unitarianism dissolved the ability to believe in anything, that Eros whispered promises it could not keep, that symbolism led him to an abyss beneath surface forms, that idealism failed to take account of feeling. In the years between 1918 and 1922, partially under the influence of Ezra Pound, whose Penelope was Flaubert, Eliot made a last-ditch effort to accept art as a substitute for religion. In a 1919 review, he sounds more like an apostle for art than a literary critic. The romantic, claims Eliot, tends to relate everything to himself. This devotion to one's self and one's caste "will not do in literature. The Arts insist that a man shall dispose of all that he has, even of his family tree, and follow art alone."[18] By alluding to some of the most difficult words Christ ever spoke, Eliot indicates that the cost of discipleship in the arts is high indeed. His words ring true, for unlike the rich young ruler, Eliot at this stage had left father and mother, country and profession, in order to devote himself to his new master and "follow art alone."

Eliot's devotion to literature is evident enough in the essays collected in 1920 in *The Sacred Wood*. That book became a textbook for those who insisted on the autonomy of art, on the self-referential nature of texts, on the irrelevance of belief, or even of life, to art. In 1928, just after his conversion, Eliot issued the second edition of *The Sacred Wood*. The preface to this edition indicates that he had become uneasy with the implications of these early essays, especially as developed by his friend, I. A. Richards. Poetry, Eliot claims in the 1928 preface, has been greatly overrated. It is not, as Arnold claimed, a "criticism of life." "And certainly poetry is not the inculcation of morals, or . . . of politics; and no more is it religion or an equivalent of religion, except by some monstrous abuse of words."[19] What is

18. T. S. Eliot, "A Romantic Patrician," Rev. of *Essays in Romantic Literature*, by George Wyndham, *Athenaeum* 4644 (2 May 1919): 266–67.

19. T. S. Eliot, *The Sacred Wood: Essays on Poetry and Criticism*, 2nd ed. (London:

THE MIND OF EUROPE

poetry? In a striking about-face, Eliot now announces that "poetry is a superior amusement." And he tries to reconnect this amusement with belief. Poetry "has something to do with morals, and with religion, and even with politics perhaps, though we cannot say what" (*SW*, viii, x).

Eliot makes several other attempts to dissociate himself from the implications of his early work, especially as developed by Richards. In the 1929 essay on Dante, for example, he describes as incomprehensible Richards's statement that in *The Waste Land*, poetry is completely severed from belief (*SE*, 230). In "The Modern Mind," he takes on Richards for asserting that "poetry is capable of saving us." He ends by placing Richards with Arnold: "salvation by poetry is not quite the same thing for Mr. Richards as it was for Arnold; but so far as I am concerned these are merely different shades of blue" (*UPUC*, 131).

Eliot's uneasiness with the rise of the New Criticism, especially with Richards's *Principles of Literary Criticism* and *Science and Poetry*, stems from the fact that Richards took *The Sacred Wood* and *The Waste Land* as primary texts. To some extent, Eliot's postconversion rebukes of Richards are an attempt to clarify his own life. He had been sincerely trying, in the years leading up to *The Waste Land*, to make poetry his Penelope, to make art the still point of his turning world. For years, he had been working on some method that would enable him to construct a great poem without using a framework borrowed from religion or philosophy. In "Prufrock," he had tried using Christian ritual, and in "Gerontion," Bradleyan philosophy. Both seemed in special ways inadequate. In *The Waste Land*, instead of borrowing a framework, Eliot borrows a method. Using the comparative method of modern science, particularly of anthropology, he tries to force the reader to construct the abstraction that will serve as the framework of the poem.[20] It is Eliot's great attempt to create an autonomous work of art, a work in which an aesthetic order is collaboratively constructed by the poet and his reader.

Methuen & Co., 1928), ix. Subsequent references will be indicated in the text, abbreviated as *SW*.

20. For a fuller discussion of the method by which Eliot forces the reader to construct the abstraction, see "The Case of the Missing Abstraction: Eliot, Frazer, and Modernism" in this volume.

Within a short time of finishing *The Waste Land*, Eliot had initiated the dialogue that led to his entry into the Christian Church. He had begun with the Arnoldian position that belief was impossible, but religion or some substitute was essential. He had tried Bergsonianism, Eros, aestheticism, humanism, idealism, and had seriously considered Buddhism. But in the end, Christianity was the only scheme satisfying both his intellectual and his emotional needs, the only scheme permitting him to unify his life and his art; or, as he came to say, the Christian scheme was the only one that worked. Of poetry, his most serious substitute for religion, he came to say in "East Coker" that "The poetry does not matter." From a position of "art for art's sake" in 1910, Eliot in 1951 came to say:

> For it is ultimately the function of art, in imposing a credible order upon ordinary reality, and thereby eliciting some perception of an order *in* reality, to bring us to a condition of serenity, stillness, and reconciliation; and then leave us, as Virgil left Dante, to proceed toward a region where that guide can avail us no farther. (*OPP*, 94)

Eliot's quest for truth was complicated, as complicated as his mind and his personality. He did not try one scheme at a time, neatly and in sequence. Both in substance and in sequence, his schemes overlapped. Moreover, in taking seriously one substitute and then rejecting it, he did not obliterate it from his mind. His mind was like the mind he describes in "Tradition and the Individual Talent," "a mind which changes, and . . . this change is a development which abandons nothing en route" (*SE*, 6). This change does not superannuate either humanism or aestheticism or Buddhism, but includes them, at least residually, in an ever increasing complexity of intelligence and feeling. The pattern of his inclusive and cultivated imagination is rich and strange, and finally, elusive. His Christianity, certainly, cannot be equated with any handbook definition, but it is Christianity just the same. His substitutes for religion cannot be treated simply as stations on the way to the church; they did lead to the church, however, and to know them is to become aware of the complexity and richness of his Christian assent.

139

Keeping Time in Time

Eliot's Struggle with Form in *The Waste Land* and *Four Quartets*

The poems of T. S. Eliot can be thought of as a series of experiments by a scrupulous artist searching for form in a formless age. Major moments in his quest can be measured by the form realized in such works as "The Love Song of J. Alfred Prufrock," "Preludes," "Sweeney Among the Nightingales," *The Waste Land, Ash-Wednesday,* and *Four Quartets*. In order to understand his achievement in *Four Quartets,* in major respects the apogee of his struggle with form, the reader must approach the poem comparatively, with some sense of the poet's early experiments and of his long journey as an artist. Each poem, to use Eliot's own language, should be seen as a new start, a new attempt to address the old problem of form. Eliot's poetry should also be seen in the context of the aesthetic challenge to which it is in precise ways a response. In *The Waste Land,* Eliot responds by formulating the "mythical method"—i.e., a method of re-collecting fragments and reconstructing wholes by use of a Darwinian reference point myth from Sir James G. Frazer. In *Four Quartets,* Eliot advances a different method, one based on repetition and relation-in-itself rather than on juxtaposition and reconstruction; in the latter masterpiece, he uses a key pattern instead of a key myth. In changing from a linear mythic model to a diachronic / synchronic and musical / mythic model, he anticipates in striking ways the work of Claude Lévi-Strauss.

I

The notion of a structure lacking any center represents the unthinkable itself.
—*Jacques Derrida*[1]

1. Jacques Derrida, *Writing and Difference,* trans. Alan Bass (Chicago: University of Chicago Press, 1978), 279.

140

The notion that creating or perceiving order depends on the existence of a reference point (or center) is crucial to understand form in art. This notion was a given in Western art before the twentieth century, and its problematization is part of the crisis of modernism. The herculean effort to cope with the loss of a shared reference point, involving ingenious attempts to retrieve or to discover or to create substitutes, characterizes modernism in all of the arts. The modernist preoccupation with form is a corollary of dispensationalism, the view that history can be best understood if analyzed into several giant blocks, each of which is identified with some overarching idea or assumption about fundamentals. Mallarmé, Yeats, Eliot, and Pound are profoundly dispensationalist; Spengler, Kuhn, McLuhan, and Foucault also worked from a dispensationalist analysis of history. The most influential contemporary dispensationalist is Derrida. In *Writing and Difference,* he divides Western intellectual history into two giant eras, each characterized by an assumption about Being or presence. His first dispensation includes the entire history of Western thought before (roughly) the twentieth century, which he claims was erected on an acceptance of "Being as presence in all senses of this word" and must be thought of as "a series of substitutions of center for center." In the late nineteenth century, he continues, a "rupture" occurred in the history of thought. Derrida associates the rupture with the "Nietzschean critique of metaphysics," the "Freudian critique of self-presence," and the "Heideggerean destruction of metaphysics." After these destructive discourses, "it was necessary to begin thinking that there was no center."[2]

Major writers responded in different ways to the collapse or disappearance of what Derrida calls the center. Yeats in *A Vision* made up a mythology to serve as a reference point for his poetry, and Joyce in *Ulysses* retrieved a Homeric reference point. Stevens creates a reference point by the simple act of introducing difference, as when in "Anecdote of the Jar" he transforms a "slovenly wilderness" into an orderly kingdom by the simple act of placing an artifact on the hill. The jar, a totally *other,* facilitates definition by creating difference and at the same time creates order by serving as a focal point. The jar was not made for the use to which Stevens puts it; it was at hand, how-

---

2. Derrida, *Writing and Difference,* 278–80.

THE MIND OF EUROPE

ever, and in a pinch, it sufficed. This 1923 poem shows Stevens playing *bricoleur*, to borrow the term Lévi-Strauss used for mythmakers in *The Savage Mind*. A *bricoleur*, in the translator's gloss, is a "kind of professional do-it-yourself man"[3] who works with whatever he has around the house, tools and materials that were not designed for the use he puts them to, but that can be adapted through cleverness and trial and error for his purpose.

Eliot typically analyzes the modernist crisis in terms of a mythic *absence* in contemporary life. "The present situation is radically different from any in which poetry has been produced in the past: namely, . . . now there is nothing in which to believe, . . . Belief itself is dead" (*UPUC*, 130). Most of his poems from "The Love Song of J. Alfred Prufrock" through *Four Quartets* are conscious experiments in achieving form apart from dependence on a fixed center. His solution is different in each case, although his achievements in each poem become platforms for beginning again. His most strenuous effort, perhaps, came in *The Waste Land* with the use of what he called the "mythical method." Because the form that unfolded in the *Quartets* has many traces of this often misrepresented method, I will describe it briefly before taking up form in the *Quartets*.

II

These fragments I have shored against my ruins.—*The Waste Land*

In his 1923 review of Joyce's *Ulysses*, Eliot addresses himself in specific terms to the problem of creating order in the absence of a center or reference point. He says that the greatest challenge facing the modern artist is finding "a way of controlling, of ordering, of giving a shape and a significance to the immense panorama of futility and anarchy which is contemporary history" (*SP*, 177). Joyce met this challenge by retrieving a reference point and by forcing the reader to use it. In attempting to clarify Joyce's achievement, Eliot draws a clear distinction between "material" and "method" in art. The material is "actual life," that of the artist (including his emotional life) and of his moment in history. The method is how one deals with it. Eliot

---

3. Claude Lévi-Strauss, "The Structural Study of Myth" (1955), trans. Claire Jacobson and Brooke Grundfest Schoepf, in *The Critical Tradition*, ed. David H. Richter (New York: St. Martin's Press, 1989), 17.

goes on to maintain that an artist is not responsible for material, which is given, but for method, which must be discovered or invented. In "Four Elizabethan Dramatists" (1924), he again distinguishes between material and method and goes on to claim that the modern malaise is a result of the fact that artists and audiences share no abstractions, no mental constructs in which to anchor their material (*SE*, 91–99). Joyce's significance for Eliot is that in the absence of a shared abstraction, he arbitrarily selected one and built it into the text of his novel. Joyce overcame his obstacles by "using a myth . . . manipulating a continuous parallel between contemporaneity and antiquity" (*SP*, 177).

Eliot insists that the mythical method was made possible by breakthroughs in the social sciences. "Psychology . . . , ethnology, and *The Golden Bough* have concurred to make possible what was impossible even a few years ago. Instead of narrative method, we may now use the mythical method" (*SP*, 178). The fact that most critics dismiss or misinterpret this statement makes it necessary to explain it briefly. Frazer was one of those scientists who extended Darwin's thesis (evolution) and Darwin's method (comparative study of fragments) into the social sciences. As Darwin had attempted to discover the origin of species and chart the descent of man, Frazer and his contemporaries tried to discover the origin of religion and chart the descent of gods. They wished to show a single evolutionary sequence in the development of religion from primitive to modern, and as Darwin had postulated a common ancestor for human beings, they postulated a common ancestor for all religions. They believed in the original unity of human consciousness and in the continuous evolution of that consciousness from prehistory to the present. And they believed that although the common ancient myth had broken up in prehistoric times, it could be reconstructed through a comparison of its remaining fragments.

The Golden Bough began as an attempt to explain a single myth. This myth is evocatively narrated on the first page of the first volume, and through twelve volumes of data, it never passes from Frazer's one-track mind. His work may seem to be a hodgepodge of primitive customs, but it is a thoroughly systematic attempt to explain the myth of the golden bough. He tracked this myth by collecting innumerable analogies and by carefully comparing them. He found no analogies to the myth as a whole, but he did find analogies to parts of it. So he dissected the myth into small pieces and collected analogies to each part. Through comparison and analysis of thousands of pieces of myths, he was able to construct ever more comprehensive myths. He then used these consciously constructed abstractions as reference points for understanding the fragments with which he had begun. In this way, he moved backward toward primitive unity.

Frazer's conclusion, consistent with his Darwinian beginnings, is that all myths, including the myth of the golden bough, derive from a parent myth, which he tries to reconstruct. His method involves privileging a single myth and keeping it constantly in mind as a reference point.[4] The omnipresence of one myth enabled him to manipulate comparisons between contemporaneity and antiquity, and through continuous comparison and contrast, to generate the parent myths that contain and unify both the reference point myth and the assembled fragments. By focusing on the myth of the golden bough, Frazer was able to shape and control his material, the fragments of futility and anarchy littering human history.

Frazer's method, then, more or less duplicates Darwin's. It is *scientific,* not mythical. Frazer used the inductive method; that is, he collected samples and then generalized from them; he then used the generalizations as a means of understanding the samples with which he had begun. A careful reading of the *Ulysses* review shows that Eliot was using "mythical" in his own way, as a near-synonym for scientific or comparative or inductive, or at least as a term for the scientific method as transformed by its application in the arts. Other scientists were quick to use Frazer's method of generating abstractions through the comparative study of fragments. Jessie Weston used it in *From Ritual to Romance* to construct a parent myth behind the Grail legends. In the notes to *The Waste Land,* Eliot acknowledges his debts to both Frazer and Weston.

In the *Ulysses* review, Eliot argues that Joyce's method "makes the modern world possible for art" (*SP,* 178) by allowing the artist to be true to both chaos and order. On the surface, Joyce in *Ulysses* and Eliot in *The Waste Land* pay their respects to contemporary his-

4. For a detailed discussion, see "The Case of the Missing Abstraction: Eliot, Frazer, and Modernism" in this volume.

144

tory and to their personal lives—that is, to their "material." But like Frazer, these artists anchor their material in carefully chosen abstractions. Frazer brings his pet myth and takes special care to keep it always in his reader's mind. He names his work—all twelve volumes—*The Golden Bough,* and in the first few paragraphs, he explains the myth and tells what he wants to discover about it. He proceeds to his thesis by constantly comparing and contrasting his fragments with each other and with his reference point myth, and by constructing abstractions suggested by this process.

Similarly, in *Ulysses* and *The Waste Land,* unity derives from reference to an abstraction brought by the artist: in Joyce, the Ulysses legend; in Eliot, the wasteland myth. As in Frazer, the reference point myth is kept in the reader's mind throughout the work. In *Ulysses,* the myth is suggested by the title and kept in the reader's mind by the presence of parallel actions and characters. In *The Waste Land,* the myth is suggested by the title and the notes and is reinforced by fragments of the myth within the poem. The artist does not bring the reference point myth in its entirety; rather he brings pieces of it and the necessary hints for reconstructing it. In *Ulysses,* it exists as a whole and may be recovered by reading the *Odyssey* in a good translation. In *The Waste Land,* the myth is more elusive. The monomyths of Weston and of Frazer exist only as reconstructions generated by using the comparative method, and Eliot's background myth is only loosely theirs. Eliot assumes a reader who is willing to take the fragments on the surface of his poem and re-collect them (both remember where they came from and gather them up again). Each reader of *The Waste Land* will construct a variant of Frazer's monomyth, a variant that will be composed anew with every reading.

III

> Except for the point, the still point,
> There would be no dance, and there is only the dance.
> —*"Burnt Norton" II*

The question of form in *Four Quartets* can only be addressed by referring to Eliot's concern with the case of the missing abstraction. Between 1922 and 1934–42, the concern is evident not only in the poet's evolving convictions about art but also in the larger convictions shaping his life. Two personal events (complementary in some ways) are particularly relevant to his continuing quest for order in life and in art. The first is the disintegration of his marriage and the second is his entry into the Church of England. In accepting the Christian position, he willed to believe that there really is a Center, a shared Center, whether it is named or unnamed, recognized or unrecognized, acknowledged or ignored. His focus changes from reconstructing a shared reference point to glimpsing a universal pattern.

Three aspects of structure in the earlier poem can be traced in the later one. The first has to do with the method of creating order, of finding a reference point. The basic principle of structure in *The Waste Land* is the juxtaposition of fragments that can be re-collected and organized by reference to a privileged myth. The basic principle in *Four Quartets* is repetition, the function of which is to permit the emergence of a common pattern beneath particulars. The second aspect of structure represents a more radical departure from *The Waste Land*. In his earlier masterpiece, Eliot focuses on fragments and on the reconstructions they make possible; in *Four Quartets*, he focuses not on fragments or experiences or ideas, but rather on relations between them, on the gaps opened by intersection and difference. Thus, in the *Quartets*, a focus on betweenness, on what is absent or "not there," causes relation-in-itself to emerge as the most important presence of the sequence. The final aspect of structure has to do with the identification of a reference point. In *The Waste Land*, Eliot solved the case of the missing abstraction by encouraging his readers to refer his fragments to a single myth borrowed from Frazer and his colleagues in comparative religion. In *Four Quartets*, Eliot anchors his texts not in a myth, but in a pattern, one archetypally presented in the Christian doctrine of the Incarnation.

IV

> You say I am repeating
> Something I have said before. I shall say it again.
> —*"East Coker"* III

> The function of repetition is to render the structure of the myth apparent.
> —*Claude Lévi-Strauss*[5]

The reader opening *Four Quartets*, like the reader opening *The Waste Land*, is immediately confronted with fragments. But the frag-

---

5. Lévi-Strauss, "The Structural Study of Myth" (1955), in *The Critical Tradition*, 877.

ments differ greatly in content and in how they are to function within the overall structure of the poem. The fragment introducing *The Waste Land* is from the *Satyricon*. It is one of many bits and pieces of an ancient original—a myth once present, now absent, and forever lost in the dark backward abysm of time. The Sibylline shard is the first of many fragments of this Ur-myth, a rough and abstract approximation of which can be constructed by the reader. The fragments introducing "Burnt Norton" (and thus *Four Quartets*) are philosophical principles attributed to the pre-Socratic thinker Heraclitus. The first can be translated as "Though there is but one Center, most people live in centers of their own"; the second as "The way up and the way down are one and the same." These fragments are not morsels of myth or shreds of a story, but philosophic principles having integrity in themselves. The first refers to a common point of stillness and the second to a common pattern of movement. As one reads and rereads *Four Quartets,* these fragments will come to be understood as imperfect realizations of a complex encompassing both, as part of an ever present but usually imperceptible pattern. In *Four Quartets,* then, the missing abstraction is not something to be constructed, but something to be experienced in miniature, to be half-heard or half-glimpsed. The pattern emerges through repetition.

Repetition is the most important structural principle in *Four Quartets.* Eliot seemed to have discovered the principle *qua* principle while he was working on "East Coker," which he began as a new poem "in succession to 'Burnt Norton.' "[6] In Book X of *The Republic,* Plato reveals what happens when one begins a sequel. "God . . . made one bed in nature and one only; two or more such beds neither ever have been nor ever will be made by God." This is so because "even if he had made but two, a third would still appear behind them of which they again both possessed the form, and that would be the real bed and not the two others."[7] In beginning "East Coker," Eliot intended to write a two-poem sequence. But as Plato's explanation of why God could have made only one bed indicates, it is impossible to duplicate something without causing a third to arise above the two. In writing a sequel to "Burnt Norton," the poet generated an abstrac-

6. Helen Gardner, *The Composition of* Four Quartets (New York: Oxford University Press, 1978), 16.

7. Plato, *The Republic,* trans. Benjamin Jowett (Oxford: Clarendon Press, 1953), 10.597c.

tion encompassing both the first poem and its sequel, an abstraction to which each individual poem could be compared and by which each could be judged. This abstraction arising from the two works assumes a life of its own, a life in certain ways superior to the individuals who generated it. Eliot discusses Elizabethan drama in similar terms by arguing that all of Shakespeare's plays are one play. When critics write of Shakespearean tragedy, of course, they are generally referring to the abstraction in the mind of the reader-spectator who knows all of the individual plays.

Repetition carries the risk of becoming *mere* repetition. "It ['East Coker'] may be quite worthless," Eliot confided to John Hayward, "because most of it looks to me like an imitation of myself."[8] Nevertheless, he persisted, and as he worked on "East Coker," he came to think in terms of a four-part sequence.

> The idea of the whole sequence emerged gradually. I should say during the composition of "East Coker." Certainly by the time that poem was finished I envisaged the whole work as having four parts which gradually began to assume, perhaps only for convenience sake, a relation to the four seasons and the four elements.[9]

At first "East Coker" takes its shape from an abstraction rising above "Burnt Norton," but increasingly this abstraction is balanced by a second one, an "idea of the whole," an imaginative construct comprehending and accommodating four poems, two of which were not much more than vague requirements emerging from the poet's sense of symmetry. Relating each poem to one of the four seasons and one of the four elements became a poetic convenience, a part of the frame for his four meditations and also part of the justification for seeing them as one poem. The idea of the whole, constantly being revised and refined as he worked, became a still but always moving reference point. In one sense, he had solved the case of the missing abstraction by forcing the work itself to generate the abstraction by which it was to be guided, understood, and finally, judged.

As the first poem in the sequence and retrospectively the model for the other three, "Burnt Norton" is not related in any direct sense to a

8. Gardner, *The Composition of* Four Quartets, 16–17.
9. Gardner, *The Composition of* Four Quartets, 18.

148

previous work; nor is there any "idea of the whole" to which it could have been related. In Lyndall Gordon's view, the main reference point in "Burnt Norton" is the idea of a perfect life, generated by Eliot's attempt to understand the troubles in his personal life at the same time that he was working on *Murder in the Cathedral,* a play about a martyr and a saint.[10] The actual text of the poem originated from lines cut from the play, lines in which Becket is confronted by a tempter who suggests a return to the past as a way to escape the dangerous present: "The Chancellorship that you resigned / When you were made Archbishop—that was a mistake / On your part— still may be regained." In this scene requiring a reexamination of the whole of life in the light of the present moment, a priest responded in the following words:

> Time present and time past
> Are both perhaps present in the future.
> Time future is contained in time past. . . .
> What might have been is a conjecture
> Remaining a permanent possibility
> Only in a world of speculation. . . .
> Footfalls echo in the memory
> Down the passage which we did not take
> Into the rose-garden.[11]

These beautiful lines, only slightly modified, now form the opening paragraph of "Burnt Norton."

Eliot visited Burnt Norton, a country house in Gloucestershire, in 1934, just as he was emerging from the long night of his first marriage. With him was Emily Hale, a woman with whom he had once been in love and perhaps intended to marry. It seems likely that on this summer day in the rose garden, Eliot, guilt-torn and exhausted by years of unhappiness and by a painful separation from his wife, experienced a temptation to deny the present by returning to the road not taken in 1914, a temptation exactly analogous to the temptation faced by Thomas à Becket that generated the lines now opening "Burnt Norton." The temptation to try to go back and take a different

10. See chapter three of Lyndall Gordon, *Eliot's New Life* (New York: Farrar Straus Giroux, 1988).

11. Gardner, *The Composition of* Four Quartets, 82.

149

road, to cancel history and create an alternative present, constitutes an intersection among the lives of Becket, Christ, and Eliot. This intersection and the might-have-been life that it brought to Eliot's attention are part of the abstraction he uses in writing "Burnt Norton."

Eliot's meditation is resumed and completed in the other three *Quartets,* begun some five years after "Burnt Norton." The experience memorialized by the moment in the rose garden becomes the first of many examples of a point of intersection between time and timelessness, of a fragment of time that takes its meaning from and gives its meaning to a pattern, a pattern at once in time, continuously changing until the supreme moment of death completes it, and also out of time. Since individuals live and have their being only in fragments, they can never quite know the whole pattern, but in certain moments they can experience the pattern in miniature. These timeless moments in time—"the moment in the rose-garden, / The moment in the arbour where the rain beat, / The moment in the draughty church at smokefall" ("Burnt Norton" II)—provide for Eliot the means to conquer time. This moment of sudden illumination, in and out of time, Eliot associates with the Word-made-flesh, the Incarnation; and also with the word-made-art, poetry. The part / pattern configuration, especially in these three dimensions (personal experience, religious illumination, art), emerges through repetition; the pattern is both the main subject and a major principle of form in *Four Quartets.*

In *Four Quartets,* Eliot solved the case of the missing abstraction both for himself and for his reader by allowing the poem itself to generate the pattern that undergirds it and give it meaning. On the simplest level, the abstraction is born from the multiplicity of meditations, all four different, and yet obviously all of a kind. Just as Frazer abstracted one myth from many; just as the listener abstracts a Mozartian symphony, heard only in the mind's ear, from the actual symphonies; just as the spectator abstracts a Shakespearean tragedy, performed only in the theater of the mind, from the various tragedies; so the reader of *Four Quartets* inevitably if unconsciously abstracts an Eliotian quartet. This poem in the mind is private to each reader, but because it is generated by the text all readers share, it agrees to a remarkable extent with the abstractions constructed by other readers. The poem in the mind is at once spatial (it exists all at once in mental space) and temporal (it is always changing). "The knowledge imposes a pattern, and falsifies, / For the pattern is new in every moment" ("East Coker" II). In order to perceive the pattern, one must temporarily spatialize it. Such spatialization inevitably falsifies, but necessarily so because it is the only way to glimpse the still point at the center of all movement.

The *Quartet* in the mind emerges automatically because each of the *Four Quartets* explores the same general subject; each is named for a place; and each has approximately the same form. The general subject of the sequence is time and human existence in and out of time. Valerie Eliot says that her husband considered affixing as an epigraph to the entire sequence the line from *Pickwick Papers*, " 'What a rum thing time is, ain't it Neddy?' "[12] Thus a modern "philosopher", such as Dickens's Mr. Roeker, would have balanced the ancient Heraclitus. The overall exploration of time and eternity includes an exploration of parallel antitheses, such as movement and stillness, change and changelessness, part and pattern. Each poem in the sequence explores these intertwined mysteries. The meaningfulness of Eliot's treatment is immeasurably enriched by the fact that the form of the sequence is itself a perfect illustration of the twin mysteries.

The poems in Eliot's meditation are also parallel in being named for places. The first, of course, is named for the manor house in Gloucestershire visited by Eliot and Emily Hale. The title of the second, "East Coker," refers to the village in Somersetshire from which in the seventeenth century Eliot's family had immigrated to America, and to which, after his death, Eliot's own ashes were to be returned. The mystery of beginnings and ends—"In my beginning is my end"—"In my end is my beginning"—in and out of history is explored in this *Quartet*. The third poem takes its title from a treacherous group of rocks, the Dry Salvages, located off the coast of Cape Ann, Massachusetts where Eliot had passed his childhood summers. These rocks, the cold and seemingly limitless ocean in which they are anchored, and the great Mississippi River of his childhood are the major symbols in this meditation. The last *Quartet* takes its title from a tiny village in Huntingdonshire, Little Gidding, which in the seventeenth century had been a community of dedicated Christians under

12. Gardner, *The Composition of* Four Quartets, 28.

151

the leadership of Nicholas Ferrar. Eliot, who visited Little Gidding in 1936, admired the example of this small group that had renounced position and wealth for a life of work and prayer. Each of these four places is associated with Eliot's part / whole pattern, with his stillness / movement theme. He insists on the importance of specific places as he does of specific moments. The timeless moment, in fact, can only occur in a specific place—a rose garden, a draughty church, a rain-washed arbour. The places permit glimpses of what is beyond place; they constitute, in a special sense, a way to transcendence. "Only through time time is conquered" ("Burnt Norton" II); only through place place is conquered.

As all the *Quartets* explore the same theme, as all point to a specific place, so all have the same general form. The first part of each consists of a meditation on time and consciousness, arranged as a statement / counterstatement / recapitulation. The second consists of a highly structured poetical passage followed by a relatively prosaic passage, both on the general subject of being trapped in time. The third explores implications of the first two in terms of a journey metaphor, of some concept of movement of the self in and out of time. The fourth is a brief lyric or prayer. The fifth begins with a colloquial passage and then ends with a lyric that secures closure by returning to the beginning and collecting major images. The fifth section in each *Quartet* incorporates a meditation on the problem of the artist who must still move in stillness, keep time in time (both continuously move in step, and continuously be still).

Repetition is not only evident in the overall skeleton or frame of *Four Quartets*. It is also present within the sequence within each *Quartet* and within each section as Eliot organizes his system of echoes. "East Coker" III provides a clear example of Eliot's focus on repetition as a way of beginning to understand and attempting to communicate what ultimately is beyond both understanding and communication. The poet offers three parallel similes for human existence, each containing a parallel realization of emptiness. The first is that human existence is like a play in which one becomes aware of the unreality of the scene only between the acts when the props are rolled away. The second compares life to a ride on a train that stops between stations, replacing movement and talk with stillness and silence and forcing the passengers to notice the empty faces of their fellow travelers. The third image adds the suggestion that in illness, under ether, one becomes aware of one's own emptiness.

Eliot continues with a series of parallel images regarding the insight made available by waiting receptively in darkness. His images—running streams, winter lightning, garden laughter—are *about* echoes. In turn, they *are* echoes—echoes of "Burnt Norton" and, more basic, echoes of something (becoming / being) that cannot be seen or heard or experienced except through echoes. At this point, the poet turns to the reader with a strikingly prosaic and arguably perverse confession.

> You say I am repeating
> Something I have said before. I shall say it again.
> Shall I say it again? ("East Coker" III)

In a series of parallel and incantatory paradoxes, he resumes his echo of himself by echoing St. John of the Cross; then he repeats himself again, echoing Heraclitus with three paradoxes summarizing his position that the way of self-denial and the way of self-fulfillment are one and the same. The experience of catching an echo of laughter, of ecstasy in a garden (the personal rose garden, the mythic hyacinth garden, the theological Eden), is repeated time and again in *Four Quartets*. The echo requires agony but points beyond it to a redemption of ecstasy. The exercise of and the insistence on repetition in "East Coker," then, is part of the poet's deliberate attempt to instruct his reader on the principle he used to construct his poem and the principle by which it is to be appreciated.

The last poem, like the first one, presents special difficulties in a sequence largely dependent on the power of repetition. By the time he came to "Little Gidding," Eliot had mastered his structural principle and his theme, but as Helen Gardner's work on the composition of the poems makes clear, he had far more trouble with this poem than with the other three. A "final" poem in a sequence that is about both movement and stillness could by its very perfection privilege stillness and thus blur the twin mysteries the poet was trying to hold in balance. "Little Gidding" had at once to accommodate itself to the pattern generated by the existing poems and to crown that pattern by adding a work that would enable the quartet in the mind of both the poet and the reader to keep realizing itself. The emergence of a new and, in one sense, a final abstraction from the creation of "Little Gidding" risked subverting the basic premises explored in the work as a whole. The challenge was to complete what was in essence always in progress, to close what was always already open. The poet accomplishes this in part by making his conclusion a repetition of his beginning, by returning to the images of "Burnt Norton" I and deepening the significance of the laughter by the children in the garden. He points beyond the garden by pointing back to it; he takes us beyond our first world by enabling us to know it for the first time; he completes his line by taking us in a circle that is at once a movement and a completion of movement, a return and a new start. The return, however, does not take us back to the exact place from which we started; nor does it take us to a resting place, but to a beginning that moves toward an end, which in turn is a beginning.

The importance of repetition as structure and theme in *Four Quartets* is inseparable from the musical analogy suggested by the title. The musical analogy is not the focus of this paper, but it must be noted that musical form reveals structure through repetition at the same time that it resists reduction to specific meaning. The theme, development, and recapitulation of musical form are perfect for the interplay between pattern and movement which is at the heart of *Four Quartets*. Musical structure is at once diachronic (temporal, linear, related to melody) and synchronic (simultaneous, vertical, related to harmony), and thus it contains within itself one of the primary mysteries Eliot is working with in *Four Quartets*. Eliot's use of repetition and his appropriation of musical form have much in common with Lévi-Strauss's analysis of myth and music. The function of repetition, Lévi-Strauss maintains in "The Structural Study of Myth," is to reveal the structure of myth. In his studies of the myths of South American Indians in *The Raw and the Cooked*, Lévi-Strauss attends carefully to repeated elements in different versions of one myth and is able thereby to discern the underlying structure or pattern of the myth. In *Four Quartets*, Eliot repeats many versions of a single pattern, a pattern that emerges as such simply by being repeated with variations. In *The Raw and the Cooked*, Lévi-Strauss claims that music "is the only language with the contradictory attributes of being at once intelligible and untranslatable."[13] He thus organizes his text as a

13. Claude Lévi-Strauss, *The Raw and the Cooked*, trans. John and Doreen Weightman, vol. 1 of *Mythologiques* (New York: Harper and Row, 1969), 18.

piece of music with an overture followed by a theme and by variations with interludes and a coda. Lévi-Strauss includes in his text
analogues to many other musical forms, including a short symphony,
a toccata and fugue, and a rustic symphony. In the overture (introduction), he justifies his use of the musical analogy in language that
with very few changes could be applied to *Four Quartets*. The corre-
spondences between Eliot's work in *Four Quartets* and Lévi-Strauss's
work on myth can be explained partially in terms of Eliot's mastery
of the social scientists whose work Lévi-Strauss was using and in
terms of Eliot's comprehension of the problems of language and
myth that Lévi-Strauss was to take up and extend in his own particular scientific discipline.

V

The way up and the way down are one and the same.—*Heraclitus*

The error of traditional anthropology, like that of traditional linguistics, was to
consider terms, and not the relations between them.—*Lévi-Strauss*[14]

From the first lines of "Burnt Norton"—"Time present and time past
/ Are both perhaps present in time future"—through the last line of
"Little Gidding"—"And the fire and the rose are one"—Eliot in *Four
Quartets* forces his reader to attend to opposites, to paradoxes,
puzzles, and contradictions. Thus, the way up and the way down are
one and the same, the end is the beginning and the beginning the
end, the darkness is the light, the stillness is the dance, and the
fire and the rose are one. Eliot's focus on contraries, everywhere apparent, could be illustrated with any number of passages. In "East
Coker" III, for example, he uncompromisingly insists on his oppositions.

> And what you do not know is the only thing you know
> And what you own is what you do not own
> And where you are is where you are not.

He continually points to what is *not* there, to what is not said, not
heard, not known, not understood. This insistence on absence contributes to the pattern of oppositions, for it is presented as simulta-

14. Claude Lévi-Strauss, "Structural Analysis in Linguistics and in Anthropology,"
quoted in *Critical Theory Since 1965*, ed. Hazard Adams and Leroy Searle (Tallahassee:
University Presses of Florida, 1986), 808.

neously an insistence on presence. The focus on opposites, similarly, is itself a part of the pattern, for it is also a focus on reconciliation.

Attention to Eliot's obsession with polarity in *Four Quartets* reveals a major principle of form in this sequence. By simultaneously emphasizing disparate terms, Eliot actually displaces focus from the terms themselves to the relation between them. For example, in the paradox that in a special sense summarizes the entire sequence—"the fire and the rose are one"—the terms themselves (fire, rose) disappear as separate terms and are replaced by the relation between them that enables the poet to predicate identity. Eliot's habit of focusing on contraries as one way to overcome them goes back at least to his studies on F. H. Bradley in graduate school.[15] Bradley's destruction of metaphysics in *Appearance and Reality* is based partly on the view that although one can only conceive of things or ideas in terms of what they are not (that is, dualistically), one is inevitably nudged by this way of seeing into an ongoing dialectical process that transcends oppositions.

Eliot's tendency in his later work to think in terms of opposites rather than of fragments can be associated with his movement beyond the linear Darwinian models that had been so useful in his early work. In *The Waste Land*, he had adapted the comparative method of Frazer and the social scientists to formulate a working model for "making the modern world possible for art." The reference point in the poem is an ancient unified myth, an ancestor to which all contemporary myths can be related through descent. In *Four Quartets*, Eliot moves beyond the evolutionary model and anticipates a spatial / temporal model somewhat similar to the one outlined in the late forties, fifties, and sixties by Lévi-Strauss. In *The Raw and The Cooked*, the first of his four-volume *Mythologiques* (1964–1971), Lévi-Strauss argues that the mythic mind sees in terms of binary oppositions, whereby a primary opposition is nature (the raw) and culture (the cooked). In analyzing myth, Lévi-Strauss breaks the story down into various elements. He then generalizes the concrete elements into binary opposites, and he ends by claiming that the purpose of myth is to produce a model capable of overcoming opposition. Thus he

15. See "T. S. Eliot and the Revolt Against Dualism: His Dissertation on F. H. Bradley in Its Intellectual Context" in this volume.

sees mythmaking as a primitive form of dialectic. But Lévi-Strauss's ambitions go beyond the primitive mind. He begins with ethnographic experience, but he universalizes his findings. His stated purpose is to draw up an inventory of all mental patterns, to discover the hidden structure of the human mind, and to describe how it works.[16]

Four Quartets came before *The Raw and The Cooked*, and thus there is no question here of influence. But certainly Eliot in his great meditation sees reality in ways that overlap with those later outlined by Lévi-Strauss. The poet and the anthropologist had a number of important theoretical models in common, including Hegelian dialectic and Darwinian evolution. Eliot's doctoral studies included systematic work in the social sciences, and his journalistic activity contains evidence of continuous and highly informed interest in comparative religion, sociology, psychology, and anthropology. Eliot based his "mythical method" primarily on Frazer, and Lévi-Strauss begins "The Structural Study of Myth" (1955) with an 1898 quotation from Franz Boaz, a contemporary of Frazer who used roughly the same method. Lévi-Strauss's epigraph, taken from Boaz's introduction to James Teit's "Traditions of the Thompson River Indians," refers to the precise method Eliot adapted for *The Waste Land*. "It would seem that mythological worlds have been built up only to be shattered again, and that new worlds were built from the fragments." Like Lévi-Strauss, Eliot begins with consideration of models drawn from linear evolution and ends with a synchronic model.

Eliot's focus on binary opposites in *Four Quartets* tends, then, to direct his reader away from terms qua terms to the relation that both unites and separates them. From a slightly different point of view, Eliot may be seen as alerting his reader to the point at which opposites almost or momentarily touch, to intersections or gaps between such polarities as time and eternity, and to the possibilities that are opened by these intersections. The first part of "Burnt Norton" I, for example, introduces age-old puzzles about the meaning of time and eternity, about linear and cyclical patterns in time. The second part describes an experience, the first of many in *Four Quartets*, in which the opposition between time and timelessness is resolved, not through synthesis, nor through dialectic, but through intersection. In

16. Lévi-Strauss, *The Raw and the Cooked*, 10.

this moment of intersection between time and eternity in a rose garden (a gift, not an achievement), this moment of echoed joy, time and eternity meet and overlap in such a way that both their sameness and their difference are apparent. Laughter echoes from "our first world" (childhood, first love, Eden, and more), a world that in being "first" was in time, and in time was lost. But as a world "round the corner" just beyond "the first gate," a world into which the reader is invited by the thrush, that world is present and eternal. Even after the bird says "Go, go, go . . . human kind / Cannot bear much reality," the children's laughter and the bird's song and the unheard music continue to echo in the garden of the poem ("Burnt Norton" V, "Little Gidding" V). And in one of many lines in which the poet addresses his reader directly. "My words [containing the hidden laughter] echo / Thus, in your mind" ("Burnt Norton" I). The "leaves," then, continue, both in time and out of time, to "contain" the laughter of the might-have-been children. And the figured leaves, the dancing leaves, refer in a repeated pun to the leaves of the book of this poem.

A recurrent example of the intersection between time and eternity can be seen in section III of "Burnt Norton," "East Coker," and "The Dry Salvages." In this central part of the poems, a horizontal temporal journey through the darkness unexpectedly intersects with a vertical journey into the darkness that leads paradoxically into the light. A train ride on metalled rails suddenly reveals an alternative journey that is not progression but descent, descent that is also ascent. Section V of each quartet points to another intersection, here between words as words (in time) and words as art (both in and out of time). Eliot again is pointing not to terms or words, but to the cracks between words as the placeless "place" where meaning might be found, as the place to go in order to get beyond time and place.

Another way to approach Eliot's emphasis on relation is to notice his fascination with intermediate states. The voices of the hidden waterfall and of the children in the apple tree within the last part of "Little Gidding" are "half-heard" in the "stillness / Between two waves of the sea." "Betweenness" or relation-in-itself is also important in the earlier poems, and "betweenness" is at the heart of "The Hollow Men."

> Between the idea
> And the reality

> Between the motion
> And the act
> Falls the Shadow

The poet continues with several other parallel statements all emphasizing the relation between opposites, the gap opened by noticing polarities. The shadow also falls between the conception and the creation, the emotion and the response, the desire and the spasm, the potency and the existence, and the essence and the descent. The effect here and throughout *Four Quartets* is to displace focus from term to relation. Eliot's modus operandi in the *Quartets,* then, leads readers to an absence or a gap or a puzzle and then leaves them there to reflect on what can only be guessed, glimpsed, imagined, half-heard. This method is reminiscent of Socrates' method whereby he systematically nonplussed his auditors or led them to an aporia or a fertile impasse.

VI

Though there is but one Center, most people live in centers of their own.—*Heraclitus*

The hint half guessed, the gift half understood, is Incarnation.
—*"The Dry Salvages" V*

An essential part of Eliot's approach to form in *The Waste Land* is his appropriation of a specific myth as a reference point. The myth of choice, Frazer's Ur-myth, is privileged by its presentation as the original myth from which all others descended and from which all others evolved into fragments; it is privileged by its prior-ity in time and its total comprehensiveness. Frazer constructed his monomyth by tracing myths and mythic fragments back through time to a reconstructed hypothetical abstract parent myth. An essential part of Eliot's approach to form in *Four Quartets* is to make problematic all imaginable reference points. "Where is the summer, the unimaginable / Zero summer?" he asks in "Little Gidding" I. The overall sequence can be seen as a radical critique of linear models such as Frazer's monomyth and, at the same time, a critique of cyclical models such as the one outlined in Yeats's *A Vision.* In the very first lines of "Burnt Norton," the poet calls into question both linear and cyclical notions of time and complicates any concept of poetic structure based on traditional models.

159

Eliot's reevaluation of the relationship between past and future includes a critique of the theory of evolution. This critique, implicit throughout the sequence, is explicit in "The Dry Salvages" II.

> It seems, as one becomes older,
> That the past has another pattern, and ceases to be mere
>   sequence—
> Or even development: the latter a partial fallacy,
> Encouraged by superficial notions of evolution,
> Which becomes, in the popular mind, a means of disowning the
>   past.

The use of "seems," "mere," "partial," and "superficial" cancels any suggestion that linear movement is rejected outright. But Eliot does reject the popular notion of evolution, which sees the past as primarily a prelude to the present or as a stage in the development of the race, and he clearly rejects the idea that the present is the highest stage in evolution. He subverts, in brief, the very notions that Frazer, an unabashed positivist, had used in constructing his monomyth, because such concepts oversimplify the present and undercut the reality that the past and future are part of an always present pattern.

Eliot's abandonment of the strenuous metaphysics of high modernism was accompanied by his move toward a position rooted in Christian humility. The "center" in his new system is not a key myth but a key pattern. The pattern is "common" not because, as in Dante, it is shared or known by the general public; not because, as in Frazer, it is a common ancestor of all beliefs, but because it exemplifies both a universal and an individual pattern that is new in every moment. He introduces the pattern in "Burnt Norton" and reiterates it throughout that poem and its successors. In "Burnt Norton" II, he describes his newfound center (or wisdom or meaning, depending on how one translates Heraclitus) in terms of a dance between stillness and movement.

> At the still point of the turning world. Neither flesh nor fleshless;
> Neither from nor towards; at the still point, there the dance is,
> . . . .
> Except for the point, the still point,
> There would be no dance, and there is only the dance.

The key principle or pattern is both diachronic and synchronic, linear and cyclical at once. It is an idea of presence in which past and future, time and timelessness, intersect and are reconciled—not once and for all, but again and again. In the passage from "The Dry Salvages" II quoted above, the poet describes the intersection as "moments of happiness," of "sudden illumination" in which lost experience is restored "In a different form, beyond any meaning / We can assign to happiness." The past, including the prehistoric experience of the race, does not cease to exist, but continues, like a buried stream, to move beneath and as part of the present; moreover, the past is sometimes vividly revived in moments that are in and out of time. Beginning with the experience in the rose garden of "Burnt Norton," many versions of the moment of illumination are presented in the *Quartets*. None of these moments is in itself complete or perfect; each is suggestive, hint-ful—a pledge rather than a full realization of transcendence.

The intersections of time and eternity in *Four Quartets* operate on many levels, including the personal, the aesthetic, the religious, the racial, and the cultural. All of the intersections are religious in the radical sense; that is, they function quite literally as re-binders, re-unifiers (re-ligare). They are not specifically or necessarily Christian, but as Eliot says in "The Dry Salvages" V, the supreme example of the key pattern is the meeting of time and eternity, becoming and being, in the Incarnation of Christ.

> The hint half guessed, the gift half understood, is Incarnation.
> Here the impossible union
> Of spheres of existence is actual,
> Here the past and future
> Are conquered, and reconciled.

This passage describes the principle of incarnation that Eliot adopts as his reference pattern in *Four Quartets*. It is dynamic and open-ended; it contains both past and future, although unlike the monomyth, it faces forward and stimulates the reader to do the same. The reader, compounded of spirit and flesh, mind and matter, provides another example of the principle of incarnation. The poem, in which words move in and out of time, in which words intersect with pattern, is in many ways the most immediate instance of this principle for the sensitive reader.

Again, the principles behind *Four Quartets* can be elucidated by comparing and contrasting Frazer's monomyth in *The Golden Bough* with Lévi-Strauss's "key myth" in *The Raw and The Cooked*. The paradigm changes in the shift from biology to geology, from one temporally focused to one allowing for a far more complex play between temporal and spatial levels. Lévi-Strauss chooses a myth of the Bororo Indians of central Brazil as his "key myth" not because he considers it ancient or superior or central, but because he intuits that it richly exemplifies a pattern he believes is present in many times and places. In *Four Quartets*, Eliot begins with a moment in a rose garden, a moment of happiness or illumination. He did not choose it for its antiquity or its universality, but for its richness in a specific present situation. That it is one version of a pattern present in the Edenic and many other myths corroborates the choice as a fine one. The experience in the rose garden occurs within time and yet suggests the intersection between time and the timeless. It is present, and yet it points to "our first world" and by implication to paradise; it is on several levels both an end and a beginning. It is privileged structurally by appearing first and last in the poem and by being repeated; and because it is associated with such motifs as Eden, first love, salvation, and transcendence, it is thematically charged. The experience in the rose garden, finally, is a hint-ful incarnation, a pledge of a principle that in *The Dry Salvages* he half-guesses and half-understands to be the Incarnation.

In *Four Quartets*, to summarize, Eliot remains interested in the problem of form he had struggled with in his early work. The poetry he writes in response to that challenge changes, however, for as he indicates in "East Coker" V, "one has only learnt to get the better of words / For the thing one no longer has to say, or the way in which / One is no longer disposed to say it." By mastering the mythical method, he outgrew the emotions and ideas that the method had enabled him to express, and he was forced in the *Quartets* to make a new start "with shabby equipment always deteriorating." His attitude toward reference points changes, a change that makes all the difference in his art. Traditionally, the reference point was a given in art. In the early twentieth century, the reference point was made up or brought or constructed. In *Four Quartets,* the reference point is both there and not there. "Where is the summer, the unimaginable / Zero summer?" ("Little Gidding" I). In the face of the aporias opened by human experience, Eliot cultivates and masters a poetic that requires accepting absence (gaps) as openings to transcendence in life and in art.

Mastery and Escape: Eliot's
Dialectical Imagination

The Education of T. S. Eliot

Modernism is one of those troublesome terms that nobody likes but everybody uses. Its congenital imprecision forces thoughtful critics to begin with an apology or, at least, with a definition. In this brief essay, modernism refers to the response in the arts to the epistemological crisis that occurred in Europe and America in the late nineteenth and early twentieth centuries, a crisis in "knowing" precipitated in large part by nineteenth-century biology (evolution) and twentieth-century physics (quantum theory). This slippery beast can be described more precisely as the seemingly abrupt collapse in many fields at once of shared assumptions about the world, assumptions that for several centuries had constituted the frame of reference enabling people to make sense of experience. As an awareness of and a response to the falling apart of traditions, modernism is in essence a religious crisis, because religion is in its essence a resistance to falling apart, a conscious effort to hold Humpty-Dumpty together.

The artists who knew the crisis firsthand described it often enough. In lines that refuse to go away, Yeats cries in "The Second Coming," "Things fall apart; the centre cannot hold." The present time, Eliot laments in "The Modern Mind," "is radically different from any in which poetry has been produced in the past: namely, . . . now there is nothing in which to believe, . . . Belief itself is dead" (*UPUC*, 130). "The modern problem," Auden explains in plain prose in "The Example of Yeats," is "living in a society in which men are no longer supported by tradition without being aware of it."[1] As with other necessities of life—food, say, or water—awareness is a sign of need, and obsession a sign of disaster. When present beneath conscious-

---

1. W. H. Auden, "Yeats as an Example," *Kenyon Review* 10, no. 2 (1948): 191.

ness, the tradition supports and nourishes; when absent beneath consciousness, its absence surfaces as itself a presence, a terrifying presence with teeth and claws. It either feeds us, or it feeds on us. In Eliot's
striking image in "Gerontion": "The tiger springs in the new year. Us
he devours."

The artist, by nature interested in order, by profession dependent
on it (at least as a possibility), must in this situation choose or create
some center, some reference point; the poet must focus on some "jar
in Tennessee," as Wallace Stevens puts it in a famous poem, to make
possible perceiving the world as ordered. Eliot and Auden, after
experimenting with various options, chose Christianity; Yeats, on the
other hand, created his own myth, a bizarre but internally consistent
system that enabled him to cope with contemporary history, with
that nightmare (to use Joyce's image) from which these giants were
struggling to awake. Christianity, of course, was the underlying tradition that had held things together. Its disappearance, not as an
object of conscious individual belief, but as the glue holding Western
civilization together, is the subject of some of the most famous poems
of this century, poems as diverse as Yeats's "The Second Coming"
and Eliot's *The Waste Land*. The poet's focus in each of these high
modernist poems on a special "jar in Tennessee" enables him to perceive order in the panorama of futility and chaos, in Eliot's language,
that is contemporary history.

Piers Gray's *T. S. Eliot's Intellectual and Poetic Development: 1909–
1922* does not mention the word "modernism," but it focuses on the
growth of Eliot's mind in the crucial decade leading up to modernism's annus mirabilis, 1922, the year not only of *The Waste Land*, but
also of Joyce's *Ulysses*.[2] Gray's title, though unimaginative, promises
a guided tour of the labyrinthine streets of Eliot's mind; and more
important, of the rag-and-bone shop where between 1909 and 1911,
alone and unaided, he was making the poems that were to make
history, poems like "The Love Song of J. Alfred Prufrock" and "Preludes." Gray shows Eliot confronting what Auden names "the modern problem" and working through the implications of one alternative after another.

2. Piers Gray, *T. S. Eliot's Intellectual and Poetic Development 1909–1922* (Sussex: Harvester Press, 1982).

The chronological limits of Gray's book encompass the years that arguably are the most important in Eliot's intellectual and poetic development—the years of his formal education at Harvard, the Sorbonne, and Oxford; of his early masterpieces, the first great modernist poems to be written in English; of his collaboration with another eminent modernist, Ezra Pound; of his marriage to a nervous English girl, Vivien Haigh-Wood. His early essays were written during these years, including "Tradition and the Individual Talent," the most celebrated piece of literary criticism in this century. And in these years, the poem of the century was forming itself in his bones.

Gray's subject, the effect of Eliot's education on his poetry and criticism, is often remarked but seldom discussed in a systematic way. The poet's relation to Irving Babbitt and to F. H. Bradley has been discussed in scattered essays, but these discussions have not been particularly illuminating. In the early seventies, two book-length attempts at intellectual biography appeared. John Margolis's *T. S. Eliot's Intellectual Development: 1922–1939,* based primarily on Eliot's *Criterion* commentaries, is a useful account of the poet's intellectual interests *entre deux guerres.* Anne Bolgan's *What the Thunder Really Said* relates Eliot's doctoral studies to the making of *The Waste Land.* Bolgan's work grew out of her collaboration with Eliot in preparing his dissertation for publication.

Gray's analysis is based largely on published philosophical and poetic texts long known to have been assimilated by Eliot, e.g., Bergson's *Matter and Memory* and Bradley's *Appearance and Reality.* But Gray did have privileged access to one fascinating and previously unstudied document: a seminar paper on the interpretation of primitive ritual read by Eliot on 9 December 1913 in Josiah Royce's seminar at Harvard. Gray quotes, with Mrs. Eliot's permission, large chunks of this handwritten manuscript. As background to the development of high modernism's most famous (or infamous) method, the "mythical method" of *The Waste Land* and *Ulysses,* this material is itself worth more than the price of Gray's book.

Gray's approach to intellectual biography is straightforward. He focuses on certain late nineteenth- and early twentieth-century figures—Laforgue, Bergson, Royce, Frazer, Durkheim, and Bradley—who were indisputably important in the growth of Eliot's mind. Approaching these "mentors" one at a time in the order in which Eliot encountered them, Gray tries to pinpoint the unique contribution each made to Eliot's intellectual development. To show the difference they made, he offers a "before" and "after" picture of Eliot's mind with respect to each. And to substantiate his belief that each enabled Eliot to make a poetic leap, he offers some midair shots of this daring young intellectual gymnast.

Gray does not peddle any precise thesis regarding Eliot's intellectual development, but he does proceed on certain assumptions regarding the nature of Eliot's mind. For example, he assumes, and he is surely right, that Eliot's mind is like the one described in "Tradition and the Individual Talent," a mind that develops and changes but abandons nothing en route, a mind that does not superannuate Laforgue as it moves on to Bergson and Frazer, a mind that becomes more and more complicated, more and more comprehensive.

Gray also assumes, though he does not say so, that Eliot is threading his way through the modernist dilemma. Even as an undergraduate, Eliot is seen to be preoccupied with questions that concern the self, questions about disorientation, displacement, self-possession, self-consciousness, and consciousness of consciousness. Eliot's discovery of Laforgue, who had polished to a high sheen his own awareness of the discrepancies between the surface life and the hidden life, the social self and the inner self, amounts to a discovery of himself that permits a poetic breakthrough. Almost immediately, though, Eliot leaps beyond Laforgue. Beneath the surface, Laforgue sees the Ideal—mysterious, but positive; but beneath the brittle surface of politesse, Eliot glimpses horrors that send him scampering back to the drawing room. Shuddering at the horror of being civilized when the traditions supporting civilization have crumbled, Eliot moves gingerly on to Bergson. But Bergson, like Laforgue before him and like all his successors, gives with one hand and takes back with the other. His insights on memory and intuition permit breakthroughs in art but lead spiritually and intellectually into a dead-end logic of defeat. And so it goes with the other masters who appear and, like April, whisper promises they cannot keep. Gray ends with Eliot's temporary refuge in Bradley, a philosophic giant who had asked himself Eliot's overwhelming questions and had come up with formal principles to deal with them. Using Bradley's doctrine of the systematic nature of truth, Gray discusses "Gerontion" and *The Waste Land*. The Bradleyan terms he appropriates, "comprehensiveness" and "coherence," are specifically applicable to Eliot's needs, and generally applicable to all those in his age who wanted more than anything else to connect, even if they ended by connecting nothing with nothing. Gray concludes with chapters that should be much better than they are. In the last, "The Coherence of the Poetry of Incoherence," he takes on "Gerontion" and *The Waste Land* but adds little to what we knew before he appeared. He has found some keys but seems too tired to slip them into the lock.

Both the weaknesses and the strengths of Gray's book may be related to its origin as a dissertation. His transitions tend to be graceless (to begin with, the next step is, it is important to note), and his outline is almost visible. Gray frequently relates background material in detail that suggests he himself is wading through it in search of the stone that will permit him to step over into Eliot's poetry. Gray's bibliography is a long one that includes most of the basic materials, but omits a few obvious studies. He does not include, for example, Anne Bolgan's *What the Thunder Really Said*, an important book on the influence of Royce and Bradley on Eliot.

These slight weaknesses notwithstanding, Gray's book is an important contribution to modernist studies. The validity of his emphasis on the range and complexity of Eliot's mind and on the intelligent comprehensiveness of his poetry is undeniable. The importance of the intellectual masters Gray elects to discuss is also beyond dispute. And in general, the soundness of his analyses is apparent. Unlike many critics who pick up their philosophy from handbooks, Gray seems to have acquired his from the philosophy texts in question. Everything considered, *T. S. Eliot's Intellectual and Poetic Development* is valuable because it adds substantially to our understanding of T. S. Eliot. Gray has clarified to a great extent the unfolding mind of a poet who in subsequent centuries will be taken as a foremost representative of the twentieth century. To demand more when so much has been given would be less than civil.

T. S. Eliot and the Revolt Against Dualism

His Dissertation on F. H. Bradley in its Intellectual Context

In 1915 and 1916, T. S. Eliot wrote a Ph.D. dissertation on the episte-mology of F. H. Bradley. Some critics, such as Hugh Kenner, be-lieve that Bradley is important only for flavor. "Bradley has an attrac-tive mind, though he has perhaps nothing to tell us. He is an experi-ence, like the taste of nectarines or the style of Henry James."[1] Eliot himself commented on the relationship several times and in every instance downplayed its importance.[2] Once, however, when writing about Bradley in an unselfconscious way, focusing on Bradley's gen-eral significance for an audience that knew nothing of his own debts to the philosopher, Eliot was unambiguous in his testimony that a close study of Bradley's work is transformative. In an obituary arti-cle, he insists that Bradley had

> the finest philosophic style in our language, [one] in which acute intellect and passionate feeling preserve a classic balance. . . . [Upon] those who will surrender patient years to the understand-ing of his meaning . . . his writings perform that mysterious and complete operation which transmutes not one department of thought only, but the whole intellectual and emotional tone of their being. To them, in the living generation, the news of his death has brought an intimate and private grief.[3]

By the time Eliot finished his dissertation in 1916, he had surrendered those patient years. Those who know of his own lifelong struggle to

---

THIS PAPER is a revision of a speech given at Duke University on 15 February 1988.

1. Kenner, *The Invisible Poet*, 63.

2. For example, Eliot says in the 1964 preface to his dissertation that he does not pretend to understand it, although he admits that his "prose style was formed on that of Bradley" (*KE*, 10–11).

3. T. S. Eliot, "A Commentary," *Criterion* 3, no. 9 (October 1924): 2.

172

nurture both intellect and feeling and to preserve them in classic balance will find the tribute moving and convincing.

But what of the dissertation? Did the patient years surrendered to following Bradley's meaning make a difference in Eliot's poetry and his literary criticism? In several articles written between 1979 and 1986, I maintained that Bradley profoundly influenced both the shape and the content of Eliot's work; and in *Reading The Waste Land: Modernism and the Limits of Interpretation* (1990), Joseph Bentley and I demonstrate through a close reading of *The Waste Land* that an awareness of Bradley's ideas can be enormously helpful in understanding Eliot's contribution to modernism. Several recent critics have also focused on the relevance of Eliot's early work on Bradley. Sanford Schwartz, for example, clearly demonstrates in *The Matrix of Modernism* (1985) that an awareness of Eliot's early philosophical studies, especially of his work on Bradley's epistemology, is immediately helpful in understanding Eliot's criticism and his position in the modernist revolution.

The context into which I would like to put Eliot's dissertation is what the *Times Literary Supplement*, in a leading article in September, 1926, called "The Dethronement of Descartes." After describing the last three hundred years in Western philosophy as a development of Cartesianism, the writer claims that Descartes and the great physicist-philosophers of the seventeenth century had been dethroned by the physicists and philosophers of the early twentieth, ushering in a new dispensation in intellectual history. Eliot, an occasional contributor to and regular reader of the *TLS*, had made the same point some months earlier in his Clark Lectures at Trinity College, Cambridge. After quoting a passage from *Meditations* (the sixth), he maintains that Descartes's crude reasoning is behind the pseudoscience of epistemology that has haunted the Western mind for the last three centuries.[4] Eliot's focus is on poetry, the *TLS* writer's focus is on philosophy, but both are focused on the twentieth-century's rebellion against the seventeenth, and both identify the deposed monarch as Descartes. A few years earlier in 1921, Eliot had

---

4. T. S. Eliot, *Varieties of Metaphysical Poetry: The Clark Lectures at Trinity College, Cambridge 1926 and The Turnbull Lectures at The Johns Hopkins University 1933*, ed. Ronald Schuchard (London: Faber and Faber, 1993), 81.

reviewed Grierson's *Metaphysical Lyrics and Poems of the Seventeenth Century*, a review included in *Selected Essays* under the title "The Metaphysical Poets." His dispensational analysis of English poetry in that review is explicitly based on the realization that in the seventeenth century, something "happened to the mind of England." That something was the triumph of dualistic thinking, and that triumph produced, to use Eliot's phrase, "a dissociation of sensibility."

> The poets of the seventeenth century . . . possessed a mechanism of sensibility which could devour any kind of experience. . . . In the seventeenth century a dissociation of sensibility set in, from which we have never recovered. (*SE*, 247)

Mind and matter, thought and feeling, subject and object, fell apart; poets thought and felt by starts and fits. In phrases now famous, Eliot claims that before Descartes took over the Western mind, poets could feel their thoughts and think their feelings. They could feel their thoughts as immediately as they could smell the odor of a rose.

A brilliant account of Descartes' dethronement is given in A. O. Lovejoy's *Revolt Against Dualism*. Lovejoy argues that Western thought has been dominated for three centuries by the assumptions of Descartes, Locke, and Newton. These geniuses all believed that the subject and the object were separable, that objectivity was possible and even necessary for understanding the world. But early twentieth-century philosophers, in Lovejoy's account, joined in an attempt to escape from this epistemological dualism of subject and object as well as from the parallel psychophysical dualism of mind and matter.[5] The realization that subject and object are connected in a systematic way and that mind and body are aspects of a single world is in effect a dethronement of Descartes. Lovejoy's argument, articulated in 1929, anticipates the work of such intellectual historians as Thomas Kuhn, Gerald Holton, and Jacob Bronowski.[6] His thesis, like theirs, is helpful in approaching modern thinkers in many fields. Most of the figures who shaped the twentieth-century mind, figures

5. Arthur O. Lovejoy, *The Revolt Against Dualism: An Inquiry Concerning the Existence of Ideas* (1929; rpt. La Salle, IL: Open Court, 1955), 1–4.

6. See Thomas S. Kuhn, *The Structure of Scientific Revolutions*, 2nd ed (Chicago: University of Chicago Press, 1970); Gerald Holton, *Thematic Origins of Scientific Thought: Kepler to Einstein* (Cambridge: Harvard University Press, 1973), and Jacob Bronowski, *The Common Sense of Science* (Cambridge: Harvard University Press, n.d.).

as diverse as Freud, Heisenberg, Picasso, Royce, and Eliot, have in common an about-face on the subject-object question and the mind-matter question; they all try to discredit the dualism that arbitrarily splits the world into pieces. Russell and the neorealists refuse to give up the subject-object distinction, but they too join in rejecting the division of the world into mind and matter.

Russell is, of course, important in Eliot's personal revolt against dualism. He was Eliot's teacher at Harvard and his benefactor in the early London years. In the fall of 1915, while Eliot was writing his dissertation on Bradley, he and his bride moved in with Russell. At this time Russell was specifically involved in trying to overcome the distinction between mind and matter, maintaining, for example, that sense-data are the ultimate constituents of matter; on the other hand, he was strenuously holding to the dualism of subject and object. Russell's general point of view at this time is preserved in *Mysticism and Logic,* a book that Eliot reviewed, in the process displaying an in-depth knowledge of Russell's work.[7] There can be no doubt that Eliot learned much from Russell; at the same time, there can be no doubt of Eliot's early and fundamental dissent, already clearly evident in the dissertation. In chapter IV, he analyzes Russell's realism and concludes by rejecting Russell's dualism:

> The curious dualism of Mr. Russell . . . which has much in common with obvious, though I can hardly think correct, interpretations of Plato, will not hold good of a world which is always partially in time, but never wholly in time, with respect to any of its elements. (*KE,* 101)

For a detailed and slightly different account of Eliot's indebtedness to Russell, I recommend Richard Shusterman's *T. S. Eliot and the Philosophy of Criticism* (1988). Shusterman's discussion of the philosophical underpinnings of Eliot's literary criticism is valuable, despite his overstatement of Russell's importance in Eliot's development. By all accounts, of course, Eliot's situation in late 1915 was extraordinary. He was a close student of both Bradley and Russell; he had studied with Bradley's friend and disciple Harold Joachim and with Russell himself. And now, while writing a dissertation explaining and in general defending Bradley against Russell, Eliot found himself face

7. T. S. Eliot, "Style and Thought," *Nation* 22, no. 25 (23 March 1918): 768–69.

to face with Russell across the breakfast table. Moreover, as the husband of a fragile wife to whom both (each in his own way) were devoted, Eliot must have found life to be a kaleidoscope of brilliant and fluctuating patterns.

The subject of this paper, however, is not Russell, but Bradley, one generation older, living in seclusion at Oxford, and generally considered as the greatest living philosopher. Bradley was a trailblazer in intellectual history, with insights anticipating and paralleling those of Heisenberg in physics and Picasso in painting. He was an unflinching leader in the revolt against dualism; and from the beginning of his career, he was a radical skeptic who rejected the notion that there is such a thing as objectivity or objective truth. Like all idealists, he believed that everything is connected to everything else in a systematic way and that everything is part of a single all-encompassing whole. He believed, consequently, that every perspective is partial and incomplete and thus, to use his terminology, an appearance.

Bradley is labelled an idealist, and often a "Neo-Hegelian," labels that are true in a sense but very misleading to the casually informed. He began his work with one foot in German idealism but with the other firmly planted on the ground, the ground being British empiricism. His distinction is that he forged these two traditions into a synthesis, a synthesis preserving the intellectual *and* the experiential—in Eliot's words, intellect and feeling. Bradley believed, with Hegel, that reality is an all-encompassing unity; but he disagreed with Hegel's first principle, that is, with the notion that the real is of the nature of thought, that it is intellectual—to use a Hegelian vocabulary, that the real is the rational.

> Unless thought stands for something that falls beyond mere intelligence, . . . a lingering scruple still forbids us to believe that reality can ever be purely rational. It may come from a failure in my metaphysics, or from a weakness of the flesh which continues to blind me, but the notion that existence could be the same as understanding strikes as cold and ghost-like as the dreariest materialism.[8]

Bradley believed that the real *includes* the intellectual, but like Locke and the British empiricists, he believed that everything begins

8. Bradley, *Principles of Logic*, 2:590–91.

and ends in experience. As Eliot correctly stated in his 1927 review of *Ethical Studies*, "Bradley is thoroughly empirical, much more empirical than the philosophers he opposed" (*SE*, 403). The philosophers he opposed, of course, lived in a world dominated by Newton and Descartes, and to them, experience consisted of a subject, who does the experiencing, and an object, which is experienced; to them, experience has two parts, mind and matter. Bradley retained their commitment to experience but dropped their dualism. Like Wordsworth, he believed that the universe is a living whole, that mind and matter, subject and object, are parts of a single whole. Bradley changed subject and object from nouns to adjectives, from things-in-themselves to the subjective and objective aspects of experience.

One must understand Bradley's empiricism to understand his work. It is best to think of him not as an idealist but as an idealist-empiricist, as much a part of British empiricism as of German idealism. In keeping with his Lockean roots, Bradley claims that "Everything is experience" and also that "experience is one." "There is but one Reality," he insists, "and its being consists in experience. In this one whole all appearances come together."[9] Now we are compelled by language to think of experience as "my" experience, or as some other person's experience. To the extent that we think of it in this way, we are missing Bradley's point and lapsing into dualism. He is not speaking of experience as something that is experienced by an experiencer but as something that simply is, as a complex that encompasses experiencer and experienced. The Absolute is experience, and it systematically includes everything that exists or can be imagined to exist. We can, with minimal distortion, think of Bradley's Absolute as a complete inventory of all experiences that have ever existed or will ever exist. This means, of course, that his Absolute itself does not yet exist in its completeness and will do so only in the moment when all experience is finished and comprehended. In that moment, it will also cease to exist.

The revolt against dualism is immediately helpful in understanding *Appearance and Reality*, the main Bradleyan text behind Eliot's dissertation. Bradley's field here is metaphysics, which he defines on his first page as "the attempt to know reality as against mere appearance." For unsuspecting literary critics, this definition will be

9. Bradley, *Appearance and Reality*, 405, 403.

congruous with a common literary theme, the opposition between appearance and reality, such as one finds in the plays of Shakespeare or the poems of Dickinson. But let us, briefly, take a closer look. Bradley's book is divided into two parts, one on appearance and one on reality. The first is a devastating attack on traditional ways of attempting to understand truth or first principles. Thinking by its very nature divides reality into this and that, into temporal and spatial, into body and soul, into mind and matter, into subject and object. All of these divisions collapse under scrutiny into self-contradiction. The second part of Bradley's book is called "Reality," and for the casual reader, it will promise Bradley's alternative to appearance. But instead of an alternative, the reader finds the disconcerting suggestion that appearance and reality are not opposites at all. An appearance is reality in any less than comprehensive aspect. Bradley's reality is not an abstraction lying behind the appearances in the external world. "The Absolute *is* its appearances, it really is all and every one of them,"—not all totalled together, but all unified.[10]

Eliot's dissertation springs to life when it is understood in the context of the revolt against dualism. His purpose is to explain and to some extent to defend Bradley's epistemology. Now epistemology, the investigation of how we know what we know, is by definition dualistic. It involves a systematic analysis of subjects and objects and their relations. The central Bradleyan insight, however, is that the world is one, that reality is one, that dualism always leads to self-contradiction; and in fact, Bradley argues that there can be no such thing as epistemology, and Eliot agrees with him. The epistemology that Bradley and Eliot reject is the activity of that name fathered by Descartes and nurtured by Kant. Ten years later, in the Clark Lectures, long after Eliot had abandoned philosophy as a career, he speaks scornfully of epistemology as a pseudo-science.[11] But in the dissertation, he says he is trying to elucidate and criticize Bradley's "theory of knowledge." At any rate we must insist, as Lovejoy does, that knowing is part of being human, and that denying one has a theory of knowing clearly indicates that one is theorizing about knowledge. Eliot's dissertation, then, is the attempt by a man who

10. Bradley, *Appearance and Reality*, 431.
11. See Eliot, *Varieties of Metaphysical Poetry*, 81.

does not believe in epistemology to explain the epistemology of a man who denies that epistemology exists.

In the opening chapter, Eliot tries to get behind the dualism implicit in his subject by grounding Bradley's theory of knowledge in something that is not dualistic. He does this, first, by making the case for Bradley's all-encompassing empiricism. "Reality, . . . the ultimate criterion which gives meaning to all our judgments, . . . is our experience" (KE, 32). He proceeds by positing "immediate experience" as a predualistic unity, as a precognitional condition, arguing that epistemology can only begin after we have fallen away from this unity. We are forced, Eliot says, "in building up our theory of knowledge, to postulate something given upon which knowledge is founded" (KE, 17). That something given, "immediate experience," is a knowing-and-being-in-one that precedes subjects and objects. Epistemology or the speculation on subjects and objects, experiencers and experienced, follows and builds upon "immediate experience" (KE, 16).

The first chapter also argues that knowing is self-transcendent, that it reaches beyond itself and is taken up in a larger unity. Eliot thus situates "epistemology" in the realm of "appearance," in the dualistic realm of relations. "Thinking" emerges from and moves toward feeling or experience, and in his own analysis of subjects and objects, Eliot is always careful to indicate his awareness that his activity is sandwiched between the beginning and the end. His conclusion in the last paragraph of chapter one is:

> We are led to the conception of an all-inclusive experience outside of which nothing shall fall. If anyone object that mere experience at the beginning and complete experience at the end are hypothetical limits, I can say not a word in refutation for this would be just the reverse side of what opinions I hold. (KE, 31)

The second chapter of Eliot's dissertation takes up the question of what Lovejoy calls psychophysical dualism, or as the chapter title puts it, the "Distinction of Real and Ideal." The main point of the chapter is that such distinctions are invalid, mainly because the real and the ideal are dependent on each other for existence. They are systematically intertwined in such a way that if one appears, the other does, and if one dissolves, the other cannot survive. Eliot admits that immediate experience falls apart of itself into subjects and

179

objects, mind and matter, but he insists that this dualism is "tentative and provisional, a moment in a process" (*KE*, 32). The process, ever repeated, never ending, is the movement from the unity of immediate experience to the unity of transcendent experience. Distinctions such as real and ideal are relative and depend upon focusing on one part from one point of view, a process that automatically generates an opposite, an other-than. Epistemology, the study of subjects and objects, then, can only be carried on from some relative and shifting point of view.

The next three chapters of Eliot's dissertation are deconstructions of two approaches to knowledge, that of the psychologist, who thinks in terms of mental content and external reality (mind and matter), and that of the epistemologist, who thinks in terms of subjects and objects. Eliot criticizes the psychologist by adopting the epistemologist's stance or point of view. Then shifting his point of view, he criticizes the epistemologist by adopting the psychologist's point of view. He evaluates idealism from the point of view of realism and vice versa. His point is that neither is right, that both are relative, that either can be reduced to its so-called opposite. Eliot's philosophical skepticism and his dialectical rhetoric make it possible to find statements that support opposite points of view, statements that contradict each other. This will not disturb those who understand his method and his position, stated at the opening of his last chapter, that every theory depends on adopting some point of view, and that every point of view is no more than one point of view. The fact is that any epistemology can be undermined fatally simply by shifting one's point of view. Standing foursquare on Bradley's argument, Eliot concludes:

> No [valid] definition can anywhere be found to throw the mental on one side and the physical on the other; . . . the difference between the mental and the real, or . . . the personal and the objective, is one of practical convenience and varies at every moment. (*KE*, 84)

We divide the world into mental and physical, but "the mental resolves into a curious and intricate mechanism, and the physical reveals itself as a mental construct" (*KE*, 154). Both Bradley and Eliot are attempting to show that all thinking is relational, that any truth can be dissolved into its opposite, and that since thinking takes place in a space between mere experience and complete experience, it can only proceed from one limited point of view or another. Thinking is always relative, always tentative, never final.

In the last chapter of his dissertation, Eliot drops the dialectical method and summarizes his own conclusions. Although he objects to a number of points from Bradley's *Principles of Logic*, he accepts the validity of the major arguments in *Appearance and Reality*. "I believe," he says, "that all of the conclusions that I have reached are in substantial agreement with *Appearance and Reality*" (*KE*, 158). Eliot specifically affirms the following Bradleyan positions.

1. Reality is experience. His own words: "From first to last, Reality is experience" (*KE*, 165).

2. Reality is one. To quote Eliot: "We are forced to the assumption that truth is one, and to the assumption that reality is one" (*KE*, 168).

3. Reality is all-comprehensive. The clearest one-sentence statement of this is in his first chapter: "We are led to the conception of an all-inclusive experience outside of which nothing shall fall" (*KE*, 31).

4. Reality is systematic. For it to include everything and still be *one* thing, it *must* be systematic. This simply means that everything is connected to everything else, and that any "new fact" that comes into being instantly becomes part of something bigger than itself, part of a system of reality. Eliot's words:

> Facts are not merely found in the world and laid together like bricks, but every fact has in a sense its place prepared before it arrives, and without the implication of a system in which it belongs the fact is not a fact at all. (*KE*, 60)

5. All relations are internal. Eliot says that he is compelled to accept the "most important" doctrine of the internality of relations (*KE*, 153). The compulsion comes from logic. If everything is a systematic part of one thing, then all relations or connections are between fragments or parts, and relations are inside the all-comprehensive totality. This is important in part because it means that nothing has its meaning alone, that no action is isolated in its significance. Any change or adjustment or development in any one part changes the whole. In the opposite doctrine, the one Eliot denies, entities are complete in themselves. Thus, relations connecting them are external to each entity, and moreover, changes in any one entity affect only that one entity.

6. Finally, Eliot says he is also compelled to accept the idea of degrees of truth, degrees of reality (*KE*, 153). "The only real truth is the whole truth," he says (*KE*, 163), but the fact that no one can know the *whole* truth does not mean no one can know truth. Partial truth is truth, to a degree. He maintains that everything, including falsehoods, errors, and hallucinations, is part of reality. Eliot illustrates this by discussing the reality status of the bear that a frightened child "thinks it sees" in its bedroom. "It is . . . not altogether true or altogether false to say that the child sees a bear." The doctrine of degrees of truth allows him to accept both the bear in the nursery and the bear in the woods as real without requiring him to agree that they have the same status in truth and reality (*KE*, 115–16). Or, to take an example that forms part of Eliot's argument with Russell, references to the "present king of France" are and are not references to something that exists. The doctrine of degrees of reality permits him to distinguish the "present king of France" from the present king of a country like England that still has a monarch. Both are real, though not in the same way (*KE*, 127ff). All imaginable truth, then, is partial, although some truths are fuller than other truths.

These principles are everywhere evident in Eliot's literary and social criticism and also in his account of history. No doctrine is more important than the doctrine of wholeness, no word more ubiquitous in his prose. In talking about other writers, for example, he insists that the plays of Shakespeare are one play, the novels of James one novel, that none of these works have meaning alone, that all are *systematically* connected. Otherwise, of course, he could not consider many plays as *one* play, many novels as *one* novel. All six of the points just outlined are prominent features of Eliot's doctrine of tradition and the individual talent. Tradition involves the historical sense, which

> compels a man to write not merely with his own generation in his bones, but with a feeling that the whole of the literature of Europe from Homer and within it the whole of the literature of his own country has a simultaneous existence and composes a simultaneous order. (*SE*, 4)

Eliot describes the relation between artists within the tradition as well as between the tradition and individual artists. By doing so, he provides a textbook example of the doctrines of the internality of relations and the systematic nature of the whole.

> No poet, no artist of any art, has his complete meaning alone. . . . You . . . must set him, for contrast and comparison, among the dead. . . . The necessity that he shall conform . . . is not onesided; what happens when a new work of art is created is something that happens simultaneously to all the works of art which preceded it. The existing monuments form an ideal order among themselves, which is modified by the introduction of the new . . . work of art among them. The existing order is complete before the new work arrives; for order to persist after the supervention of novelty, the whole existing order must be . . . altered; and so the relations, proportions, values of each work of art toward the whole are readjusted. . . . Whoever has approved this idea of order . . . will not find it preposterous that the past should be altered by the present as much as the present is directed by the past. (*SE*, 4–5)

What keeps this from being preposterous is the doctrine of internal relations. If every artist is related within an organic and systematic whole, then any alteration in any part changes both every other part and the whole itself; similarly, any change in any part of one's body affects not just that part but other parts and the person as a whole. Thus one can say not only that *The Divine Comedy* alters *The Waste Land,* but also that *The Waste Land* alters *The Divine Comedy* and the tradition in which both participate. Eliot's notions about organic wholes and systems of art are repeated in the opening paragraphs of "The Function of Criticism" (*SE*, 12–13).

These ideas are also helpful in reading Eliot's poetry. "Gerontion" and the so-called quatrain poems were written on the heels of the dissertation, and the principles Eliot accepted from Bradley's philosophy are everywhere apparent. To take "Gerontion" as an example: One of its major subjects is history; and Eliot brings in everything from the war between the Greeks and the Persians at Thermopylae, several centuries before Christ, to the First World War and the treaty at Versailles in 1919, the very year he was writing the poem. Not only does he bring in everything, he forces the reader to see that everything is systematically connected, that all relations are internal, fragment to fragment, both within history and within the poem; and he

183

compels the reader to connect these whirling fragments into a unity. His use of allusion and juxtaposition, his collapse of time and space, his comprehensiveness and complexity—all of these and more are inseparable from Bradley's ideas. Eliot incorporates other complicated influences, of course. Frazer is there, and so are Théophile Gautier, Ezra Pound, and others. But Bradley is at issue here, and Bradley is of the essence. The structure of the poem is based on the Bradleyan principle of the systematic nature of truth, on self-transcendence of parts always leading toward greater, more inclusive wholes. The last lines of the poem—"Tenants of the house, / Thoughts of a dry brain in a dry season"—provide the major structural clue. Eliot has composed the poem as a complex of houses within houses within houses, all decayed, all crumbling. Gerontion's dry thoughts are contained in his dry brain, which is contained in his desiccated body, which is contained in his crumbling house in his rocky yard in war-torn Europe in Western civilization over thousands of years, and all of these are contained in a whirling cosmos. Both the content and the form of the form illustrate Bradleyan principles.[12]

The epistemology, or theory of knowing, outlined and in its major points defended in Eliot's dissertation rests upon the metaphysics. All knowledge, Bradley argues, begins and ends in experience. Knowing occurs in three stages which are also three levels of experience.[13] The first and most foundational is "immediate experience," the second is "relational experience," and the most comprehensive is "transcendent experience." Immediate experience is experience that has not been mediated through the mind; it is a knowing and feeling and being in one prior to the development of logical or temporal or spatial categories. The first chapter of Eliot's dissertation, "On our Knowledge of Immediate Experience," reviews an essay by Bradley of the same title. The point of both is to postulate a starting point for knowledge, a foundation upon which knowledge can be built and to which it can return. Eliot defines this doctrine by quoting *Appearance and Reality*. Immediate experience is:

12. See "The Structure of Eliot's 'Gerontion': An Interpretation Based on Bradley's Doctrine of the Systematic Nature of Truth" in this volume.
13. For a fuller discussion of Bradley's levels of experience, see "F. H. Bradley's Doctrine of Experience in T. S. Eliot's *The Waste Land* and *Four Quartets*" in this volume.

> first, the general condition before distinctions and relations have been developed, and where as yet neither subject nor object exists. And . . . second . . . anything which is present at any stage of mental life, in so far as that is only present and simply is. (*KE*, 16)

In a later essay, Bradley defines immediate experience with even greater clarity:

> We in short have experience in which there is no distinction between my awareness and that of which it is aware. There is an immediate feeling, a knowing and being in one, with which knowledge begins; and, though this in a manner is transcended, it nevertheless remains throughout as the present foundation of my known world. And if you remove this direct sense of my momentary contents and being, you bring down the whole of consciousness in one common wreck. For it is in the end ruin to divide experience into something on one side experienced as an object, and on the other side, something, not experienced at all.[14]

As an example of immediate experience, Eliot describes the viewing of a painting in which the viewer is so absorbed that he has no consciousness of self or subject, on the one side, and painting or object, on the other. This directly experienced nonrelational many-in-one is not the viewer's experience, for he as subject and the painting as object do not yet exist. When he becomes aware of "his" experience and of the painting as other than himself, then immediate experience has dissolved into the realm of relations, of self and not-self (*KE*, 20). *Four Quartets* contains several references to immediate experience, for example, the "music heard so deeply / That it is not heard at all" ("The Dry Salvages" V).

Immediate experience is by definition transitory. As one becomes conscious of the self, of the world in itself, of surrounding people and things as other, immediate experience dissolves into the dualistic realm of subjects and objects. The intellect, which hitherto has been an undiscriminated part of experience, assumes dominance and experience becomes relational. Reality can no longer be apprehended immediately, but is filtered through the mind. Most waking experience takes place at the level of relations, as the conscious self moves

---

14. F. H. Bradley, *Essays on Truth and Reality* (1914; rpt. Oxford: Clarendon Press, 1950), 159–60.

through the day and organizes experience into working categories such as present and past, knower and known, self and other. All of these categories are abstractions from experience; all are partial. This is the level of all analytical thinking, of all philosophy, including epistemology, and this level is the major subject of Eliot's dissertation, which is in simplest terms an analysis of the nature of objects. This level is unavoidable, for to quote Eliot, "the only way in which we can handle reality intellectually is to turn it into objects, and the justification of this operation is that the world we live in has been built in this way" (*KE*, 159).

Immediate experience can be known only through reflection and intuition after it has dissolved. Time does not exist in immediate experience, but immediate experience does exist in time, for it does not last. In the following lines from "Burnt Norton," Eliot describes relational experience, the level at which we are not fully conscious because our consciousness is primarily intellectual and reductive.

> Time past and time future
> Allow but a little consciousness.
> To be conscious is not to be in time
> But only in time can the moment in the rose-garden,
> The moment in the arbour where the rain beat,
> The moment in the draughty church at smokefall
> Be remembered; involved with past and future.
> Only through time time is conquered. ("Burnt Norton" II)

If immediate experience were all that one had, in a paradoxical way, one would not even have *it*, for only in time can one remember immediate experience and thereby in a sense begin to conquer time.

A third level, in Bradley's view, a transcendent experience, permits a return of sorts to the wholeness and unity of immediate experience. Immediate experience exists before relations, but transcendent experience exists after or above relations. Immediate experience dissolves of itself into relational experience, but relational experience resists resolution into the higher monistic experience. The villain is the discursive intellect, and the transcendence of relations such as self and other or space and time becomes largely a matter of reforming the discursive intellect from a servant of division and fragmentation to a partner in the achievement of wholeness. Whereas immediate experience is characterized by a *knowing* and feeling in one that comes before intellection, transcendent experience is characterized by a *thinking* and feeling in one that comes after and is achieved through intellection.

This idea of transcendent experience is readily illustrated from *Four Quartets,* which in a number of passages reads like Bradley versified. The following lines are from "The Dry Salvages" II:

> We had the experience but missed the meaning,
> And approach to the meaning restores the experience
> In a different form, beyond any meaning
> We can assign to happiness.

We had the immediate experience, say, the moment in the draughty church at smokefall, but because in immediate experience one simply exists as part of a larger unity, we were not conscious of meaning. But in relational experience, by remembering and reflecting, we can approach the meaning in such a way that it will be restored in a more complex and comprehensive form. That form will be transcendent experience, and it will take us beyond the relational level where we are aware of *assigning* meanings to happiness.

The idea of transcendent experience runs throughout Eliot's literary and religious criticism. The famous notion of the unified sensibility in the essay on "The Metaphysical Poets" is one of his numerous uses of transcendent experience. A number of critics have said that when Eliot refers to "a direct sensuous apprehension of thought, or a recreation of thought into feeling" (*SE,* 246), he is referring to immediate experience. But it is clear from his terminology that he is describing transcendent experience. One of Bradley's favorite terms for transcendent experience is "felt thought." This is precisely the language that Eliot uses to distinguish between the poets of the seventeenth and the nineteenth centuries. This is a unity that comes after thought, not before it. It is a complex of feeling and thinking in one.

There is no doubt that Eliot shared this general view of relational experience as enclosed in an envelope of undiscriminated, felt, nonrelational totality. He says so in plain words at the end of the first chapter of his dissertation. To Eliot, then, as to Bradley, immediate experience at the beginning (that is, before—yet including—intellectual consciousness) and transcendent experience at the end (that is, after—yet including—intellectual consciousness) are not mere hypothetical limits to the comprehended dualistic sphere of relational experience. Together, they constitute the reality that makes possible the construction of the relational world, the everyday world of appearances.

In summary: several pervasive principles in Eliot's work directly parallel principles in Bradley's philosophy.

1. Analytical thinking shatters the unity between knowing and feeling by breaking reality into thinking subject and object of thought. Thinking is intrinsically limited in part because it can only proceed from one thinking subject, from one point of view, at a time. This means that the movement toward truth involves, not only development of one point of view, but also migration from one interpretation to another, occupation of as many perspectives as possible. A main principle associated with greater degrees of truth and reality is comprehensiveness, so the more comprehensive, the more true. These matters are evident everywhere in Eliot, but nowhere more than in the multiple points of view within his poetry. In *The Waste Land,* for example, Eliot attempts to speak through many voices, from many points of view, from many times and places, all at once.

2. Language is necessarily and profoundly reductive; moreover, its grammar and syntax skew propositions. Over and over in his dissertation, Eliot says that "when we try to press an exact meaning, we find language forcing untenable theories upon us" (*KE*, 129–30). In the first chapter, he speaks of the "embarrassment" to our theories created by the fact that we have to reduce them to words. Constantly he shows an awareness of being caught in the language trap. He says, for example, "In describing immediate experience we must use terms which offer a surreptitious suggestion of subject or object" (*KE*, 22). This suspicion of language is also evident in Eliot's poetry. Prufrock is terrified by language, and Sweeney moans "I gotta use words when I talk to you." Moreover, at the heart of each of the *Four Quartets* is an "intolerable wrestle with words and meaning." In "East Coker," for example, Eliot refers to twenty years of

> Trying to learn to use words, and every attempt
> Is a wholly new start, and a different kind of failure
> Because one has only learnt to get the better of words
> For the thing one no longer has to say, or the way in which
> One is no longer disposed to say it. And so each venture

> Is a new beginning, a raid on the inarticulate
> With shabby equipment always deteriorating
> In the general mess of imprecision of feeling,
> Undisciplined squads of emotion. ("East Coker" V)

3. Eliot's rhetoric, the way he develops his discussions, is deeply indebted to Bradley's epistemology, in which feeling is transcended in thought and then both are transcended in "felt thought" or "thought feeling" or "transcendent experience." Bradley typically focuses on opposites, deconstructs both of them, and then reclaims them in a new and unified form. Think briefly of Eliot's opposition of tradition and the individual talent and his inclusion of both in a greater tradition; or of his opposition of romanticism and classicism, and his inclusion of both in a more comprehensive framework. The ghost of Hegel hovers here, of course, but this dialectical imagination goes beyond Hegel, especially in its emphasis on experience.

4. As Eliot himself said, his prose style is modelled on Bradley's. The combination of humility and irony, of feeling and intelligence, that characterizes Bradley's writings is a hallmark of Eliot's. Both the humility and the irony are genuine; both, in fact, are necessary results of the epistemology. They come from the double awareness that one has glimpsed some light and that one can only work in the dark; from the compulsion to refute error coupled with the consciousness that one's own work is bound to be in error; from an awareness that one is making a raid on the absolute with shabby equipment always deteriorating. One of the disarming aspects of Bradley's rhetoric is that he generally concludes by calling his own theories into doubt. Thus in the *Ethical Studies*, he shows that Kant's formalism and Mill's utilitarianism are deeply flawed ethical theories. He then presents his own ethical theory based on the idea that society is a moral organism. He concludes, however, by arguing the insufficiency of all ethical theories, including the one he has just proposed. Being ethical and formulating ethical theories, he claims, are worlds apart, not because an ethical philosopher might himself be unethical, but because being anything and analyzing it are inconsistent activities.

Each of the positions I have mentioned represents a conscious and strenuous effort to overcome dualism. I am not suggesting that Eliot was dependent upon Bradley for these insights. The revolt against dualism, as Lovejoy and others have documented, was in the air in the early part of the century; moreover, Eliot had already mounted his own revolt against dualism in his poems of 1909–11. It must be noted, however, that Eliot found in Bradley an elegant and convincing argument against every type of dualism and that he surrendered several patient years to a sympathetic reading of Bradley's work. In spite of the closest personal and intellectual involvement with a formidable neorealist (Russell), Eliot explicitly endorsed many of Bradley's ideas in his dissertation, ideas that remained to color all of his subsequent work, including *Four Quartets*.

F. H. Bradley's Doctrine of Experience in T. S. Eliot's *The Waste Land* and *Four Quartets*

The criticism of T. S. Eliot is sometimes used to authorize a rigorous formalism. Such doctrines as the irrelevance of personality, of belief, of context, were extensions of positions outlined in *The Sacred Wood* (1920) and *Selected Essays* (1932). Eliot himself, however, was never a formalist. He winced at being celebrated by I. A. Richards as the artist who had purged poetry of its context in life (*SE*, 230). He believed, moreover, that people should bring special knowledge to the reading of texts. In order to collaborate with the poet in the making of a poem, readers must be willing to close the book and dwell awhile with Ezekiel and Dante, among many others. Readers must be willing, according to Eliot, to prepare for reading a poem as a barrister prepares for presenting a court case.

Most readers of Eliot are particularly handicapped by an inadequate knowledge of modern philosophy. Eliot, an immensely learned poet, studied in prestigious universities where some of the most illustrious names in the history of philosophy were among his teachers. At Harvard University, his teachers included George Santayana, Josiah Royce, and Bertrand Russell; at the Sorbonne, Henri Bergson. At Merton College, Oxford, his tutor was Harold Joachim, the colleague and disciple of F. H. Bradley, generally considered (even by Russell) as the greatest living philosopher.[1] Like many in his generation, Eliot was attracted to Bradley's thought and in 1916 completed a Ph.D. dissertation entitled "Experience and the Objects of Knowledge in the Philosophy of F. H. Bradley." This document, "the work of an expert," according to Royce (*KE*, 10), represents the culmination

---

1. T. S. Matthews, *Great Tom: Notes Towards the Definition of T. S. Eliot* (New York: Harper & Row, 1973), 35.

191

of Eliot's investigation into possible answers to the epistemological crisis precipitated around the turn of the century by the new physics. The dissertation was published in 1964 as *Knowledge and Experience in the Philosophy of F. H. Bradley.*

Eliot's meticulous study of philosophy, particularly of the epistemological idealism of F. H. Bradley, is directly relevant to the poetry he was writing. His dissertation centers on an inquiry into the self, more precisely, on whether it is possible for the self to know anything outside itself. The poems from "The Love Song of J. Alfred Prufrock" through *The Waste Land* explore in their own way the murky caverns of the isolated self. In spite of the fact that Eliot inescapably filtered his interpretation of the self through Bradleyan idealism, most commentators on the poet have not taken Bradley very seriously. Hugh Kenner's casual summary of the Bradleyan element in Eliot's art is perhaps typical: "Bradley has an attractive mind, though he has perhaps nothing to tell us. He is an experience, like the taste of nectarines or the style of Henry James."[2] This is the essence of critical chic; it is also unadulterated nonsense.

A superficial knowledge of Bradleyan idealism has led to serious misreadings of Eliot's representation of the self in *The Waste Land.* The most concentrated passage on the egocentric predicament in the entire poem occurs in part V, "What the Thunder Said."

> *Dayadhvam:* I have heard the key
> Turn in the door once and turn once only
> We think of the key, each in his prison
> Thinking of the key, each confirms a prison
> Only at nightfall, aethereal rumors
> Revive for a moment a broken Coriolanus

These lines on isolation are associated with the following quotation from Bradley's *Appearance and Reality* that Eliot included in *The Waste Land* notes, themselves a part of the poem:

> My external sensations are no less private to myself than are my thoughts or my feelings. In either case my experience falls within my own circle, a circle closed on the outside; and, with all its elements alike, every sphere is opaque to the others which surround it. . . . In brief, regarded as an existence which appears in a

2. Kenner, *The Invisible Poet,* 63.

soul, the whole world for each is peculiar and private to that soul.[3]

This quotation is usually read by literary critics as an authorization for a solipsistic interpretation of the poem. A general reason for this mistaken reading is the popular assumption that all idealists, ergo Bradley, ergo Eliot, are solipsistic by definition. This assumption comes from a failure to differentiate Bradleyan idealism from that of George Berkeley and G. W. F. Hegel. In fact, both Bradley and Eliot explicitly refute solipsism—Bradley in chapter 21 of *Appearance and Reality* and Eliot in chapter 6 of his dissertation. A more specific reason for the misreading of Bradley is a failure to understand certain technical definitions in his philosophy. "My own circle," the "soul," "experience," and the "opaque centre" are often read as referring to the self or ego. Read in this way, Bradley's statement is virtually a definition of solipsism, or of the position that the self can know nothing but its own states, or that the self is the whole of reality. The truth is that none of the terms in the above quotation is equivalent to the self. To Bradley, the self is unreal in that it can exist only as an abstraction.

It may be assumed that the misreading of one quotation in *The Waste Land* notes is a matter of small consequence in understanding Eliot. This assumption would be a serious mistake. In the first place, the Bradley quotation is part of an extremely concentrated passage on a crucial subject in Eliot's early poetry—the isolation of the self. Second, the spatial structure of *The Waste Land*, in which readers are expected to see the entire poem in a moment, simultaneously, as they see a painting, means that an awareness of the Bradley quotation must be in the minds of readers if they are to understand, say, the beautiful lyric that opens the poem—"April is the cruellest month." Finally, the doctrine to which the Bradley quotation refers is important in Eliot's work from "Gerontion" through *Four Quartets*.

The critic who has probably done most to popularize the misreading of the Bradley quotation is J. Hillis Miller. In *Poets of Reality*, Miller uses this quotation as part of his evidence that Eliot, at least through *The Waste Land*, was a solipsist. Repeatedly, he speaks of Eliot's "reduction of all to mind." "Everything is already subjective for Eliot,

3. Bradley, *Appearance and Reality*, 306.

and the mind can never bump into anything other than itself, anything stubbornly recalcitrant to its devouring power to assimilate everything."[4] In supporting this allegation by an appeal to Bradley, Miller is guilty of begging the question. It is not Bradley who has convinced him that Eliot is a solipsist; it is his own excellent and usually irrefutable analyses of the texts of the early poems. Miller shows that J. Alfred Prufrock is trapped in the labyrinthine alleys of his own mind, and he assumes, like many lesser critics, that Eliot must have been. Certainly, the Prufrockian persona is solipsistic, but clearly his subjectivity is diagnosed as a disease. Miller's thesis that Eliot was a "subjective idealist" cannot be corroborated from Eliot's use of Bradley in *The Waste Land.* That passage from *Appearance and Reality* actually has nothing to do with solipsism, a fact that will be clear enough when its technical terminology is clarified.

The common assumption that all idealists are solipsists presupposes that epistemological idealism, that is, the position that the object of knowledge is dependent on the existence of the perceiving subject, is a monolithic category; actually, epistemological idealism encompasses great heterogeneity. Some idealists believe that the knower creates the object in the process of knowing it. This view, called "subjective idealism," is often attributed to Berkeley, who expressed it in a famous formula—"*esse est percipi*," that is, "to be is to be perceived." Bradley consciously rebelled against this kind of idealism. He believed that the subject or self and the object or not-self come into existence simultaneously. It is as incorrect to say that the knower creates the object as to say that the object creates the knower. Both are concurrent products of a process, and either is inconceivable without the other. Eliot also rejected this kind of idealism. His most famous early poem, "The Love Song of J. Alfred Prufrock," suggests that the consequences of subjective idealism are devastating.

Another important view, called "transcendental" or "critical idealism," is that the knower transforms and shapes the object in the process of knowing it. Kant, the most significant representative of this view, held that the mind contributes as much to reality by knowing an object as the object itself contributes by its materiality. Kant's

4. J. Hillis Miller, *Poets of Reality: Six Twentieth-Century Writers* (Cambridge: Harvard University Press, 1974), 159–60.

194

epistemology is dualistic in that it puts an impassable gulf between the knower, on the one side, and the object-in-itself, on the other. Bradley explicitly rejects all dualism. His position is that the knower and the known coincide in a unity that includes them both. In Bradleyan idealism, subject and object are changed from nouns to adjectives, that is, subject and object as independent entities are replaced by the subjective and objective aspects of a greater whole. Again, Eliot, like Bradley, rejected dualism, the desire for wholeness being the basic impulse of his life and art.

Finally, some idealists conceive of all reality, including the knower and the known, as belonging to an all-encompassing whole or totality. This view, called "absolute idealism," is the position of Hegel in the early nineteenth century and Bradley in the early twentieth. Bradleyan idealism is not, however, British Hegelianism. It is an original native movement, rooted principally in a reaction against British empiricism, particularly the epistemological dualism of John Locke (theory of representative perception) and the epistemological solipsism of Bishop Berkeley (subjective idealism).

Bradley, then, was the same general kind of idealist as Hegel. At the same time, he differed in striking ways from his great German predecessor, and one of those differences is important to acquit Bradley (and Eliot) of the charge of solipsism. This difference is related to Hegel's so-called panlogism. For Hegel, the Absolute, the ultimate and all-inclusive reality, was the actualization of Mind, that is, it was of the nature of thought. Bradley unequivocally rejects Hegelian rationalism, because, for one thing, it swallows up the glory of the experienced world. In *Principles of Logic,* Bradley eloquently denies Hegel's mentalism.

> Unless thought stands for something that falls beyond mere intelligence, . . . a lingering scruple still forbids us to believe that reality can ever be purely rational. It may come from a failure in my metaphysics, or from a weakness of the flesh which continues to blind me, but the notion that existence could be the same as understanding strikes as cold and ghost-like as the dreariest materialism. That the glory of this world in the end is appearance leaves the world more glorious, if we can feel it is a show of some fuller splendour; but the sensuous curtain is a deception and a cheat, if it hides some colourless movement of atoms, some spec-

tral woof of impalpable abstractions, or unearthly ballet of blood-less categories. . . . Our principles may be true, but they are not reality. They no more *make* that Whole which commands our devotion, than some shredded dissection of human tatters *is* that warm and breathing beauty of flesh which our hearts found delightful.[5]

Bradley, then, insists that thought cannot "make" anything and that reality is nonmental. It is simply a misuse of words to call him a solipsist.

To understand what Bradley does believe reality to consist of, it is necessary to examine the most important word in his vocabulary. That word, also Bradley's key term in the passage Eliot quotes in *The Waste Land* notes, is "experience." And experience is the name Bradley gives to the absolute.

> Everything is experience, and also experience is one.[6]
>
> Experience is the same as reality. The fact that falls elsewhere seems, in my mind, to be a mere word and a failure, or else an attempt at self-contradiction. It is a vicious abstraction whose existence is meaningless nonsense, and is therefore not possible.[7]
>
> There is but one Reality, and its being consists in experience. In this one whole all appearances come together.[8]

Bradley is using the word "experience" in his own unique way, and some caution is required if one is to follow his argument. As Eliot implies in his dissertation, it is perhaps easier to understand what experience is not than to understand what it is. "We must be on guard . . . against identifying experience with consciousness, or against considering experience as the adjective of a subject" (*KE*, 15). More simply, we must avoid thinking of experience as "my" experience, or as any person's experience. To the extent that we think of it in this way, we are failing to comprehend Bradley's Absolute. He is not speaking of experience as something that is experienced by an experiencer, but as something that simply is, as a complex that encompasses experiencer and experienced. The absolute is pure experience, and it systematically includes all objects that can be said to be real.

5. Bradley, *Principles of Logic*, 2:590–91.
6. Bradley, *Appearance and Reality*, 405.
7. Bradley, *Appearance and Reality*, 128.
8. Bradley, *Appearance and Reality*, 403.

Perhaps the most crucial point in Bradleyan idealism is just this: the absolute is not mental but empirical; it is not grounded in thought but in experience. To quote G. Watts Cunningham, "It is not, as William James mistakenly supposed, a 'marble temple shining on a hill'; it is . . . inextricably involved in the dust and dirt of things."[9] Bradley's experience is not an abstraction lying behind the appearances in the external world. "The Absolute *is* its appearances, it really is all and every one of them"[10]—not all totalled together, but all unified.

The experience mentioned in *The Waste Land* is not, however, Bradley's "absolute experience"; it is "immediate experience," a special category within absolute experience. Bradley divides experience into three categories: "immediate experience," "relational experience," and "transcendent experience."[11] Immediate experience is a direct experience of knowing and feeling and being in one prior to the development of logical or temporal or spatial categories. This doctrine is immensely important in Bradley's thought. Both his epistemology and his ontology are hinged upon this single idea. This is one way that he defines it.

> We in short have experience in which there is no distinction between my awareness and that of which it is aware. There is an immediate feeling, a knowing and being in one, with which knowledge begins; and, though this in a manner is transcended, it nevertheless remains throughout as the present foundation of my known world. And if you remove this direct sense of my momentary contents and being, you bring down the whole of consciousness in one common wreck. For it is in the end ruin to divide experience into something on one side experienced as an object, and on the other side, something, not experienced at all.[12]

In his dissertation, Eliot gives as an example of immediate experience the viewing of a painting in which the viewer is so absorbed that he has no consciousness of self or subject, on the one side, and painting or object, on the other (*KE*, 20). This directly experienced nonrela-

---

9. G. Watts Cunningham, "English and American Absolute Idealism," in *History of Philosophical Systems*, ed. Vergilius Ferm (New York: Philosophical Library, 1950), 317.

10. Bradley, *Appearance and Reality*, 431.

11. Immediate experience is Bradley's term for prerelational consciousness. Relational experience and transcendent experience are my own terms for Bradley's concepts of relational consciousness and suprarelational consciousness.

12. Bradley, *Essays on Truth and Reality*, 159–60.

tional many-in-one is not the viewer's experience, for he as subject and the painting as object do not yet exist. When he becomes aware of "his" experience and of the painting as other than himself, then immediate experience will have dissolved into the realm of relations, of self and not-self.

The suggestion that Bradley is solipsistic derives partially from a confusion between "my" experience and immediate experience. When Bradley argues that everything is constituted by experience, he does not mean the experience of any self; he means pure undifferentiated experience. Both the self and the not-self are mere fictions, simple "intellectual constructions"[13] according to Bradley. To attribute either one to the agency of the other is an error, because each is dependent for definition upon the existence of the other. In other words, it is simply impossible to think of a self unless one has simultaneously in mind an idea of a not-self.

Immediate experience takes place within what Bradley calls "finite centres." A finite center is not a self or a knower, for immediate experience is prior to such distinctions. To return to Eliot's example, a finite center is rather the whole complex uniting the viewer, the painting, and all other elements of that situation. It is a *center* of being and feeling in one; it is *finite* because it breaks up into relational consciousness.

The idea of immediate experience existing in opaque, impenetrable finite centers is of the essence in the passage from Bradley that appears in *The Waste Land* notes. Perhaps the doctrine can be elucidated with reference to experience in the theater. In a 1923 memorial essay on the music hall comedienne Marie Lloyd, Eliot says that the working man in Marie's audience unconsciously collaborates with her in the performance of her act (*SE*, 407). This working man, in Eliot's view, is directly in touch with a reality characterized by a knowing and feeling in one, uncontaminated by the divisions and relations of thought. This experience is not *his* experience, for he, as a self, does not even exist. He and the music and Marie Lloyd and all other constituents of that perfectly unified situation make up a finite center. In this particular music hall, this working man's situation is more or less replicated by the situations of other members of the

13. Bradley, *Appearance and Reality*, 465.

audience. Each person in the audience has his or her own finite center, which is both unique and private, even though its contents will parallel to a great extent the contents of finite centers of persons in adjoining seats. Marie Lloyd, whose situation is in obvious ways different from that of any one member of the audience, has her own finite center, the contents of which will overlap to a small extent elements in the finite centers of other people in this same theater. But the fact that the finite centers contain parallel contents does not mean that finite centers interpenetrate. Each complex of thought and feeling, each nonrelational center of immediacy, is private and impenetrable. As Bradley explains, "Finite centres of feeling, while they last, are (so far as we know) not directly pervious to one another."[14] In another place, he tells us why this is so: "The immediate experiences of finite beings cannot, as such, come together; and to be possessed directly of what is personal to the mind of another, would in the end be unmeaning."[15] All of these finite centers are penetrated by "reality," but as the quotations from Bradley show, they are not penetrated by other finite centers. The very idea of otherness is inconsistent with the nonrelational unity that is immediate experience. Eliot insists in the Marie Lloyd essay that the actress is not expressing her own personality (*SE*, 406). In truth, at this point (immediate experience), she has no personality to express, for she does not exist as self any more than her audience exists as not-self.

It is the nature of immediate experience to fall apart. It breaks up because intelligence, existing heretofore as an undifferentiated part of pure experience, suddenly assumes dominance. Consciously, the intellect begins to structure and organize the elements that, like itself, had been undiscriminated in immediate experience. Reality can no longer be apprehended directly, as a unity, but must be approached through the tortuous streets of thought in terms of relations. This is the level of such dualisms as the self and the not-self, of the knower and the known, of mind and matter, of the here and there, of the now and then. All of these necessarily dualistic concepts are abstractions from reality; all are unreal. It is no wonder that Bradley denies solipsism so energetically, for solipsism is being locked in one half of an

14. Bradley, *Appearance and Reality*, 464.
15. Bradley, *Appearance and Reality*, 303.

abstraction. Only intelligence, only thinking, could create such an absurd prison.

A third level, in Bradley's view, transcendent experience, permits a return of sorts to the wholeness and unity of immediate experience. Immediate experience exists before relations, but transcendent experience exists after or above relations. Immediate experience dissolves of itself into relational experience, but relational experience resists resolution into the higher monistic experience. The villain is the discursive intellect, and the transcendence of relations such as self and space and time becomes largely a matter of reforming the discursive intellect from a servant of division and fragmentation to a partner in the achievement of wholeness. Whereas immediate experience is characterized by a *knowing* and feeling in one that comes *before* intellection, transcendent experience is characterized by a *thinking* and feeling in one that comes *after* and is achieved through intellection. Obviously, it is this level of experience that Eliot refers to in "The Metaphysical Poets" as " a direct sensuous apprehension of thought, or a recreation of thought into feeling" (*SE*, 246). One of Bradley's favorite terms for transcendent experience is "felt thought." In a famous passage, Eliot uses this concept to distinguish between the poets of the seventeenth and the nineteenth centuries: "Tennyson and Browning are poets, and they think; but they do not feel their thought as immediately as the odour of a rose. A thought to Donne was an experience; it modified his sensibility" (*SE*, 247).

That Eliot shared this general view of relational experience as enclosed in an envelope of undiscriminated and felt nonrelational totality need not be deduced from his literary criticism; it is explicit in his dissertation. In the first chapter, he explains Bradley's immediate and absolute experience and then unambiguously states his concurrence. "If anyone object that mere experience at the beginning and complete experience at the end are hypothetical limits, I can say not a word in refutation, for this would be just the reverse side of what opinions I hold" (*KE*, 31). To Eliot, then, as to Bradley, immediate experience at the beginning, that is, before (yet including) intellectual consciousness, and transcendent experience at the end, that is, after (yet including) intellectual consciousness, are not mere hypothetical limits to the comprehended dualistic sphere I am calling relational experience. Together, they constitute the reality that makes possible all abstraction or, in other words, that makes possible our construction of the relational world, the everyday world of straw.

An awareness of Bradley's three levels of experience is essential in understanding the quotation from *Appearance and Reality* (306) that Eliot included in *The Waste Land* notes. That passage, quoted in full earlier in this essay, has nothing to do with solipsism. "My experience" is not the experience of any self, but immediate experience. "My own circle" is not my self, for my self as such does not even exist. The plumber collaborating with Marie Lloyd, for example, is no solipsist. "The circle closed on the outside" is not his self, but the finite center, including "all its elements alike"—himself, his sensations, Marie Lloyd. These elements—and this is a crucial point—do not yet exist in themselves; they are "alike," that is, they are part of an undifferentiated whole. Another basic point is that "soul" in this passage does not mean any individual self or ego; in Bradley's simple words: "a soul is a finite centre."[16] This finite center will dissolve into relational experience, but while this center of immediate experience lasts, it is peculiar to that working man. It is a world, different from all the worlds surrounding it, and yet, it is partially the universe.

Ironically, critics who have misinterpreted the Bradley quotation as a statement of solipsism may have taken their cue from Eliot himself. The poet pointed them in that direction by appending the note to a line in the poem that clearly refers to the self locked in a prison. Moreover, Eliot's association of Dante's Ugolino and Shakespeare's Coriolanus with this part of *The Waste Land* seems to support a solipsistic interpretation. Did Eliot then misunderstand the Bradleyan statement? There is ample evidence that he understood it all too well. In an October 1916 article in the *Monist*, Eliot quotes and discusses the very same passage from *Appearance and Reality* that he later put in *The Waste Land* notes. He emphasizes in this article the importance of distinguishing "self," "soul," and "finite centre."

> The self is a construction in space and time. It is an object among others, a self among others. . . . The soul (as in the passage quoted at length) [the same passage quoted in *The Waste Land*] is almost the same as finite centre. The soul, considered as finite centre, cannot be acted upon by other entities, since a finite centre

16. Bradley, *Essays on Truth and Reality*, 414.

is a universe in itself. . . . The finite centre, so far as I can pretend to understand it, *is* immediate experience. (*KE*, 204–5)

The correct reading of the Bradley quotation raises a question about Eliot's intent when he juxtaposes two notions of self that seem contradictory, when he appends to poetic lines that present the self as the only knowable reality a doctrinal statement that cancels the reality of the self.

The lines from "What the Thunder Said" that Eliot associates with the Bradley quotation are part of the second command of the thunder, the *Dayadhvam* command cited earlier in this essay. There are four important allusions in this passage—two that are identified in the lines themselves and two that are identified in the notes. Together they constitute a highly concentrated statement on solipsism—its origin and perpetuation in discursive thought and its possible dissolution in Bradleyan experience. The four allusions are to the *Upanishads,* Dante's *Inferno,* Bradley's *Appearance and Reality,* and Shakespeare's *Coriolanus.* From the *Upanishads* comes the sound of the thunder, "Da," expanded by the listener to *Dayadhvam*—to sympathize. The other three allusions are generally considered parallel in meaning, all referring to solipsism. Supposedly, the juxtaposition of these allusions to *Dayadhvam* is ironic, since sympathy is essentially a reaching out beyond the self. This interpretation, however, is based on a mistaken reading of Bradley and on a superficial reading of Shakespeare, neither of which is parallel to the Dante passage.

The Bradley quotation is related most closely to the lines, "We think of the key, each in his prison / Thinking of the key, each confirms a prison." In Bradley's doctrine of experience and reality, it is "thinking" that dissolves immediate experience, which is real, into relational or intellectual experience, which is unreal. In *The Waste Land* manuscript, the connection between "thinking" and solipsism is even clearer—"Thinking of the key, each has built a prison" is Eliot's earlier line. Solipsism originates, then, in discursive thought, especially thought about the self and the not-self. It is also perpetuated by thought: "thinking of the key," the essence of intellectual consciousness, confirms the prison of the self and makes it impregnable. As long as the intellect is dominant, as long as reality must be filtered through mind, so long will abstractions such as self and not-self, subject and object, reign in a kingdom of appearances.

One key, however, will unlock the prison of self. That key, hidden in the Bradley quotation from *Appearance and Reality,* is immediate experience. According to Bradley, immediate experience is both the judge of solipsism and the guarantor that it can be transcended:

> Immediate experience, however much transcended, both remains and is active. It is not a stage which shows itself at the beginning and then disappears, but it remains at the bottom throughout as fundamental. And, further, remaining it contains within itself every development which in a sense transcends it. Nor does it merely contain all developments but in its own way it acts to some extent as their judge.[17]

Immediate experience remains and is active as a "felt" (in contrast to a "thought") background of wholeness; it persists throughout the plurality and fragmentation that characterize relational experience. It is this background existence of immediate experience that acts as the judge of such dualistic abstractions as solipsism.

Immediate experience remains not only as a "felt" background but also as an object of thought, the contemplation of which can reveal the nature of the Absolute. "From such an experience of unity below relations we can rise to the idea of a superior unity above them. Thus we can attach a full and positive meaning to the statement that Reality is one."[18] By recognizing (literally, knowing again) the nature of immediate experience, "we are led," as Eliot puts it, "to the conception of an all-inclusive experience outside of which nothing shall fall" (*KE,* 31). Although in a sense immediate experience is transcended (otherwise it could never be the subject of this essay), it is precisely because immediate experience "both remains and is active" as a present felt background and as an object of analysis that it constitutes the key to the prison of the self.

Obviously, an understanding of Bradley's quotation complicates the standard interpretation of the second command of the thunder. In brief, Eliot first presents a traditional suggestion for breaking the prison of self—*Dayadhvam.* Next he alludes to Ugolino thereby relating solipsism to pride, to human intelligence, and to grotesque distortions of religious myth. The tower in which Ugolino and his chil-

17. Bradley, *Essays on Truth and Reality,* 161.
18. Bradley, *Appearance and Reality,* 462.

dren are sealed to starve is, of course, a metaphor for solipsism. More important as a metaphor for solipsism is Ugolino's confinement in hell, the ultimate prison without a key. Dante's despicable sinner knows the key turns once only, for even the exit of death is blocked in this prison of damned souls. Juxtaposed to the Dante allusion is the account of the origin of solipsism and also the suggestion that the self may or may not become Ugolino's prison, depending on how one manages the intellect.

The final allusion in this passage, to Shakespeare's *Coriolanus,* concerns the difficulty of transcending the self. *Coriolanus* dramatizes the conflict between a heroic noble patrician—an "eagle," a "tiger"—and a base and ignoble populace—"the mutable rank-scented many" (III.i.66), as dependable as "hailstones in the sun" (I.i.174).[19] The title character resembles Ugolino in that he is proud and a traitor, but he is unlike Ugolino in more important ways. Ugolino was ignoble, Coriolanus noble. Ugolino exploited his country; Coriolanus served his country, repeatedly risking his life for his people. Ugolino's betrayal was tit for tat; Coriolanus's banishment total injustice. Ugolino fell because he could not sympathize, Coriolanus because he could not compromise. In fact, Coriolanus is broken precisely because he *does* sympathize. He calls off the attack against Rome with full knowledge that this act of compassion will be "most mortal to him" (V.iii.189). Eliot's reference to Coriolanus is ambiguous.

> Only at nightfall, aetheral rumours
> Revive for a moment a broken Coriolanus

Coriolanus has reached beyond self; his eyes have been made to sweat compassion. For recompense, he is broken to pieces. And although revival is mentioned, the fragility and perhaps failure of his revival is underscored by the diction—"aethereal," "rumours," "only at nightfall," and "for a moment." "Aethereal rumours" would be akin to April's promises or the thunder's reassurance or the song of the hermit thrush, all of which give hope for a revival that is not to be.

What the reader of the *Dayadhvam* passage ends with is the time-honored Eastern precept for transcending the self, Ugolino's blatant refusal to sympathize and his consequent damnation, Bradley's philosophic suggestion of a possible transcendence, and Coriola-

19. William Shakespeare, *Coriolanus* (New York: Signet, 1966).

nus's fruitless compliance with the traditional precept. There are many possible interpretations of these juxtaposed allusions. An obvious one is the apparent suggestion that since traditional precepts from religion and psychology have failed us, we should substitute more sophisticated precepts from philosophy. This is far too simple, however, for Bradley's transcendent experience is highly problematic. Even in Bradley, it is only a possibility. In Eliot, tinged with despair, it is barely a possibility. One objection that appears in Eliot's technical discussions of Bradleyan idealism, one note of dismay in Eliot's literary and social criticism, is that Bradley greatly underestimated the difficulty of achieving transcendent experience. Perhaps immediate experience, like April, is cruel, promising what it cannot deliver; perhaps transcendent experience is, after all, no more than an aethereal rumor.

Bradley's influence on Eliot did not end with *The Waste Land*; it persisted throughout his career, though probably as a "felt" rather than a "thought" element. Parts of *Four Quartets* that have been considered almost hopelessly obscure are more accessible to those who understand Bradley's doctrine of experience.

> We had the experience but missed the meaning.
> And approach to the meaning restores the experience
> In a different form, beyond any meaning
> We can assign to happiness. ("The Dry Salvages," II)

The "meaning," being intellectual, was not comprehended in the immediate experience. Awareness of the meaning takes away the immediate experience of wholeness. The task becomes finding an "approach to the meaning" that will, by reforming the discursive intellect, restore the immediate experience "in a different form" (transcendent experience), "beyond" assignable meaning, that is, beyond intellectual analysis.

Another passage from *Four Quartets* that is explicable in terms of Bradley's experience occurs in "Burnt Norton" II.

> To be conscious is not to be in time
> But only in time can the moment in the rose-garden,
> The moment in the arbour where the rain beat,
> The moment in the draughty church at smokefall
> Be remembered; involved with past and future.
> Only through time time is conquered.

Time, being a relation, does not exist in immediate experience, but immediate experience exists by definition in time. "Its own tendency and nature," Bradley explains, "is to pass beyond itself into the relational consciousness."[20] Paradoxically, Bradley argues that immediate experience, "however much transcended, both remains and is active" as a "felt" background allowing transcendence. The experience in the rose garden was a moment of direct consciousness of reality. Time was not in this experience; yet the experience was in time, for it has been lost. Although this experience has been dissolved by time, it remains in time as a means to conquer time. As a felt totality, the experience in the rose garden remains as a judge of the present; as an object of memory, it remains as a guide to transcendence. While *Four Quartets* cannot be reduced to a versification of Bradley, Eliot's great philosophical poem is deeply indebted to Bradley's ideas.

The relationship between Eliot's philosophical studies and his poetic intuitions and concepts is complex. The Harvard poems of 1910–11, written several years before Eliot's work on Bradley, indicate that the poet was independently critical of the solipsistic conclusion. Eliot's critique of solipsism, in fact, can be understood apart from his philosophic studies. The richest understanding, however, will be reserved for readers who are willing to prepare themselves for the experience of reading the poetry. Readers who come armed only with the ABC book from which they learned to read, to borrow a metaphor from Mallarmé, will not achieve a very profound understanding. In the case of Eliot's poems, readers should bring some knowledge of Bradley, for Bradley is a part of everything Eliot wrote after 1914. Even sophisticated and learned readers who are ignorant of neo-idealism are apt to misinterpret those great poems on the egocentric predicament.

20. Bradley, *Appearance and Reality*, 462.

Modernism and Belligerence

With *Skepticism and Modern Enmity,* Jeffrey M. Perl has emerged as a major analyst and chronicler of Western culture. His first book, *The Tradition of Return: The Implicit History of Modern Literature* (1984), was a painstaking examination of post-Renaissance culture with attention to the ideology that was institutionalized by Burckhardt in the nineteenth century—the ideology of rebirth or return. Perl's account of the dynamic between cultural change and the simultaneous commitment to ancient texts / values, with *Ulysses* as his major case study, culminated in penetrating insights about the mindscape of the early part of this century. *The Tradition of Return* concludes with an open invitation for someone to join the author and others in a sustained conversation on the meaning of the structure within modern cultural politics.

Perl's new book, *Skepticism and Modern Enmity,* opens with a poignant allusion to that invitation: "Given the silence that is the condition of our working lives, we respond, each, to our own invitations."[1] For the listener fortunate enough to be within earshot, the Perl-to-Perl conversation brings a brilliant analysis of twentieth-century ideological struggles. Perl calls his project a description of modern ambivalence and a history of the enmities through which this ambivalence has been expressed. Enmity in modern culture is not so much a result of the inability to reach consensus, he claims, but of the deep need to evade it, to evade that perfect consensus that would be, in the language of T. S. Eliot, annihilation and utter night. Perl expects to continue exploring modern conflict and consensus in future vol-

1. Jeffrey Perl, *Skepticism and Modern Enmity: Before and After Eliot* (Baltimore: Johns Hopkins University Press, 1989), xiv.

umes, and if the level of discourse in his published work is any indication, he will deliver sequels both provocative and illuminating.

Skepticism and Modern Enmity is a tightly coiled book with thesis within thesis, history within history within history, prophecy within prophecy. The primary thesis is focused on twentieth-century literary enmities (e.g., modernism-postmodernism) and, of enormous interest, the relation of these enmities to politics, war, and more specifically, to the Holocaust. This thesis is contained within a more comprehensive and to some extent parallel one regarding the dynamic play of antitheses in post-Renaissance culture (e.g., humanism–antihumanism); at the same time, the thesis on the twentieth-century both frames and contains the story of T. S. Eliot, a complex figure omnipresent on the front lines of this belligerent century's art and politics. All of these stories are systematically related; in Perl's argument, all are variants of one story, a story of polarities and antitheses that descend from ambivalence and depend on each other for existence. The history of post-Renaissance culture, the history of modernism, and the history of Eliot all reveal themselves to be patterned by irresolvable and necessary oppositions.

The five-centuries war inaugurated by the dissolution in the early Renaissance of the Christian and medieval synthesis continues with no victor, a situation Perl describes more in terms of mutual dependence than mutual antagonism. The Renaissance was inseparable from the humanist impulse to return to ancient texts. And as Hugh Kenner has argued, modernism—the movement of Eliot, Joyce, Stravinsky, and Picasso—was also an expression of the humanist impulse. At the heart of postmodernism is a recoil from humanism and the classical tradition, but as Perl persuasively maintains, those who have led the rebellion are conspicuously dependent on the values and the traditions they are trying to invert. For postmodernists, Perl claims, "the chief obsession has been the influence of parents." And the parent most vilified has been the poet who had been most celebrated. Eliot remains, nevertheless, the central figure to those who misread and attack him. Harold Bloom, for example, bases his Oedipal theory of literary history on his own relationship to Eliot.

Skepticism and Modern Enmity is a major contribution to our understanding of the complicated and elusive Mr. Eliot. Following an account of Eliot's reception into the canon and of the extraordinary abuse formulated to banish him, Perl demonstrates by his examination of Eliot's philosophical papers (published and unpublished) that the supposed czar of reactionary positions (tradition, orthodoxy, Anglo-Catholicism, Royalism) was a radical skeptic. In the process of completing the course work for a Ph.D. in philosophy at Harvard University Eliot generated a number of notebooks in philosophy and comparative (especially Asian) religion. Several scholars have been allowed to study these materials, but Perl is the first to use them to describe the unfolding of Eliot's mind and the first to contextualize those materials in the larger sweep of post-Renaissance intellectual history.

Using quotations from Eliot's student papers, Perl is able to clarify the poet's famous (or infamous) contrariety, his seemingly endless ability to occupy two opposing camps at the same time. Unsympathetic critics typically accuse Eliot of speaking out of both sides of his mouth, and sympathetic ones try to synthesize the contradictions or to relate them to his midlife conversion to Christianity. But Perl shows that Eliot was philosophically not at all self-contradictory. Eliot accepted the self-contradictory nature of human existence and stubbornly refused to take any position that would exclude its opposite. Perl fatally undermines the "proof-text" approach to Eliot. One can very easily find quotations to support a claim that Eliot contradicted himself, easier still texts to "prove" that he was narrow-minded and dogmatic. Perl demonstrates that Eliot was aware that he was speaking from a particular perspective (not necessarily his own), that part of his strategy for embarrassing single points of view was a migration from one perspective to another. The poet's purpose was to illustrate the relative and conventional nature of all graspable truth.

Eliot's disenchantment with Western philosophic traditions and his long studies in Asian religion prepared the way, in Perl's account, for the poet's conversion to Christianity. The poet found in Buddhism forms of thought congenial to his skepticism and his relativism—to his views that human truth is a construct, that everything beneath the sun is contingent, and that to exist is to be in relation to other things. In Buddhism, Eliot found a religion that accepted contradiction and transcendence, one that associated salvation with liberating oneself from presuppositions. The "end" of our explorations, as Eliot describes it in *Four Quartets,* "Will be to arrive where we started / And know the place for the first time." It is clear from Eliot's few comments on conversion that he considered skepticism, relativism, and a sort of dialectical transcendence as fundamental in his own religious inclinations. He defined conversion, in fact, as "the arrival of skepticism" and the "erasure of prejudice." Both Eliot's philosophy and his religion involve the acknowledgment that "facts" are constructs from some point of view. Eliot did not believe there is no truth; on the contrary, he steadfastly maintained there are many truths. He rechristened "skepticism" as "humility" and made it the cornerstone of his religious faith. Humility, in the language of *Four Quartets,* is endless. And he rechristened "tradition" as "orthodoxy," a concept often misread as an expression of cultural absolutism but one that is exactly the opposite: "an expression of radical skepticism in regard to any one philosophical position" (Perl 1989, 63). The hidden advantage of tradition, as Perl argued in an earlier essay in *The Southern Review,* is that it speaks with many discordant voices. Eliot chose the Anglican Church in part because it has a definite theological position and yet tolerates a multitude of voices, Catholic and Protestant, past and present, living and dead. Attention to Eliot's religion must focus, not only on what he believed, but also on *how* he believed it. Skepticism and relativism are related to the latter; they are not beliefs but attitudes toward belief.

Perl describes Eliot's transformation from a philosopher to a man of letters and examines his social, religious, and political odyssey as he moved *entre deux guerres.* In the late twenties, Eliot began to recoil from politics as he had earlier recoiled from philosophy, an impulse inseparable from his distrust of theory. Both politics and philosophy, in their search for truth, tend to prolong rather than to resolve disputes, to divide rather than to unite. Eliot's characterization of his own political position as "royalist" is clarified by Perl's association of it with the poet's resistance to ideology. The poet was not, as is commonly claimed, against popular participation in government, but against majoritarianism. Perl discusses the importance of the idea of "consensus" in Eliot's thought, particularly in the thirties, and goes on to argue in his last section that the war had a profound influence on the modernists who survived it. Eliot, Picasso, Stravinsky, and other modernists understood that they were implicated in the failure of consensus resulting in the war; and in all of them (even Picasso, a connoisseur of violence), sentiment is liberalized. Eliot in particular came to deplore the "germanism of sensibility" that had led to the destruction in Europe and to praise democracy as the best form of government. The war also educated Eliot on the importance of the Jews, and after the war he gave speeches on *German* radio maintaining that Europe could not survive without the literature of Israel. Perl discusses the changes in Eliot's understanding of cultural unity and maintains that the poet retreated in significant ways from the inclinations that had made him a pioneer of modernism. Perl's analysis of the complicated relation between ethics and aesthetics concludes that Eliot's late work has greater moral than aesthetic significance. "Eliot's last plays, like Picasso's last paintings, efface their own self-portraits" (Perl 1989, 133). Perl locates the cause for modernists's retreat in the postwar world within a "conditional surrender" and the change in Eliot within a "conversion to mediocrity as a criterion of accomplishment" (Perl 1989, 158).

Important to the experience of reading *Skepticism and Modern Enmity* is the awareness of voice or point of view. Parodying Eliot's 1927 announcement that he tended to be an Anglo-Catholic in religion, a classicist in literature, and a Royalist in politics, Perl announces in the preface that he is Jewish in religion, of the American mainstream in politics, and unclear about what "classicism" means. Perl's statement also parodies a parody, for another Jewish critic, Harold Bloom, recently described his own position as Jewish in religion, liberal in politics, and romantic in literature. As a critic and as a Jew, Perl implicitly positions himself as Bloom's son; and as a scholar who has reflected in depth on Eliot, Joyce, and other modernists, he explicitly positions himself as a mediator between them (especially Eliot) and Bloom. Perl addresses, not only his own generation, but also Bloom and other founders of postmodernist culture. The genius of Bloom's theory in *The Anxiety of Influence* resides partly in the impossibility of addressing the theory without confirming it, at least in outline, as I suspect Perl knows too well. Bloom and Eliot's other rebellious children are perhaps unlikely to study this brilliant family history. As Max Planck once said (in a passage quoted by Perl), new ideas do not gain credence because they convince their opponents but because their opponents die and are replaced by a new generation.

211

Perl's relation to his material is felt throughout the book. He knows modernism intimately and at first hand, and he knows postmodernism even more intimately. He is a champion of neither, and in fact comes across as ambivalent, skeptical, moral, and concerned about modern culture. His exploration of the "final solution" and of its relation to both modernism and postmodernism is penetrating and authentic in a way that an analysis by a Christian could not be. His analysis of the association of modernism and anti-Semitism, and particularly of Eliot's alleged anti-Semitism, is moving and helpful.

Skepticism and Modern Enmity is a brilliant contribution to modern studies. Its elegant argument is at once familiar and new, and it will have a profound effect on any reader who surrenders to it. The book, though, is difficult at times, because it makes extraordinary demands on its reader. The complexity is related in part to the subject and in part to the style. I am reminded of my initial experience in reading the *Areopagitica*. The first sentence seemed so complicated that I temporarily gave up. But having returned and devoted myself to it, I felt more than rewarded for my efforts. Perl's book has that much in common with Milton's speech. It is so difficult in spots that the reader will be tempted to walk away, but the reader who remains or returns will gain a rich understanding of our bellicose century.

Tradition and Female Enmity

Sandra M. Gilbert and Susan Gubar Read T. S. Eliot

One of the most promising aspects of feminism in general is related to values: feminists, in theory at least, make up the party of peace. They are associated with building community and enhancing conversation, with reconciliation. In practice, however, many feminists seem dedicated to perpetuating old wars. The work of Sandra M. Gilbert and Susan Gubar is a case in point. They have contributed a great deal to our understanding of nineteenth- and twentieth-century women novelists and, in their anthology of writing by women, have rescued powerful writers from near oblivion. But their work is scarred by its presumption of a gender-based cold war. By insisting on interminable sexual warfare as an explanation of literary modernism, they limit their understanding of both men and women writers; by using binary logic, they preclude an understanding of one of their central texts, Eliot's influential "Tradition and the Individual Talent."

Gilbert and Gubar's account of feminism and modernism is developed in *The War of the Words,* the first volume of their three-volume series on twentieth-century women writers. Taking war as their controlling image, they filter everything through metaphors of conflict, enmity, and violence. Modernism, they argue, is a product of sexual battle; modernist techniques are weapons against women; literary history is an exercise designed to retrieve male heroes; tradition involves an attempt to define and protect the territory of male combatants. The series of which their book is a part also takes its title, *No Man's Land,* from the lexicon of war. A no-man's-land is a strip of land between the most advanced units of opposing armies; it refers to ground not controlled by either side, dangerously ambiguous territory in a lethal conflict. The conflict at issue is the ongoing battle of

213

the sexes energized by the late nineteenth-century rise of feminism and the emergence of women into the political and literary arenas previously dominated by men. Gilbert and Gubar describe this war in their account of women writers; in their approach to male critics, they demonstrate it—an enactment that on one level substantiates their thesis of ceaseless conflict.

Gilbert and Gubar's war plan includes war games with puns abounding. A no-man's-land, predictably, is a woman's-land, which in turn is a woe-man's-land for males. A herland ruled by powerful women fosters hostility in adversaries who fear the literalization of the no-man's-land metaphor (that is, the displacement and banishment of men) in this epic clash. They suggest that the literary and cultural no-man's-land in the battle between the sexes is being progressively occupied by women who proceed to expel the fallen and to redefine as the new no-man's-land part of the ground formerly held by men, both literally and metaphorically.

The methodology of *The War of the Words,* the discovery and manipulation of binary oppositions, mirrors the title metaphor. Focusing the war on verbal conflict, Gilbert and Gubar advance by generating warring terms. Their major polarity is male / female, and all of their many other oppositions are assigned to one of these opposing categories. Their thesis, in fact, dictates that they see modern cultural and literary history in terms of battles that can be accommodated under their overarching antagonism between men and women. They privilege this opposition in order to support their understanding of history as a record of female oppression and to substantiate their thesis of sexual discord as the driving force in modern cultural history. The effect of this methodology is to demonstrate and thus to perpetuate enmity, to maintain the polarity that is necessary for their position to have any point.

The male army in the war between the sexes has many generals, but none are more important than T. S. Eliot, who gave the modernist period its name. As Conrad Aiken wrote in his obituary for this archetypal modernist, "Our age beyond any doubt has been, and will continue to be the Age of Eliot."[1] Eliot is the villain who invented modernism in his early poetry, a body of work characterized by Gil-

---

1. Conrad Aiken, "T. S. Eliot: 1888–1965," *Life,* 15 January 1965, 93.

bert and Gubar as a battlefield strewn with weary debilitated males such as J. Alfred Prufrock and Gerontion. Eliot's mangled males include the impotent Fisher King and the old blind prophet Tiresias in *The Waste Land.* What Tiresias sees, the poet remarks in his notes, is the substance of the poem. And what he sees, according to Gilbert in "Costumes of the Mind" (1980), is a nightmare of "sexual misrule, an unreal . . . City enthralled by the false prophetess Madame Sosostris and laid waste . . . by its emasculated king's infertility."[2]

Gilbert and Gubar take *The Waste Land* as a major reference point in *No Man's Land.* They allude to it frequently, beginning with the title. Eliot's metaphor points to many waste lands, one of the most obvious being a Europe devastated by the First World War. Gilbert and Gubar maintain that the war between the sexes produced its own waste land.

> To poet-critics from Lawrence, Eliot, Pound, and Williams to Ransom and Blackmur, a literary landscape populated by women, whether they were scribblers, mentors, or great artists, may have seemed like a no man's land, a wasted and wasting country that left them with what Beerbohm called "an acute sense of disgrace."[3]

Gilbert and Gubar's interest in Eliot goes beyond his writing. His troubled marriage to a talented woman with artistic pretensions becomes for them a microcosm of the early twentieth-century battle between the sexes.

The face-off with Eliot, then, is perhaps inevitable for Gilbert and Gubar. He is a massive figure in the territory they wish to conquer. His cluster of subjects in criticism—tradition, literary history, literary influence—is precisely the cluster that they deal with from a feminist perspective. Their interest is articulated in Gilbert's essay "Literary Paternity" (*Cornell Review,* 1979), expanded as the first chapter of their collaborative *The Madwoman in the Attic* (1979), and relentlessly pursued in its sequel *No Man's Land.* The centrality of Eliot in *The War of the Words* is schematized in the table of contents.

2. Sandra M. Gilbert, "Costumes of the Mind: Transvestism as Metaphor in Modern Literature," *Critical Inquiry* 7 (1980): 391–417, 401.

3. Sandra M. Gilbert and Susan Gubar, *The War of the Words,* vol. 1 of *No Man's Land: The Place of the Woman Writer in the Twentieth Century* (New Haven: Yale University Press, 1988), 155.

Without even reading the book, one can see that Eliot is in the gun sight and his most famous essay in dead center. "Tradition and the Individual Talent" is framed on one side by the war between the sexes and on the other side by the displacement of that antagonism from the social to the linguistic realm. This frame is subtly reinforced visually and conceptually by the use of "sexes" and "sexual" in chapter titles I and V, and by the alliteration between "Fighting and "Forward" in II and IV; the center is highlighted by its form and length and by its celebrity. If the subtitles are ignored, the chapter titles visually suggest a shaped verse resembling a lethal weapon such as a spear or dagger, its point tipped with "Female Talent." The first word of each title is emphasized, not only by being first, but by special coherence with other first words: Battle—Fighting—Tradition—Forward—Sexual. Analysis of the subtitles corroborates the impression that the authors' opening shots are fired before the first words of text appear.

In the table of contents, then, the battle of the sexes is established as a frame for Eliot's essay on tradition. Essentially a way of directing focus, a frame tends to stabilize what is inside, to define it, and to keep it from moving about. But this picture contains a destabilizing effect. The substitution of "female" for "individual" announces a subversive insight and directs attention back to the battle of the sexes that constitutes the frame. By playing in this way with Eliot's title, Gilbert and Gubar set up an oscillation between their conceded patrilineage and their rebellious intent. They open a gap between their insight and Eliot's; in this distant shot of the battlefield, they disclose their realization that Eliot's individual talent is male, that his tradition must be taken under siege.

The title of the central analytical chapter of *The War of the Words*, "Tradition and the Female Talent: Modernism and Masculinism," consists of a double binary opposition that plays on Eliot's terminology. Gilbert and Gubar take the complementary Eliotian terms "tradition" and "individual talent" and, with a modification of the second term, present them as opposites. In displacing "individual," they retrieve its opposite ("community"), and thus the new term "female" is associated with a cluster of values that includes "community." Gilbert and Gubar's second pair identifies modernism with masculinism, and it simultaneously calls up Eliot's opposition of modernism / romanticism. This opposition in turn suggests Eliot's classicism / romanticism. Romanticism, Gilbert and Gubar will argue, was feminized and demonized by Eliot, and classicism was masculinized. Thus his oppositions of modernism / romanticism and of classicism / romanticism are used by Gilbert and Gubar to substantiate their equation of modernism and masculinism.

The title of *The War of the Words,* then, announces the topic of literary / sexual battle, and the table of contents reveals that "Tradition and the Individual Talent" is being molded for use in the war of the sexes. The reader is pointed toward Eliot but immediately discovers that the authors have directed attention to him as the center in order to redefine him as the frame. Literally and conspicuously, Eliot serves as the frame for this thesis chapter. "Tradition and the Individual Talent," flamboyantly alluded to in the title, is quoted in one of the epigraphs: "The existing order of monuments form an ideal order among themselves, which is modified by the new (the really new) work of art among them." After forty pages of exposition of their own theories, which from time to time includes detailed discussions of Eliot's work, Gilbert and Gubar conclude the chapter with:

> Eliot's theory that new works of art alter not only our sense of the past but also our sense of what art might *be* actually seems to reflect the sexual crisis that underlies modernism. For inevitably, the "ideal order" of patriarchal literary history was radically "modified by the introduction of the new (the really new) work of art"—and, as Woolf remarked, that "really new work" was women's work. (Gilbert and Gubar 1988, 162)

This closing quotation completes the frame generated by the title and epigraph. It is of course self-reflexive, for the authors claim that they themselves are doing really new work. They are grappling with their own author-ity as critics, a necessary agon as they attempt to take the territory occupied by Eliot.

Eliot's poetry and criticism, in Gilbert and Gubar's reading, can be explained as a "reaction-formation against the rise of literary women" (Gilbert and Gubar 1988, 156). His strategy involved, first, a devaluation of women's intellect. Without making any distinction between Eliot and his narrators-characters, they remark that, in one of the drafts of *The Waste Land*, "Eliot declares that 'women grown intellectual grow dull / And lose the mother wit of natural trull'" (Gilbert and Gubar 1988, 152). The second element in Eliot's so-called war plan involved "usurpation of women's words." In a sentence that illustrates the misrepresentation created by Gilbert and Gubar's habit of coordinating disparate terms, they assert that "F. Scott Fitzgerald famously drew on material provided by his wife, Zelda, and even T. S. Eliot incorporated a few lines contributed by his first wife, Vivien, into *The Waste Land*" (Gilbert and Gubar 1988, 153). This equates Fitzgerald's use of Zelda's material with Eliot's use of Vivien's. But the first was a theft and deeply resented, while the second was a gift joyously bestowed. Eliot invited not only Ezra Pound but his wife to look over his manuscript and make suggestions. In the second section ("A Game of Chess"), Vivien marked through various words and lines and suggested alternates, with the note: "Make any of these alterations—or *none* if you prefer."[4] Some of her recommendations are excellent, a fact Eliot easily recognized. He accepted, for example, her suggestion of "pills" to replace his more general "medicine" in the line that now reads, "It's them pills I took, to bring it off." She scratched out one of his lines in the pub section, replacing it with "What you get married for if you don't want to have children," a change he accepted. A number of her comments are enthusiastically appreciative—"WONDERFUL . . . wonderful & wonderful . . . Yes . . . Splendid last lines." The tone of her marginalia makes it clear that she was delighted to be taken seriously as a reader-critic. Driven by their "battle of the sexes" metaphor, however, Gilbert and Gubar missed a point that Vivien understood very well. Eliot respected her judgment, just as he did that of Ezra Pound.

The third and fourth elements that Gilbert and Gubar discover in Eliot's strategy to "ward off the onslaught of women" (Gilbert and Gubar 1988, 131) involve more substantial distortions of his position. The third focuses on Eliot's theory of the role of the "dissociation of sensibility" in literary history. Gilbert and Gubar read this as "an

---

4. Eliot, The Waste Land: *A Facsimile and Transcript*, 15.

attempt to construct *his* story of a literary history in which women play no part." They observe that Eliot devalues those periods when women were picking up the pen, which Gilbert and Gubar call a metaphorical penis and a metaphorical sword, both essential in arming the female warrior. In exposing this "construction of a literary history that denies the reality of women writers" (Gilbert and Gubar 1988, 154–55), they note with displeasure that Eliot first feminizes and then devalues romanticism and that he openly longs for the good old days of undisguised sexism. The fourth element they see at work is the development of a sexist aesthetic that degrades feminine values of subjectivity and celebrates masculine values. Armed not only with the pen (penis, sword) but with a war chest of binary oppositions, Gilbert and Gubar concentrate their assault on Eliot's view of literary history and his modernist aesthetic.

Gilbert and Gubar's analysis of Eliot's view of literary history is based on binary "either / or" logic, with the controlling opposition being "past / present." Presenting Eliot as a nostalgic male with a sexist agenda, they bemoan his "consecration of an 'orthodox' tradition." They lament his "desire to learn 'how to see the world as the Christian Fathers saw it' " and his "yearning for a Golden Age before 'the dissociation of sensibility set in.' " They maintain that the unexpressed psychological need here is the erasure of eighteenth- and nineteenth-century history, the obliteration of the "history associated with the entrance of women into the literary marketplace" (Gilbert and Gubar 1988, 154). Gilbert and Gubar also attribute this view of literary history to the New Critics, who "were motivated by a nostalgia as strong as Eliot's for the lost power of 'the Christian Fathers,' and implicitly for the male strength associated with bygone male sexual hierarchies" (Gilbert and Gubar 1988, 155).

Several problems riddle Gilbert and Gubar's analysis of Eliot's position. The first and fatal difficulty is the radical reductiveness inherent to their generation of the binary opposition between past and present, a strategy that blinds them to Eliot's argument and purpose in "Tradition and the Individual Talent." A second problem is the murkiness created by combining in one sentence and without qualification words and phrases from essays separated by decades. Another problem is the distortion arising from positing equivalence between concepts such as "orthodoxy" and "tradition" that have quite different meanings from each other and are used to mean different things at different times in Eliot's intellectual development. A fourth problem is the misrepresentation produced by enclosing such words as "orthodoxy" in quotation marks as if *Eliot's* concept were the one being discussed. Gilbert and Gubar repeatedly convey the impression that his notion is being transported into a new context for the purpose of analysis, when in fact they have substituted their own definition for the term under discussion.

The most serious flaw in Gilbert and Gubar's work, the reliance on "either / or" logic, forces them to see not only men and women but also logical categories and abstractions of all kinds as divided into clearly defined hostile camps. Their procedure can be schematized. They typically choose a conventional problem—for example, the question of tradition in literary history. They then focus on a term—in this case, tradition—and explicitly or implicitly reduce it to a definition that is primitive in its simplicity. Finally, they leap to the opposite of their stripped-down term, creating the impression that a radical new insight has been born. Their definition of "tradition," for instance, is precisely what Eliot takes great pains in the beginning of his essay to say that tradition is *not*.

> [I]f the only form of tradition, of handing down, consisted in following the ways of the immediate generation before us in a blind or timid adherence to its successes, "tradition" should positively be discouraged. . . . novelty is better than repetition. (*SE*, 4)

If Eliot were using the same sort of binary "either / or" logic that Gilbert and Gubar are using, he would in fact come down on their side. If one must choose between past and present, between repetition and novelty, then one must take a stand for the present: novelty is *better* than repetition. The purpose of Eliot's essay, however, is to undermine binary logic and introduce a more complex and less ideological model. "Tradition" and the "individual talent" had conventionally been thought of exactly as Gilbert and Gubar project them, as opposites. But Eliot changes the "or" to an "and," changes the opposition to complementarity. What makes a writer "traditional" is not a sense of the past but of the past and present together, of the timeless and the temporal together. He insists that "the past should be altered by the present as much as the present is directed by the

past" (*SE*, 4, 5). And he does the same with other parallel oppositions: "mind of Europe" / "individual mind," "community / individual," "impersonal / personal," and "universal / particular" are
all seen as interconnected and interdependent.

Eliot's rejection of "either / or" logic is evident in his literary
criticism. It is also fundamental in his early philosophical writings.
Like his mentor F. H. Bradley, Eliot is part of the early twentieth-
century revolt against dualism. He argues in his dissertation—"Experience and the Objects of Knowledge in the Philosophy of F. H. Bradley"—that all oppositions (such as "subject / object" and "past /
present") are artificial because they are forced upon us by language
and by the structure of the human mind. (Nietzsche's quip that we
are not rid of God because we are not rid of grammar speaks to the
same point.) All binary sets, furthermore, are in time and thus are
unstable. It is impossible to settle on one ("either / or") part of a
binary opposition, Eliot argues, because both are necessary for either
one to be defined. Interestingly, Eliot's theory insists on difference
but suggests that unity can be imagined. He maintains, in fact, that it
is impossible not to imagine some immediate or primary grounding
of difference and / or some transcendence of it. Dwelling in difference (both parts of a binary set) is inseparable from being finite, from
the human condition. To a thoughtful and sensitive individual, however, difference always points beyond itself.

Reliance on conflictual rhetoric and on binary logic precludes an
understanding of Eliot's argument in "Tradition and the Individual
Talent." The perspective that he cultivates in order to appreciate the
temporal and the timeless and also the temporal and the timeless
together is concealed by such an approach. The blindness that is a
corollary of Gilbert and Gubar's methodology makes it impossible
for them to see the complexity and subtlety of his thinking. While
undercutting black and white polarities, he recovers multiple shades
of gray. Moreover, he facilitates consensus without obliterating difference. In his dissertation, he substitutes for the truth / falsity polarity the notion that truth must be understood, not absolutely, but in
"degrees." He argues for a living whole that must be accepted on
faith (no one mind can grasp the whole), a whole that respects multiple voices, multiple perspectives. Eliot's "both / and" mentality has
much in common with Blake's speculation about "Heaven and Hell"
and Nietzsche's reasoning about "Apollo and Dionysus." Gilbert

221

and Gubar, presumably, would be forced by their rhetoric to choose either "Heaven" or "Hell," either "Apollo" or "Dionysus."

Although the major distortions in Gilbert and Gubar's critique of Eliot can be associated with binary oppositions, other misrepresentations are evident. To support their working assumption that Eliot idealized the past and rejected the present, they argue that he equated the age before the "dissociation of sensibility set in" with the world of "the Christian Fathers." His concept of "unified sensibility," they suggest, stemmed from "a desire to learn 'how to see the world as the Christian Fathers saw it.'" By combining a quotation from a 1921 review of an anthology of seventeenth-century poetry with one from a 1939 essay on the state of Europe moving toward a world war, Gilbert and Gubar document their position that Eliot was nostalgic, that he was sick with "yearning for a Golden Age" (Gilbert and Gubar 1988, 154). This nostalgia, they argue, resulted from a sense of "belatedness" toward the romantic tradition and an anxiety about female writers. The combination of Eliot phrases on different subjects from different time periods is psychologically naive, for it ignores or trivializes the enormous life and mind shaping events of the 1920s and 1930s, including the constant illness of his wife, the breakup of his marriage, his entry into the church, his growing concern with social and religious issues, and his cumulative gloom about political solutions. But even if these phrases had been written in the same year, they would not support Gilbert and Gubar's argument that he idealized the past and rejected the present.

When returned to their contexts in "The Metaphysical Poets" and *The Idea of a Christian Society,* the fragments Gilbert and Gubar quote exhibit intense concern with the present. In the former, Eliot is trying to sort out how "poets in our civilization, as it exists at present," can write poetry that reflects a "unified sensibility," a sensibility that consists of both intellect and feeling (and by implication both male and female) (*SE,* 241–50, 248). In the latter, Eliot is trying to come to terms with the options available to a civilization on the brink of war. The "Christian Fathers" snippet quoted by Gilbert and Gubar does not advocate a simple return to the past but a harvesting followed by a loop back to the present.

> We need to know how to see the world as the Christian Fathers saw it; and the purpose of reascending to origins is that we

should be able to return, with greater spiritual knowledge, to our own situation. We need to recover the sense of religious fear, so that it may be overcome by religious hope.[5]

His primary concern was with the here and now (with Europe and America in 1939) and with the possibility of gaining insights into the contemporary crisis by examining the past.

Another problem with Gilbert and Gubar's procedure lies in their concern with Eliot's "consecration of an 'orthodox' tradition." Given the title of their chapter "Tradition and the Female Talent" and their frequent references to Eliot's 1919 essay, one would assume that the "tradition" at issue is the "tradition" outlined in "Tradition and the Individual Talent." But prefacing the word "tradition" with "orthodox" in quotation marks introduces considerable confusion. "Orthodoxy" is not a special term for Eliot until the 1930s and 1940s, and by that time, his interests have drastically changed and his definition of "tradition" has also changed. In the first chapter of *After Strange Gods* (1934), he carefully defines "tradition" and "orthodoxy." Tradition is "a way of feeling and acting which characterizes a group throughout generations; . . . it must largely be unconscious." It is a handing over of habits, whether good or bad. Tradition is "a by-product of right living, not to be aimed at directly." But while tradition is "of the blood," orthodoxy is "of the brain." It has to do with the "exercise of conscious intelligence," with judgment. In this period of Eliot's life, tradition is associated with feeling, and orthodoxy is associated with thought. They are at once opposites and complements.[6] The reference to Eliot's "consecration of an 'orthodox' tradition," then, seems to be sheer nonsense or a rhetorical smoke bomb in this war of words.

The blindness precipitated by Gilbert and Gubar's rhetoric keeps them from recognizing those aspects of Eliot's thinking that support feminism. Although he does have respect for the past, he consistently makes the present his point of reference. His theory authorizes and empowers the newcomer, male or female.

> No poet, no artist of any art, has his complete meaning alone. . . . You must set him, for contrast and comparison, among the dead. . . . The necessity that he shall conform, that he shall co-

5. T. S. Eliot, *The Idea of a Christian Society* (London: Faber and Faber, 1939), 63.
6. T. S. Eliot, *After Strange Gods: A Primer of Modern Heresy* (New York: Harcourt, Brace, 1934), 31–32.

> here, is not onesided; what happens when a new work of art is created is something that happens simultaneously to all the works of art which preceded it. The existing monuments form an ideal order among themselves, which is modified by the introduction of the new (the really new) work of art among them. . . . for order to exist after the supervention of novelty, the *whole* existing order must be . . . altered; and so the relations, proportions, values of each work of art toward the whole are readjusted; and this is conformity between the old and the new. . . . the past should be altered by the present as much as the present is directed by the past. (*SE,* 4, 5)

Gilbert and Gubar make much of Eliot's reference to "conformity"; but despite their allusion to this very passage in the closing paragraph of "Tradition and the Female Talent," they seem to have missed his clear definition of conformity as an adjustment triggered and controlled by the present, by the newcomer, by the individual talent. This theory predicts that the marginalized or the newcomer can make all the difference. The appearance of a great woman epic poet, for example, would shatter the existing tradition; she would *alter* Dante and Milton; she would force reconsideration of Homer as the inevitable precursor in Western literature. (The word "precursor," of course, literally and necessarily takes the present as a reference point.) Empowered by Eliot's notion of tradition, she would dispose of some precursors, alter others, and create entirely new ones.

Modernism, especially as abstracted from Eliot's early work, also comes under attack in *The War of the Words.* Gilbert and Gubar claim that when the feminist issues are factored in to classic modernism, one dis-covers

> an entirely different modernism. And it is a modernism constructed not just against the grain of Victorian male precursors, not just in the shadow of a shattered God, but as an integral part of a complex response to female precursors and contemporaries. Indeed, it is possible to hypothesize that a reaction-formation against the rise of literary women became not just a theme in modernist writing but a motive for modernism. (Gilbert and Gubar 1988, 156)

The repeated "not just" in this passage divulges the authors' realization that this is not "an entirely different modernism." It is at once

224

a confirmation of the high modernism associated with Eliot and a modification of it. The modification, though overstated, is nevertheless significant. Although Gilbert and Gubar are less than persuasive in presenting a "new" modernism, they do point to the importance of accounting for the presence of women in the literary marketplace.

Gilbert and Gubar's strategy in regard to modernism (as in their critique of tradition) involves the manipulation of binary oppositions. In assessing the values associated with classic modernism, for example, they find a "nature / culture" opposition, and in reading Eliot's early poems, they place him firmly on the side of culture. (This overlooks an enormous body of evidence associating modernists such as Eliot, Picasso, and Stravinsky with primitivism; and indeed, the evidence of poems such as "The Love Song of J. Alfred Prufrock" is that Eliot was sick of culture.) Gilbert and Gubar substantiate their claim with commentary on "Cousin Nancy" and "The Love Song of J. Alfred Prufrock." Their reading of "Cousin Nancy" illustrates once again the reductive effect of a model of logic that depends upon conflict. Eliot, they argue,

> frankly satirizes the specious modernity of the liberated Miss Nancy Ellicott, who not only "smoked / And danced all the modern dances" but also, as if to destroy the earth itself, "Strode across the hills and *broke* them." Even the poem's allusive conclusion implicitly censures this aggressive protoflapper. (Gilbert and Gubar 1988, 31)

The conclusion of the poem is: "Upon the glazen shelves kept watch / Matthew and Waldo, guardians of the faith, / The army of unalterable law." Gilbert and Gubar continue their analysis:

> Though Eliot presents Matthew (Arnold) and Waldo (Emerson) ironically, as fragile "guardians of the faith," the fact that they are identified with the "army of unalterable law" which defeats "Prince Lucifer" in Meredith's "Lucifer in Starlight" suggests that Eliot sees the rebellious Nancy as a diabolical upstart whose breaking of nature (the hills) also threatens to break the grounds of culture. (Gilbert and Gubar 1988, 31)

Gilbert and Gubar's rhetorical strategy forces them into seeing the narrator and Nancy as representatives of God and Lucifer, good and evil, and of course male and female, enemies in the war of the sexes. But to describe their relationship in this way is to misrepresent it. The narrator is not so much hostile to Nancy as to her culture, to that against which she is rebelling. The narrator and Nancy are of the same generation ("cousins"), and both are rebelling in their own way against their elders and against the culture epitomized by Arnold and Emerson. Blind to Eliot's use of irony, Gilbert and Gubar assume he is on the side of Arnold and Emerson while against the "diabolical" Nancy. It is true that he treats her somewhat playfully, but the effect is to underscore the fragility and pathetic decadence of Arnold and Emerson, for him the symbols of Boston's two great religions: Culture and Unitarianism. It is bizarre to place Eliot on the side of "culture" in this poem. The representatives of culture are Arnold and Emerson; they and not Cousin Nancy are the objects of his irony.

Gilbert and Gubar devote particular attention to the aesthetic of modernism, and again, they set up a shoot-out of warring phrases. The binary opposition they focus on is "impersonal / personal" with its coordinate antitheses of "thought / feeling" and "classical / romantic."

> The Eliotian theory . . . that poetry involves "an escape from emotion" and "an escape from personality" constructs an implicitly masculine aesthetic of hard, abstract, learned verse that is opposed to the aesthetic of soft, effusive, personal verse supposedly written by women and Romantics. (Gilbert and Gubar 1988, 154)

Stylistic characteristics are translated into sexual terms, whereby precision equates with "hard" (masculine) and vagueness with "soft" (feminine). Again, their conflict-driven methodology forces them to choose between thought and feeling and forces them to classify styles as misogynist or feminist. The lenses they have chosen blind them to Eliot's point regarding the importance of feeling one's thoughts and thinking one's feelings, to his repeated conviction that fruitfulness is only possible through a combination of masculine and feminine values. By polarizing intellect and emotion, Gilbert and Gubar eliminate all of the complexities in Eliot's literary-philosophical-psychological discussion and completely miss the point of his critique of Descartes. They revert, in fact, to just the kind of reductive Cartesian rhetoric he was resisting.

Gilbert and Gubar also discuss the techniques of classic modernism and conclude that they are instruments of sexism. The twin strategies of modernism, to use their own terminology, are "excavation" and "innovation." In another misappropriation of Eliot's essay on tradition, they define "excavation" as using fragments of the "mind of Europe" in order "simultaneously to counter and to recover the noble fatherhood of precursors from Homer to Dante and Shakespeare." "Innovation" refers to the "use of puns, allusions, phrases in foreign languages, arcane and fractured forms . . . to occult language so that only an initiated elite can participate in the community of high culture" (Gilbert and Gubar 1988, 156). The most famous work using these diabolical strategies is of course *The Waste Land.* To clinch their argument regarding a sexist intent, they quote Joyce's quip that *The Waste Land* ended once and for all the idea of "poetry for ladies."

To their credit, Gilbert and Gubar sometimes rise above the reductive confrontational mentality that tarnishes their work in *No Man's Land.* When working within the feminist camp, they drop the military metaphor and try to build bridges. In "The Mirror and the Vamp," for example, they survey contemporary feminist literary politics and argue that differences are not evidence of a war but of a stimulating dialogue. Playing on M. H. Abrams's distinction between mimetic and expressive aesthetic theories in *The Mirror and the Lamp,* Gilbert and Gubar classify contemporary feminists as "mirror critics" or "vamp critics." Mirror critics consider criticism "a space in which to capture the shifting historical images of gendered reality," while vamp critics consider criticism a space for "expressive autonomy as well as for rebelliously anti-rational and anti-hierarchical impulses that have been repressed but not erased by patriarchal culture."[7] Instead of using metaphors that pit these critics against each other in a "war of words," Gilbert and Gubar maintain that both mirror and vamp critics are valuable partners in an empowering conversation. The mirror critic and the vamp are interrelated, like tradition and the individual talent, and neither should try to destroy the other. The question driving their meditation of course is an Eliotian one. Should feminist criticism be considered as continuous with tradition or as a repudiation of the past? Their answer, again analogous to Eliot's in "Tradition and the Individual Talent," is that feminist literary criticism should be considered as a product of the West-

---

7. Sandra M. Gilbert and Susan Gubar, "The Mirror and the Vamp," in *The Future of Literary Theory,* ed. Ralph Cohen (London: Routledge, 1989), 144–66, 145.

ern tradition and as a disruption of it. Rejecting binary logic, they discover both continuity and rupture within the feminist community; they embrace both mimetic and expressive theories, both classical and romantic tendencies. Like Eliot in "Tradition and the Individual Talent," Gilbert and Gubar in "The Mirror and the Vamp" revisit inherited categories and force readers to attend to ways in which these categories are restrictive.

Gilbert and Gubar's enmity toward male critics (especially male precursors) is ambivalent and psychologically complex. It is not simply the opposite of love or of good will. And although it does not fit neatly into Harold Bloom's model of the anxiety of influence, it does involve at a profound level an anxiety regarding their own critical authority. Gilbert and Gubar's preoccupation with their seat at the literary table can be seen from how frequently they announce in their titles kinship with an influential male predecessor (Eliot, Abrams, Bloom) while indicating their feminist and subversive intent. In "The Mirror and The Vamp," for example, they place themselves in the great tradition of romantic criticism, which includes Abrams. It is interesting to note the interplay of descent and dissent here. At one and the same time, they honor Abrams and, by changing his "lamp" to their own "vamp," mischievously promise a feminist and subversive agenda. In "Tradition and the Female Talent," Gilbert and Gubar announce their ties to Eliot at the same time that they open a gap between their insights and those of the modernist poet-critic, acknowledging that his tradition both always is and never can be theirs. Their criticism, despite the weaknesses discussed in this paper, is valuable and has become part of a larger clarification of the original issues raised by their male precursors.

228

Dialectical Pedagogy: Teaching

The Waste Land

"The Second Coming" and *The Waste Land*

Capstone Texts in the Western Civilization Course

" The Second Coming" by W. B. Yeats and *The Waste Land* by T. S. Eliot are ideal companion poems to use as a capstone experience in a course in Western civilization. Both Yeats and Eliot believed that moving forward needs to be informed by looking backward, and their poems are exhibits of the proposition that the most avant-garde work in art often comes from artists who maintain a living and dynamic relationship with their cultural past. Both "The Second Coming" and *The Waste Land* deal powerfully with the state of civilization in the twentieth century; both suggest that civilization is falling apart, and each in its own way reveals the cause of the crisis. Both poems (especially *The Waste Land*) allude to central events and major texts of the last several thousand years of Western (and Eastern) civilization; the list of allusions in Eliot's poem, in fact, reads like a syllabus for a survey course in Western civilization. *The Waste Land*, furthermore, suggests that the main activity of general humanities courses, i.e., systematic retrieval of great texts, has value as a means to redeem civilization from ruin.

In his most famous critical essay, "Tradition and the Individual Talent," Eliot argues that a poet must write with Western civilization, so to speak, in his bones. He calls this presence of the past within a poet "the historical sense," and he argues that it is "indispensable for anyone who would continue to be a poet beyond his twenty-fifth year."

> The historical sense involves a perception, not only of the pastness of the past, but of its presence; the historical sense compels a man to write not merely with his own generation in his bones, but with a feeling that the whole of the literature of Europe from Homer and within it the whole of the literature of his own coun-

231

try has a simultaneous existence and composes a simultaneous order. (*SE*, 4)

One can disagree with Eliot's idea that the historical sense is universally required for poets, but one cannot dispute the fact that Eliot used it as a standard for himself and prepared himself to be a poet by saturating himself in the great texts of Western civilization. Next to Milton, Eliot is the most learned English language poet; his mind includes most of the great classics of Western civilization and is like the "mind of Europe" described in "Tradition and the Individual Talent"—a "mind which changes, . . . but which abandons nothing *en route*" (*SE*, 6). The great texts hover over everything that he wrote; but in a special and obvious sense, they literally and conspicuously constitute *The Waste Land*. Yeats was not learned in the same classical sense as Eliot, but he too was well educated and particularly in the great myths of Western civilization. As a repository of the myths of the Greeks, Hebrews, Romans, Christians, and especially the Celts, as well as a representative of his age, Yeats is invaluable in a general humanities course.

One reason for using "The Second Coming" and *The Waste Land* as capstone texts in a Western civilization course, then, is that they gather within themselves many of the texts studied in the early parts of such a course. Insofar as they focus on the same crisis from very different standpoints, they tend to be more valuable used together than alone because they tend to interpret each other. Moreover, Eliot's particular mode of re-collecting texts provides students with the joy of re-cognizing and re-interpreting the past texts at the same time that they are beginning to understand the present ones. These poems enable students to understand another point that Eliot makes in "Tradition and the Individual Talent": the new changes the old as much as the old influences the new. The *Divine Comedy*, for example, not only influenced and became a part of *The Waste Land*, but for students who study first Dante and then Eliot, *The Waste Land* actually makes a difference in the *Comedy*.

Even though the two modern poems seem made to order for use as companion capstone texts, they are seldom so used. The main reason is that they are considered too difficult for such courses. Many faculty feel uncomfortable with them; many more feel that these poems are simply too advanced for general education courses, ones usually taught in the first two years of college and often as requirements. Although both poems are in some ways endlessly complex, both are remarkably accessible to students, especially if introduced into a course that anticipates them by including great works that in a sense they recapitulate. In my experience, students find "The Second Coming" mysteriously powerful even before they have any idea of what it means. And today's students, brought up on rock music rather than on books, in one way are more prepared than their more literary elders to read *The Waste Land.* Unhampered by expectations of narrative form, they bring an immediate appreciation of discontinuous form. In fact, to the astonishment of teachers, students often take to *The Waste Land* far more naturally than to the "easier" poems of, say, Wordsworth or Frost.

Convinced that the poems by Yeats and Eliot are both invaluable and accessible, I have written the following guide for students (freshmen, for the most part) in general humanities courses of the kind so often taught in American colleges. The first part of my essay provides the context for these poems; the second offers a reading of "The Second Coming;" and the third focuses on *The Waste Land.* I assume in this discussion that students bring to the twentieth-century materials some experience with central texts of the Western past, specifically including Sophocles's *Oedipus Rex,* Matthew's gospel, Augustine's *Confessions,* Dante's *Purgatorio,* Shakespeare's *Hamlet,* Darwin's *Origin of Species* (selections), Nietzsche's *Birth of Tragedy,* Freud's *Interpretation of Dreams,* and Frazer's *Golden Bough* (selections).

I. THE AGE OF ANXIETY

The importance of such poems as *The Waste Land* and "The Second Coming" is inseparable from their value as pictures of modern civilization; and they should be considered, first of all, in the context of the civilization and the crisis that they document.[1] At the core of this crisis is a fear that Western civilization is on the edge of disaster and, in fact, may be wiped out entirely. One reason why these poems continue to speak to us so powerfully is that we are still in this crisis. We still live with the possibility that contemporary peo-

---

1. For a more detailed exposition of this crisis and the method Yeats and Eliot used to circumvent it, see "The Case of the Missing Abstraction" in this volume.

ple will destroy their universe and everything in it, that they will literally annihilate themselves and their civilization. The anxiety of our age extends from the anxiety of Eliot's and Yeats's age; both anxieties have the same roots. In the early twentieth century, when these works were written, and now, in the last decade of the century, the danger is related to incredible advances in knowledge and, at the same time, a loss of cultural memory, a collective forgetfulness about basic spiritual and humanistic resources and values.

The massive collapse of traditional values and the disappearance of people's sense of belonging to a universal human family have resulted in a pervasive cultural uneasiness. W. H. Auden calls the modern crisis a breakdown of liberal humanism, by which he means a breakdown of faith in the existence of God, in the goodness of humanity, and in the possibility of progress. This breakdown produced what Auden in a fine poem calls "The Age of Anxiety." Insofar as "anxiety" is distress or uneasiness caused by the apprehension of some certain but vague disaster, Auden's term seems appropriate. The Age of Anxiety is often said to have begun in August 1914; and it is true that the First World War had an incalculable effect on the modern mind. In that war, Western civilization began literally tearing itself to pieces on the battlefields of Europe. But the war was not primarily a beginning, not a cause of the modern spiritual crisis; rather, it was a continuation, a result of that spiritual crises.

The pervasive disillusionment characteristic of the Age of Anxiety should be associated with a radical revision, during the second half of the nineteenth century, of ideas and principles that had long served as the foundation of Western civilization. Among those most responsible for the revision are Charles Darwin, Friedrich Nietzsche, Sigmund Freud, and Sir James G. Frazer. In *On the Origin of Species* (1859) and *The Descent of Man* (1871), Darwin removed mind (human or divine) from the origin and development of life. He maintained that God, if he existed, had been absent in history; and he implied that humans, merely creatures among creatures, are not justified in considering themselves endowed with inalienable "human" rights. Like all other organisms, they are creatures of environment and chance. In *The Birth of Tragedy* (1872), Nietzsche argued that Dionysus, the dark god of wine and irrationality, is as basic to art and to life as either Socrates or Apollo, symbols of reason and light. And in a fa-

234

mous boast, Nietzsche proclaimed that "God is dead." Sigmund Freud, in *The Interpretation of Dreams* (1899), suggested a model of human nature in which the irrational and the unconscious and the violent are foundational. In *Civilization and its Discontents* (1930), he summed up his findings that people are not gentle loving creatures who simply defend themselves when attacked but are innately aggressive ones opposed to culture. The anthropologist Sir James George Frazer also contributed much to the shape of the Age of Anxiety. In *The Golden Bough* (1890), a great encyclopedia of primitive religion, he argued that religion evolved from magic and is in turn being replaced by science. He might have intended to recover scientific respectability for Christianity by bringing it into line with Darwinian evolution; but he ended by suggesting that all religions are the same religion, all heroes (Christ and Dionysus) the same hero. The disquiet produced by these thinkers was compounded around the turn of the century by physicists who called into question or denied notions of reality that had supported the Western mind for millennia. In the place of an ordered universe, scientists such as Max Planck and Niels Bohr postulated one ruled by chance, a universe consisting of tiny and unpredictable bits of energy. All of this work contributes to the intellectual background leading to the Age of Anxiety, to the disease (both disease and dis-ease) associated with the fear that Western civilization was falling apart.

The conviction that a major dispensation in history was quickly drawing to a close was not limited to artists. German historian Oswald Spengler argued in *The Decline of the West*, published in German in 1918 and in English a few years later, that civilizations are organisms that go through stages of youth, maturity, decay, and then, like all organisms, they die. As Greece and Rome flourished and disappeared, so shall we. Western civilization, in his diagnosis, is in a very late stage of decay, and death is being hastened by neglect of the spiritual (philosophy, religion, art) and by cultivation of the merely material. The British historian Arnold Toynbee similarly argued in *A Study of History*, in the 1930s and 1940s, that Western civilization is breaking down. He did not believe that civilizations automatically move through stages of growth and decay but that they stand or fall insofar as they meet or fail to meet environmental and moral challenges. Toynbee argued that Western civilization is breaking down because we resort to violence and war to solve our problems. He was part of a chorus of intellectuals who claimed that by abandoning our spiritual and humanistic values, we have lapsed into barbarism.

Yeats and Eliot were not alone, then, in their feeling that a major era in civilization was coming to an end. Eliot is often described as having expressed in *The Waste Land* the disillusionment of his age. He himself hated this sort of talk, and he once quipped that maybe he expressed his readers' illusion of being disillusioned, but that he never meant to do so. He was, he claimed, expressing his own disillusion; he was just "grumbling." But whether he meant to or not, he transformed his personal grumbling into art, expressing in a new form what many of the most intelligent and sensitive people of this century have felt. In *Ulysses* (1922), published the same year as *The Waste Land*, James Joyce put it this way: "History is a nightmare from which I am trying to awake."

II. "THE SECOND COMING"

The conviction that Western civilization is falling apart, important in most twentieth-century art, is perhaps most memorably expressed in Yeats's "The Second Coming," written in 1919 and published in 1920.

> Turning and turning in the widening gyre
> The falcon cannot hear the falconer;
> Things fall apart; the centre cannot hold;
> Mere anarchy is loosed upon the world,
> The blood-dimmed tide is loosed, and everywhere
> The ceremony of innocence is drowned;
> The best lack all conviction, while the worst
> Are full of passionate intensity.
> Surely some revelation is at hand;
> Surely the Second Coming is at hand.
> The Second Coming! Hardly are those words out
> When a vast image out of *Spiritus Mundi*
> Troubles my sight: somewhere in sands of the desert
> A shape with lion body and the head of a man,
> A gaze blank and pitiless as the sun,
> Is moving its slow thighs, while all about it
> Reel shadows of the indignant desert birds.
> The darkness drops again; but now I know

236

> That twenty centuries of stony sleep
> Were vexed to nightmare by a rocking cradle,
> And what rough beast, its hour come round at last,
> Slouches towards Bethlehem to be born?[2]

The title of this poem is taken from the Christian religion. The first coming was the birth of Christ, the Incarnation; it marked the end of one major historical dispensation and the beginning of another. According to the New Testament, Christ's Second Coming, to be preceded by a time of troubles and sorrow, will mark the end of this present age. In many interpretations, the Second Coming is also to usher in a new age, a millennium in which Christ will reign on earth and in which there will be peace. This doctrine of the Second Coming as a turning point in history can be found in Matthew 24 and other parts of the Bible.

Yeats strongly believed that civilization as we know it is coming to an end. He had a theory of history similar in some respects to that of Spengler. Like Spengler, he believed that history moves in large cycles of growth and decay. Yeats believed that these cycles last about two thousand years and that the present cycle, which began with the birth of Christ, is about to end. Because the Second Coming of Christ traditionally is considered to be a major historical intersection, the end of this age and the beginning of the next, images of it are useful for him.

The first stanza of Yeats's poem begins with an image of a falconer who has lost control of his hawk. Communication and control are lost, and things fall apart. This image is followed by a description of the historical situation when Yeats was writing this poem, a time of unprecedented violence and barbarism. These were the days of the First World War, the Russian Revolution, and civil war in Yeats's own country of Ireland.

Matthew's gospel describes the days just before the Second Coming in the following terms: "For then shall be great tribulation, such as was not since the beginning of the world to this time, no, nor ever shall be. And except those days be shortened, there should no flesh be saved" (Matthew 24:21–22). Surely, the poet cries, this anarchy

---

2. W. B. Yeats, *The Poems of W. B. Yeats*, ed. Richard J. Finneran (New York: Macmillan, 1983).

and violence and moral collapse in history must be the sign that the Second Coming is at hand. The mention of the Second Coming triggers a vision. It arises from the *Spiritus Mundi,* that is, from the "Spirit of the World." (For Yeats, the *Spiritus Mundi* is the storehouse of primitive and archetypal images, such as the Sphinx.) One would expect that the vision triggered by the phrase "the Second Coming" would be the same as that described by Matthew: "And they shall see the Son of man coming in the clouds of heaven with power and great glory" (Matthew 24:30). And one would expect that the vision of the new age would be an image of the biblical kingdom of God, where swords (implements of war) have been recycled as plows (implements of agriculture), where love and pity have banished hate. But Yeats's vision is not the Christian vision. This turning point in history will not be the Second Coming of Christ the "Prince of Peace," but the appearance of another god, a successor to Christ. Like Christ, this god will come from the Mediterranean world. But whereas Christ was a combination of the divine and the human, a perfect man, his successor in Yeats's vision is a combination of the bestial and the human, a monster with the head (intelligence) of a man and the body (passions, instincts) of a lion. In this ultimate nightmare, Yeats sees a god with a blank gaze and slowly moving thighs, a god who is the antithesis of love. This new master will be "pitiless as the sun"; that is, he will be morally neutral and radically democratic. The sun, as the Bible says, shines alike on the just and the unjust. This blond god sheds his beams equally on murderer and victim; he smiles at the same time on the gluttony of war lords and the starvation of children.

Yeats interprets his vision by saying that the Greek world was vexed to nightmare by the birth of Christ in Bethlehem. And now, interpreting contemporary history, he sees the Christian era in its own nightmare. In the famous closing image, he wonders about Christ's successor, the rough beast now slouching toward Bethlehem to inaugurate the next era of human history.

III. *THE WASTE LAND*

T. S. Eliot is of towering significance in the aesthetic and moral life of this century. The first half of the century, in fact, is often referred to as the "Age of Eliot," and the publication in 1922 of *The Waste Land* is the most important event in twentieth-century poetry.

As the distinguished critic Richard Ellmann has said, *The Waste Land* became so famous that for much of this century, the latest poetry in Arabic, Swahili, or Japanese was far more likely to have been influenced by Eliot than by earlier poets in those languages or by any other poet in English. After *The Waste Land*, Eliot turned to a different kind of poetry, of which the masterpiece is *Four Quartets*, published during the Second World War.

A wasteland, of course, is a desert or any place inhospitable to life and health. Some wastelands, such as deserts or icebergs or rocky mountains, are natural; but others, such as the used part of a coal mine, a trash dump, a city slum, or a bombed countryside, are human artifacts. And of course some wastelands are symbolic, that is, they are not "lands" but states of being. For example, a college or a marriage may be a wasteland. Eliot's poem includes references to all of these wastelands. The literal desert may be seen in such lines as "What are the roots that clutch, what branches grow / Out of this stony rubbish?" (ll. 19–20). The culturally produced wastelands may be seen in such lines as those describing the polluted river banks where the "flowers" of summer consist of "empty bottles, sandwich papers, / Silk handkerchiefs, cardboard boxes, cigarette ends" (ll. 177–78). The symbolic wastelands can be seen in the two families of part II—the miserable and fruitless couple from the upper classes, and the literally fruitful but loveless marriage of Lil and Albert, whose children are the expensive and unwanted by-product of Albert's lust.

The most important wasteland in Eliot's poem, however, is the comprehensive one that includes all of the others—Western civilization in the twentieth century, a place that is sterile and hostile to health and flourishing. Eliot's poem is his metaphor for the state of culture in the twentieth century. Like Yeats and many others of his generation, he interpreted the contemporary situation in Europe and the United States as one of moral and cultural decay. He felt that the basis of cultural unity had disappeared, that the glue that had held Western civilization together had dissolved. As Yeats describes this crisis in "The Second Coming," "Things fall apart, the centre cannot hold." The center of which Yeats writes is Christianity, which for two thousand years had held things together. But in the late nineteenth century, Christianity lost its power to unify culture, and for the first

239

time in two thousand years, the nonexistence or irrelevance of God was consciously taken as a cultural assumption. *The Waste Land* is a picture of what remains when the center is removed; it is a picture of civilization with no moral or cultural or religious center, no god-concept, no glue. It consists quite literally of hundreds of fragments of the Western present and of the Western past insofar as it had survived into the twentieth century. The text of the poem is in some ways comparable to what Bloomsbury would look like if a bomb should drop on the British Museum.

Some of the fragments in *The Waste Land* are preserved exactly. For example, "Those are pearls that were his eyes" is a line from Ariel's song in Shakespeare's *The Tempest;* and "Poi s'ascose nel foco che gli affina" a line from Dante's *Purgatorio.* Other fragments in the poem have been changed by evolution through time but can still be recognized. The pathetic song of Ophelia in Shakespeare's *Hamlet,* for example, has evolved into the popular song "Good night, ladies, we're going to leave you now" and also into the final words that contemporary people say as they leave the pub after an evening of drinking together, "Goonight Lou. Goonight May. Goonight."

Eliot's fragments at first may appear to be more or less independent, related only by their capacity to be connected on some level to a wasteland. But in fact the fragments fall naturally into groups, and a number of fragments fall into several groups at once. These fragment clusters, then, are not mutually exclusive and do not have firm boundaries. Part of the poem's meaning derives from the juxtaposition of these clusters. For example, many fragments deal with wasted landscapes and many deal with city scenes. By simply placing these fragments side by side without comment, Eliot suggests that the modern city is a wasteland. This idea is reinforced by portraying the city dwellers as sterile, loveless, and isolated. Eliot does not actually state: "London (or Paris or New York) is a wasteland," but he clearly suggests that these cities are places where life does not flourish. The accuracy of Eliot's depiction of modern urban existence may account in some part for the power of his poem.

The single most important group of fragments in Eliot's poem are those having to do with literal wastelands, for these refer to the ancient myth that provides Eliot with his title and his major symbol. The myth describes a land cursed with sterility, a land in which crops

240

will not grow, women cannot bear children, cattle cannot reproduce, etc. The sterility in the land and its occupants is connected in some mysterious way to impotence in the ruler of the land. The ruler, who is both a god and a king, has been wounded in his genitals (by such causes as war, sickness, old age), and this sexual incapacity affects his entire kingdom by depriving it of regenerative power. Just as the curse on the divine ruler has blighted his people and land, so would his healing lead to their health. The curse can be lifted if (1) a hero will come and undergo certain trials in order to find the wounded ruler and ask him certain ritualistic questions; and if (2) the healed ruler is allowed to die, a circumstance that would permit his resurrection or revitalization and the transmission of his power.

The wasteland myth is contained in the background of the Greek tragedy *Oedipus Rex*. The following description of the city of Thebes is only one ancient version of the myth of the cursed land and its suffering inhabitants.

> Thebes is tossed on a murdering sea
> And cannot lift her head from the death surge.
> A rust consumes the buds and fruits of the earth;
> The herds are sick; children die unborn,
> And labor is vain. . . . Death alone
> Battens upon the misery of Thebes.
> . . . The noble plowland bears no grain
> And groaning mothers cannot bear—[3]

The curse on the land and its inhabitants is directly related to the king's sexual health. Oedipus is guilty of the great sexual taboo of incest (as well as the sin of patricide), and the situation defined by his guilt reacts on his land. For healing to occur, certain questions have to be asked and answered. The horrible irony of this version of the wasteland myth is that Oedipus is the sexually unclean king as well as the questor who must ask the questions and purge the land.

Eliot must have encountered innumerable versions of this myth during his extensive education in philosophy, literature, and religion. In a note to *The Waste Land*, he reveals two special sources of his understanding of the myth.

---

3. Sophocles, *The Oedipus Cycle: Oedipus Rex, Oedipus at Colonus, Antigone*, trans. Dudley Fitts and Robert Fitzgerald (New York: Harcourt Brace Jovanovich, 1977), 4.

> Not only the title, but the plan and a good deal of the inciden-
> tal symbolism of the poem were suggested by Miss Jessie L.
> Weston's book on the Grail legend: *From Ritual to Romance*. . . . To
> another work of anthropology I am indebted in general, one
> which has influenced our generation profoundly: I mean *The
> Golden Bough*; I have especially used . . . *Adonis, Attis, Osiris*.

The Golden Bough by Sir James Frazer is a twelve-volume collection of
thousands of myths from all times and all places. Frazer began his
work in the generation after Darwin, and as Darwin had attempted
to discover the origin of the species and to chart the descent of man,
so Frazer tried to discover the origin of religion and to chart the
descent of the gods. He discovered that most myths have certain
features in common, and as Darwin had postulated a common ancestor for humankind, so Frazer postulated a single ancestor for all
religions. By putting together the common features of many myths,
he was able to construct what he considered to be the parent myth.
This myth had broken up over time, but its fragments persist in the
myths and religions that we know from history and in the present
world. According to Frazer, all religions, including Christianity, are
fragments of this one great myth. The myth that Frazer constructed
out of all of his fragments is the myth of the wasteland, outlined
above and taken by Eliot for the main symbol of his poem.[4]

Jessie Weston was a student of the legends having to do with the
Holy Grail, the cup Christ is said to have used at the last supper.
From her study of these legends and fragments of legends, most of
which date from the early Middle Ages, she concluded that the legends of the Holy Grail had also descended from a single parent. Like
Darwin and like Frazer, she used the fragments she had in order to
construct what she thought to be the parent legend. She argued that
the legends of the Holy Grail are, in fact, fragments of the pre-
Christian wasteland myth.

Eliot's interest in the wasteland myth, unlike that of Frazer and
Weston, is not in the myth itself. Instead, his interest lies in the myth's
power to suggest truths about contemporary life and in its claim to
support an underlying unity for modern society. Post World War I
London, where Eliot was living when he wrote the poem, contained

4. For a more detailed discussion of Eliot's use of Frazer, see "The Case of the
Missing Abstraction" in this volume.

all sorts of people, all sorts of beliefs. They seemed to have nothing in common with each other or with the poet; and although crowded together in a modern city in which they literally touched and smelled each other daily, they all seemed alone, isolated. But in terms of Frazer's thesis, all people, regardless of how separate they seem to be, are brothers and sisters; all beliefs, no matter how bizarre, are one belief. *The Waste Land* is a collection of human voices and mythic fragments such as that found in any modern metropolis. The human and mythic odds and ends of a modern city seem unconnected, but they are all related within and by the myth of the wasteland.

Eliot works mainly by suggestion, and so he does not say precisely what causes a flourishing place to become a wasteland. His use of the myth suggests a mysterious but particular relationship between the wounding of God and the existence of a wasteland. By wounding our God, we have wounded ourselves. His decay and ours are intertwined. Similarly, the myth suggests a connection between the moral and intellectual weakness of political and religious leaders and the decay of their followers. Fruitfulness in a family or a city or a civilization depends upon community, upon relations between people and their leaders. Fruitfulness also depends upon connections between people who know and love each other, who share traditions and beliefs. Yet the physical or sexual connection by itself, without traditions and beliefs and love, generates not a garden but a different type of wasteland. By using the myth, Eliot also suggests a connection between human love (eros and philia) and divine love (*agape*). The Bible makes the same connection by stating that a man who cannot love his brother, whom he has seen, cannot truly love God, whom he has not seen.

The background myth, then, suggests that what causes the wasteland is a failure to connect, a lack of love. The myth also suggests that the curse can be broken. In the myth, the healing of the land is tied to the healing of the king. His healing, death, and revitalization would lead to ours. This healing could be accomplished by undergoing certain trials and by asking certain questions about the meaning of life. The healing, interestingly, happens because the questor asks the right questions rather than because he receives the right answers. God cannot heal himself; his healing depends on a person who will conceive of and ask certain questions.

Whether readers experience *The Waste Land* as difficult or easy depends to a great extent on the expectations they bring to the work. If readers demand a story or plot, a hero or main character or main speaker, an argument or lesson; if readers demand an understanding of every line; if they demand any or all of these things, they will have a difficult time indeed. But if (as Eliot expects) readers suspend these demands and accept the poem as an arrangement of fragments from Western culture, they will have an easy time. To return to my example of Bloomsbury after a bomb has fallen on the British Museum: coming upon such a scene, one would be able to make sense out of it without understanding every fragment. In fact, one could get the basic idea just by experiencing the scene, even if one did not at first recognize any specific fragment. And then one could start reconstructing a Grecian urn by identifying a few fragments and finding complementary fragments and so forth. And one would find meaning, not just in the reconstructed fragments, but more important, in the act of reconstructing them.

Eliot's poem has suffered from the work of teachers who try to explain it line by line, layer by layer. Often the poem is introduced by presenting to the reader a list of fragments with tags showing where Eliot got them. Such a list overwhelms most readers and constitutes a barrier to understanding the poem. A better approach would be one in which the reader notices that the poem is made up of fragments of Eliot's own verse and fragments of Western civilization, realizes that these fragments (according to Frazer and Weston) were once part of one myth, and tries to understand what has happened and why. Simply knowing the myth and experiencing the bits and pieces of meaning in the poem is to most readers at once illuminating and unforgettable.

A second stage in reading this poem concerns the recognition of specific fragments. Many of the fragments are pictures and sounds of contemporary life, familiar because we see and hear them every day. Others are from other times and places; we instantly notice some in foreign languages. These fragments of contemporary and historical life have been carefully selected and arranged by the poet so that the more one knows, the richer the poem becomes. Most people will recognize some of the fragments of myth and religion and history and literature, even on a first reading. But getting the main point of the poem does not require understanding all of the fragments and

244

does not require immediate understanding of any specific fragment. Thus, the best procedure is to focus on the familiar ones and, for the time being, ignore the others.

The richness that comes from retrieving fragments (and the works from which they came) can be suggested by considering the lines "To Carthage then I came / Burning burning burning burning" (ll.307–8), lines which can be understood minimally—as part of a scene of contemporary life. The first part of this passage from *The Waste Land*, however, is a translation of the opening phrase of chapter three of Augustine's *Confessions*, which reads:

> To Carthage I came, where there sang all around me in my ears a cauldron of unholy loves. I loved not yet, yet I loved to love. . . . I sought what I might love, in love with loving. . . . For within me was a famine of that inward food, Thyself, my God, yet, through that famine I was not hungered. . . . my soul was sickly and full of sores, it miserably cast itself forth, desiring to be scraped by the touch of objects of sense.[5]

If recognized as part of Augustine's autobiography, if recovered as part of his quest for love and knowledge and truth, if understood as part of his attempt to put his loves in order, if then returned to the context of the modern city, the fragment in Eliot's montage takes on profound suggestiveness. This process of recognizing and recovering fragments and of bringing them to bear on Eliot's poem will be rewarding in itself and will lead to the heart of his deeply moral vision of Western culture. By asking such questions as why the line from Augustine exists only as a fragment, why Eliot thought the line and the tradition containing it were worth recovering, and why he put it at the end of a contemporary scene of sterile lust, readers will have begun the work of reconstruction that will lead them beyond the wasteland.

Some readers are disquieted by the foreign phrases in *The Waste Land*. The fact that they are jibberish to most of us and to most modern characters in the poem is almost as important as any meaning they have in themselves. A main point in the poem is that we are so split up by nationalism and other "isms" that we do not understand

5. Augustine, *The Confessions of St. Augustine*, trans. Edward B. Pusey (New York: Washington Square Press, 1951), 30.

each other's languages, much less each other's literature. Most of us would not recognize lines in English from Tennyson, much less lines in Italian from the *Inferno* or in German from *Tristan und Isolde;* and Eliot claims that this inability to connect to our past and to each other is a main cause of the wasteland. Mere translations of foreign phrases, such as appear in the footnotes of many teaching editions of the poem, do not solve the problem, because simply knowing the translations of lines does not permit the reconnection that Eliot considered essential. In the final analysis, recovery of meaning and reconstruction of bridges will not be accomplished by editors but by readers who take Eliot and his landmark poem seriously.

As parts of classic works available in ordinary libraries, most of the wasteland fragments are in a literal sense not really fragments. But Eliot is not concerned with what exists in libraries; he is concerned with what exists in the heads and hearts of modern readers. And to most modern people, Plato, the Bible, Augustine, Dante, Shakespeare, and most of our noblest ancestors exist only as names or as parts of lines heard in an advertising jingle or as part of a popular song ("O O O O that Shakespeherian Rag—"). Fragments in themselves have no power to unify and revivify culture; but as part of the great traditions of our common history, they have the power to help us turn our wasteland into a garden.

When Love Fails

An Approach to Teaching *The Waste Land*

Undeniably a complex and inexhaustible work, *The Waste Land* is also in many ways a simple poem with themes that are central in human experience and in Western literature. When presenting the poem to freshmen and sophomores, I focus on a single basic theme: "When love fails, a wasteland develops." I then move to more complex and more literary issues of structure and meaning. The idea that failed love has disastrous consequences is basic to all Eliot's work from "Prufrock" to *The Elder Statesman;* as presented in *The Waste Land*, this motif is so clear that almost any student can pick it up, even on a first reading.

My presentation of *The Waste Land* requires three ninety-minute class periods. In the first, I introduce the theme of failed love and its consequences, lecture on the mythic backgrounds of the poem, and lead students through a reading of the first seven lines of the poem and of the epigraph, relating these passages to the theme and to the wasteland myth. In the second class, the students and I read together and discuss three passages of the poem that illustrate failed love and its consequences—the boudoir scene and the pub scene in "A Game of Chess," and the typist-clerk scene in "The Fire Sermon." In the final class, we touch on other parts of the poem that are relevant to the theme, and we discuss why love has failed and how it can be recovered.

A crucial aspect of my approach to teaching literature involves the formulation of assignments that build common ground between me and the students. Even when they seem to be passive, when they are listening to a lecture or to the comments of their classmates, students can (and should) actively collaborate with the poet and with their teacher. To help prepare students to become my collaborators (and

Eliot's) in reading *The Waste Land*, I have designed the following assignments to go with the three classroom sessions.

In preparation for our first class on *The Waste Land*, students read the poem and a handout that I wrote to introduce them to the context of the poem, more specifically, to its relation to the late nineteenth and early twentieth-century crisis in culture and religion. I have found that cultural and religious backgrounds, when emphasized *in class*, can compete with or even overwhelm the poem itself. Yet the poem should not be taught apart from its context in culture. My solution to this pedagogical problem is the use of a brief essay discussing the collapse of Christianity as a cultural force, the collapse of a shared god-concept capable of holding civilization together. In this handout I use Yeats's "The Second Coming" to introduce the idea of civilization losing its center and falling apart. I then discuss *The Waste Land* as a picture of civilization with no moral or cultural or religious center, no god-concept. For more advanced students, I assign a second essay—"T. S. Eliot and the Revolt Against Dualism."[1] My students thus come to the first class on *The Waste Land* with an awareness that the poem consists quite literally of hundreds of fragments from the Western present and from the Western past insofar as it had survived into the twentieth century.

The text of the poem is the focus of the second assignment. I have students reread the entire poem, dividing it into nuggets of narrative or drama or song. I require them to list these nuggets by line numbers and to label each with a descriptive tag (for example, "pub scene" or "fortune-telling scene"). And I tell them not to worry about how the fragments fit together. In doing so, I am quite deliberately planting the suspicion that the fragments might fit together in some less-than-obvious way, a suspicion that often leads the better students to think about the problem of unity. Also in preparation for this class, I ask students to pair off and practice reading aloud three special fragments: lines 77–138 and lines 139–72 in "A Game of Chess," and lines 215–56 in "The Fire Sermon." These are all scenes of love in the modern world, scenes that we will read together as illustrations of the statement "when love fails, a wasteland develops." All three are dramatic, and all have obvious and traditional internal coherence.

1. Both " 'The Second Coming' and *The Waste Land:* Capstones of the Western Civilization Course" and "T. S. Eliot and the Revolt Against Dualism" are included in the present volume.

In preparation for our concluding class on *The Waste Land,* students write an essay in which they identify and discuss scenes from the poem relevant to failed love and its consequences, or to say it another way, passages suggestive of wastelands and the causes of wastelands. They may not use the fragments we have already examined in class (lines 1–7 of "The Burial of the Dead," the epigraph, "A Game of Chess," and the typist-clerk scene in "The Fire Sermon"). Completing this assignment enables students to come to their own understanding of how the poem works and how the fragments fit together. Thus they arrive in class prepared to share their insights and receptive to my attempt to pull things together. In my closing remarks, I usually discuss the mythic materials behind the poem, the poem itself, and the contemporary world in order to suggest why (in Eliot's view) love has failed and how it can be recovered.

I want now to describe what we actually do in our three classes. The main purpose of my first lecture is to introduce the mythic materials behind the poem and to relate these materials to the theme "when love fails, a wasteland develops." In this lecture, I focus on the first seven lines of the poem and on the epigraph. I take for granted that students have studied the handout and read the poem, and I begin by saying that this poem, though very complex, can be discussed in terms of a simple statement, "when love fails, a wasteland develops." A few leading questions induce students to think about what *love* means and to consider the effects of love—fruitfulness, health, happiness, transcendence. Using the spring song from the prologue to *The Canterbury Tales*—"Whan that April with his showres soote / The droughte of March hath perced to the roote—", I remind them of what they already know about the association of spring with showers, with fruit, with birds' songs, and with young people falling in love. I also use Chaucer to suggest that nature's renewal in springtime generates a desire for spiritual renewal. Not only do "smale fowles maken melodye" in April, but also "Thanne longen folk to goon on pilgrimages / . . . . . . / The holy blisful martyr for to seek."[2] After introducing Chaucer's conception of April as a time of reawakened spiritual longing, I observe that April is the time when Christians celebrate the Resurrection of Christ and anticipate their

2. Geoffrey Chaucer, "The General Prologue," *The Canterbury Tales* in *The Norton Anthology of English Literature,* 5th ed., ed. M. H. Abrams et al. (New York: Norton, 1986), 1:95.

own resurrections. From the meaning of *love,* we turn briefly to the meaning of *wasteland,* which I define as a place where life cannot exist or can exist only in a distorted way. I ask students for examples, because it is pedagogically useful for students to have a number of *wasteland* images in mind—not only deserts, but bombed landscapes, city slums, polluted lakes, and so forth.

I now turn directly to the startling variation on spring love with which Eliot begins his poem:

> April is the cruellest month, breeding
> Lilacs out of the dead land, mixing
> Memory and desire, stirring
> Dull roots with spring rain.

The presence of April, warm rain, and lilacs reveals that Eliot is not referring to a literal wasteland, that the wasteland is generated by the speaker's perception. Spring is experienced as cruel because it emphasizes by contrast the speaker's own spiritual lethargy; it nudges him with memory—vague recollections of past love, and desire—intuitive longings for new life. The dull roots in winter's wasteland breed lilacs, but the dull roots in the speaker are stirred to no purpose. Whispering promises that will not be kept, April comes across as disturbing and ironic. And unlike Chaucer's pilgrims, the speaker has no shrine and no place to go for spiritual renewal. I point out that "The Burial of the Dead," the title of part I, is an allusion to the funeral service in the *Book of Common Prayer,* a service in which the Resurrection of Christ on Easter is seen as the guarantee of human immortality. In view of the text immediately following this title—"April is the cruellest month"—the allusion to Christ as the first fruit of spring's new life is bitterly ironic.

Next, I discuss the epigraph of the poem, explaining that an epigraph, like a title, colors the entire work. I show that the overarching reference to the Sibyl of Cumae, a divinity older than Christ, is consistent with the opening perception that spring is cruel. After reviewing the story of the Sibyl as given in the *Aeneid* and in the passage in the *Satryricon* that is behind Eliot's text, we discuss what April would mean to an old and decaying being withered to the size of a cricket and imprisoned in a jar, a being who continues to age but cannot die. We also discuss what is implied by divinity's entrapment in a bottle on display for mortals' scrutiny and amusement and what is implied by the results of such scrutiny. The inspection of the Sibyl reveals impotence, not only a withered body, but also withered powers.

From the Sibyl, I move to the withered prophet Tiresias, at the center of Eliot's poem, and to ancient myths about failed prophets and wastelands. To introduce the myth of the wasteland, I use the description of blighted Thebes that appears in the opening scene of Sophocles' *Oedipus Rex*.

> Thebes is tossed on a murdering sea
> And cannot lift her head from the death surge.
> A rust consumes the buds and fruits of the earth;
> The herds are sick; children die unborn,
> And labor is vain. . . . Death alone
> Battens upon the misery of Thebes.
> . . . The noble plowland bears no grain
> And groaning mothers cannot bear—[3]

I tell the story of the fisher king and his wasteland, explaining briefly that Eliot took his version of the myth from James G. Frazer and Jessie Weston. I then move on to my major subject—what we can learn about the relation of blighted love and wastelands by attending to the mythic backgrounds of Eliot's poem.

My first point is that prosperity depends in myth on interconnectedness, and any failure to connect leads to disaster. Religion, according to Frazer, began with hard physical facts, such as the need to eat. Attempts to insure the fertility of the earth and of animals led to the development of ceremonies involving human sexuality. I use examples from Frazer of sacred prostitution and sexual orgies devised as part of primitive agricultural engineering, emphasizing the fact that in myth, the fruitfulness of the land is inseparably linked to fruitfulness of human beings and animals. I point out that in agricultural and sexual terms, it is literally true that when a connection fails, a wasteland will develop. The latter point has to do with the effects of love, that is, crops or children, but also, and of great importance, transcendence. From the sexual level, there is a move to the spiritual; in some mysterious way, lovers achieve self-transcendence or union. I show from the book of Genesis and various legends that the spiritual fruit of transcendence in some myths actually precedes the

3. Sophocles, *Oedipus Rex*, trans. Fitts and Fitzgerald, 4.

physical fruit of children. Turning to the wasteland myths, I show
that the relation between the king and the land is in certain ways
analogous to the one between husband and wife, that the king
achieves transcendence in his relation to his people, and that they
achieve unity through their relation to him. I develop the point that in
myth, health is related to a coexistence of physical fruits (crops, children) and spiritual fruit (self-transcendence, unity).

The third point about love that I draw from the mythic materials is
that in myth, horizontal love (or love between persons) and vertical
love (or love between the human and the divine) are mutually contingent and interrelated. If human beings cannot love one another,
they cannot love God. If they cannot love God, they cannot love one
another. I illustrate this from the wasteland myths but also from the
Bible. "If a man says, I love God, and hateth his brother, he is a liar;
for he that loveth not his brother, whom he hath seen, how can he
love God, whom he hath not seen? . . . He who loveth God loveth his
brother also" (I John 4:20–21). I underscore the importance of this
principle by quoting from another famous work, Samuel Taylor
Coleridge's "Rime of the Ancient Mariner." Under a curse for having
shot a fellow creature, alone on the wasteland of the cursed sea, the
old seaman notices the beauty of the water snakes.

> O happy living things! no tongue
> Their beauty might declare:
> A spring of love gushed from my heart,
> And I blessed them unaware.

The moment love springs in the heart of Coleridge's old mariner, the
curse begins to lift.

> The self-same moment I could pray;
> And from my neck so free
> The Albatross fell off, and sank
> Like lead into the sea.[4]

By the time we finish this first class, I have established the relation
between love and fruitfulness, between lovelessness and waste—in

---

4. Samuel Taylor Coleridge, "The Rime of the Ancient Mariner," in *The Norton Anthology of English Literature*, 5th ed., ed. M. H. Abrams et al. (New York: Norton, 1986), 2:343.

the myths of Frazer and Weston, in the Bible, and in a few well known works in the Western literary tradition.

The second class again takes up the theme, "when love fails, a wasteland develops," this time focussing on three dramatic passages. We read them almost as reader's theater. Depending on my knowledge of the students and their reading abilities, I either invite certain students to be actors or ask for volunteers. For the boudoir scene in the first part of "A Game of Chess," two actors are needed: a female who is willing to play the nervous desperate woman and a male who is willing to play the bored reflective partner. For the pub scene, three roles must be filled: the nonstop gossip, the friend who is trapped in this nonconversation, and the bartender who interrupts them ("HURRY UP PLEASE ITS TIME"). For the third scene, the encounter between the typist and the clerk in "The Fire Sermon," three roles must be filled: Tiresias, who speaks aside or from behind, and the two lovers who eat and make love in silence. Simply setting up these reading situations is a valuable exercise for students because doing so stimulates them to interpret the scenes and to participate in the class presentation. My role in this class session is chiefly to organize the reading and to encourage discussion afterwards. I ask a few leading questions about failed love and wastelands. My students, in general, enthusiastically relate these scenes to the theme we have been emphasizing and to the mythic backgrounds.

These discussion sessions almost always lead to interesting analogies and insights. Students are quick to notice in the boudoir scene the connection between narcissism and boredom and as quickly the special type of wasteland that characterizes this failed love scene. In the pub scene with the gossip who talks about the marriage of Lil and Albert, students usually notice the coexistence of physical fruitfulness (five children) and spiritual sterility, of sex and waste. And students also have much to offer on the scene of the typist and the clerk. They never fail to note the relevance of "April is the cruellest month" to all of these scenes, nor do they fail to note that in these scenes sex fails to produce transcendence or unity. They also quickly register the contrast between the symbolic importance of sex in the wasteland myths and in religion as well as the total desacralization of sex in the poem. To the first couple, sex is a way to kill time, analogous to a game of chess; to the second, sex is a matter of appetite, analogous (for Albert and the gossip, though not for Lil) to a steak and kidney pie; and to the typist, sex is analogous to a tedious memo (" 'Well now that's done, and I'm glad it's over' ").

Students bring to our third class period their own illustrative fragments, and we spend part of the period sharing these by relating them to failed love and to wastelands of various sorts. I occasionally ask a question or two, but I generally allow the students to lead. After they have heard my opening lecture on myth and love, read the poem three times, participated in our dramatization of the three scenes, and written a short paper on a fragment (or fragments) of their own choosing, most students have definite ideas on the poem, its relevance, its unity or lack of unity, and its value as an object of study. Most often, even those who had never heard of Eliot before this course have come to appreciate him and his achievement; and most, I have discovered, can quote parts of the poem. (I have often wondered whether these students actually memorize lines or simply remember them.) I reserve the last half hour of the period for a few concluding remarks on Eliot and the poem. Sometimes I use Eliot's essay on Baudelaire or the 1929 essay on Dante (both in *Selected Essays*) to say more about special ways in which love has failed in the modern world. Usually, I remind students that Eliot's fragments of failed love come from many times and places, that he is not simply contrasting an idyllic past with a sordid present. I often emphasize how inseparable structure and meaning are in the poem. Our attention to structure when we teach *The Waste Land* has the special value of engaging students and teachers in the collaborative reading valued by Eliot; such attention engages us in recognizing fragments apparently strewn on the poem's surface, and it engages us in re-collecting them by remembering their origins and by gathering them into our present. We and our students shore up our cultural ruins by such collaborative life-enhancing acts of reading.

Bibliography

Aiken, Conrad. "T. S. Eliot: 1888–1965." *Life*, 15 January 1965. 92–93.

Andrewes, Lancelot. *Works*. Oxford: Clarendon Press, 1854.

Auden, W. H. "Yeats as an Example." *Kenyon Review* 10, no. 2 (1948): 187–95.

Augustine. *The Confessions of St. Augustine*. Translated by Edward B. Pusey. New York: Washington Square Press, 1951.

Bolgan, Anne C. *What the Thunder Really Said: A Retrospective Essay on the Making of "The Waste Land."* Montreal: Queen's University Press, 1973.

Bradley, F. H. *Appearance and Reality: A Metaphysical Essay*. 2nd ed. Oxford: Clarendon Press, 1897.

———. *Essays on Truth and Reality*. 1914. Oxford: Clarendon Press, 1950.

———. *Principles of Logic*. 1883. London: Oxford University Press, 1928. 2 vols.

Bronowski, J. *The Common Sense of Science*. Cambridge: Harvard University Press, n.d.

Brooker, Jewel Spears, and Joseph Bentley. *Reading* The Waste Land: *Modernism and the Limits of Interpretation*. Amherst: University of Massachusetts Press, 1990.

Chaucer, Geoffrey. *The Canterbury Tales*. *The Norton Anthology of English Literature*. Ed. M. H. Abrams et al. Vol. 1. 5th ed. New York: Norton, 1986. 95. 2 vols.

Coleridge, Samuel Taylor. "The Rime of the Ancient Mariner." *The Norton Anthology of English Literature*. Ed. M. H. Abrams et al. Vol 2. 5th ed. New York: Norton, 1986. 343. 2 vols.

Conrad, Joseph. "Heart of Darkness." *Heart of Darkness, Almayer's Folly, The Lagoon: Three Tales*. New York: Dell, 1960.

Cory, Daniel. "Ezra Pound." *Encounter* 30, no. 5 (May 1968): 38.

Cunningham, G. Watts. "English and American Absolute Idealism." In *History of Philosophical Systems*, edited by Vergilius Ferm. New York: Philosophical Library, 1950.

Darwin, Charles. *The Descent of Man*. 1871. 2nd ed. London: J. Murray, 1874.

———. *On the Origin of Species by Means of Natural Selection*. London: J. Murray, 1859.

Derrida, Jacques. *Writing and Difference*. Translated by Alan Bass. Chicago: University of Chicago Press, 1978.

Drew, Elizabeth. *T. S. Eliot: The Design of His Poetry*. London: Eyre and Spottiswoode, 1950.

Eliot, T. S. *After Strange Gods: A Primer of Modern Heresy*. New York: Harcourt, Brace, 1934.

———. "Beyle and Balzac." Rev. of *A History of the French Novel, to the Close of the Nineteenth Century*, Vol. 2, by George Saintsbury. *Athenaeum* 4648 (30 May 1919): 392–93.

———. "Christianity and Communism." *Listener* 7, no. 166 (16 March 1932): 382–83.

——. *The Collected Poems 1909–1962*. New York: Harcourt Brace Jovanovich, 1963.

——. *The Complete Poems and Plays*. New York: Harcourt, Brace and Company, 1952.

——. *Four Quartets*. New York: Harcourt Brace Jovanovich, 1971.

——. *The Idea of a Christian Society*. London: Faber and Faber, 1939.

——. "Introduction." In *Pascal's Pensées*, translated by W. F. Trotter. vii–xix. New York: E. P. Dutton, 1931.

——. *Knowledge and Experience in the Philosophy of F. H. Bradley*. 1916. New York: Farrar, Straus and Company, 1964.

——. Letter to William Force Stead. 2 December 1930. Osborn Collection, Beinecke Library, Yale University.

——. *On Poetry and Poets*. London: Faber and Faber, 1957.

——. "The Poetic Drama." Rev. of *Cinnamon and Angelica: A Play*, by John Middleton Murry. *Athenaeum* 4698 (14 May 1920): 635–36.

——. Rev. of *Elements of Folk Psychology: Outlines of a Psychological History of the Development of Mankind*, by Wilhelm Wundt. *Monist* 28 (January 1918): 159–60.

——. Rev. of *Group Theories of Religion and the Religion of the Individual*, by Clement C. J. Webb. *International Journal of Ethics* 27, no. 1 (October 1916): 115–17.

——. "A Romantic Patrician." Rev. of *Essays in Romantic Literature*, by George Wyndham. *Athenaeum* 4644 (2 May 1919): 265–67.

——. *The Sacred Wood: Essays on Poetry and Criticism*. 2nd ed. London: Methuen & Co., 1928.

——. "A Sceptical Patrician." Rev. of *The Education of Henry Adams: An Autobiography*. *Athenaeum* 4647 (23 May 1919): 361–62.

——. *Selected Essays*. New ed. London: Faber and Faber, 1950.

——. *Selected Prose of T. S. Eliot*. Edited by Frank Kermode. New York: Harcourt Brace Jovanovich / Farrar, Straus and Giroux, 1975.

——. "Style and Thought." *Nation* 22, no. 25 (23 March 1918): 768–69.

——. *To Criticize the Critic and Other Writings*. London: Faber and Faber, 1965.

——. *The Use of Poetry and the Use of Criticism*. London: Faber and Faber, 1933.

——. *Varieties of Metaphysical Poetry: The Clark Lectures at Trinity College, Cambridge 1926 and the Turnbull Lectures at the Johns Hopkins University 1933*. Edited by Ronald Schuchard. London: Faber and Faber, 1993.

——. *The Waste Land: A Facsimile and Transcript of the Original Drafts Including the Annotations of Ezra Pound*. Edited by Valerie Eliot. New York: Harcourt Brace Jovanovich, 1971.

——, ed. *The Criterion: 1922–1939*. London: Faber and Faber, 1967. 18 vols.

Epstein, Jacob. *Epstein: An Autobiography*. New York: Dutton, 1955.

Flint, F. S. "The History of Imagism." *Egoist*, no. 2 (1 May 1915): 70–71.

Flint, F. S., and Ezra Pound. "Imagisme." 1913. In *Ezra Pound: A Critical Anthology*, edited by J. P. Sullivan, 198–206. Baltimore: Penguin, 1970.

Fowlie, Wallace. *Mallarmé*. Chicago: University of Chicago Press, 1953.

Frank, Joseph. "Spatial Form in Modern Literature." In *The Widening Gyre: Crisis and Mastery in Modern Literature*, 3–62. Bloomington: Indiana University Press, 1963.

Frazer, Sir James George. *The Illustrated Golden Bough*. Edited by Sabine MacCormack. Garden City, NY: Doubleday, 1978.

Freud, Sigmund. *Civilization and Its Discontents*. 1930. Translated by James Strachey. New York: Norton, 1961.

——. *The Interpretation of Dreams*. 1899. Translated by James Strachey. New York: Avon Books, 1980.

Gardner, Helen. *The Composition of* Four Quartets. New York: Oxford University Press, 1978.

Gilbert, Sandra M. "Costumes of the Mind: Transvestism as Metaphor in Modern Literature." *Critical Inquiry* 7 (1980): 391–417.

Gilbert, Sandra M., and Susan Gubar. "The Mirror and the Vamp." In *The Future of Literary Theory*, edited by Ralph Cohen, 144–66. London: Routledge, 1989.

———. *The War of the Words.* Vol. 1 of *No Man's Land: The Place of the Woman Writer in the Twentieth Century.* New Haven: Yale University Press, 1988.

Gordon, Lyndall. *Eliot's New Life.* New York: Farrar Straus Giroux, 1988.

Gray, Piers. *T. S. Eliot's Intellectual and Poetic Development 1909–1922.* Sussex: Harvester Press, 1982.

Heidegger, Martin. *Existence and Being.* Translated by Douglas Scott. Chicago: Henry Regnery, 1949.

Holton, Gerald. *Thematic Origins of Scientific Thought: Kepler to Einstein.* Cambridge: Harvard University Press, 1973.

Hulme, T. E. *Speculations: Essays on Humanism and the Philosophy of Art.* Frontispiece and Foreword by Jacob Epstein. Edited by Herbert Read. London: Routledge & Kegan Paul, 1924.

———. *Further Speculations.* 1955. Edited by Sam Hynes. Lincoln: University of Nebraska Press, 1962.

Jaspers, Karl. *Man in the Modern Age.* 1931. Translated by Cedar Paul and Eden Paul. London: Routledge & Kegan Paul, 1951.

Jones, D. E. *The Plays of T. S. Eliot.* Toronto: University of Toronto Press, 1960.

Kenner, Hugh. *The Invisible Poet: T. S. Eliot.* New York: Harcourt, Brace & World, 1959.

———. "The Urban Apocalypse." In *Eliot in His Time: Essays on the Fiftieth Anniversary of* The Waste Land, edited by A. Walton Litz, 23–49. Princeton: Princeton University Press, 1973.

Kuhn, Thomas S. *The Structure of Scientific Revolutions.* 2nd ed. Chicago: University of Chicago Press, 1970.

Lévi-Strauss, Claude. *The Raw and the Cooked.* Vol. 1 of *Mythologiques (1964–1971).* Translated by John and Doreen Weightman. New York: Harper and Row, 1969. 4 vols.

———. "Structural Analysis in Linguistics and in Anthropology." Quoted in *Critical Theory Since 1965,* edited by Hazard Adams and Leroy Searle. Tallahassee: University Presses of Florida, 1986.

———. "The Structural Study of Myth." 1955. Translated by Claire Jacobson and Brooke Grundfest Schoepf. In *The Critical Tradition*, edited by David H. Richter, 869–77. New York: St. Martin's Press, 1989.

Lewis, Wyndham. *Blasting and Bombardiering.* London: Eyre & Spottiswoode, 1937.

Litz, A. Walton, ed. *Eliot in His Time: Essays on the Fiftieth Anniversary of* The Waste Land. Princeton: Princeton University Press, 1973.

Lovejoy, Arthur O. *The Revolt Against Dualism: An Inquiry Concerning the Existence of Ideas.* 1929. La Salle, IL: Open Court, 1955.

Mallarmé, Stéphane. *Mallarmé: Selected Prose Poems, Essays, and Letters.* Translated by Bradford Cook. Baltimore: Johns Hopkins University Press, 1956.

———. *Oeuvres Complètes.* Edited by Henri Mondon and G. Jean-Aubry. Paris: Editions Gallimard, 1945.

Margolis, John D. *T. S. Eliot's Intellectual Development, 1922–1939.* Chicago: University of Chicago Press, 1972.

Martin, Wallace. "The Sources of the Imagist Aesthetic." *PMLA* 85 (March 1970): 196–204.

Matthews, T. S. *Great Tom: Notes Towards the Definition of T. S. Eliot.* New York: Harper and Row, 1973.

Michaud, Guy. *Mallarmé.* Translated by Marie Collins and Bertha Humez. New York: New York University Press, 1965.

Miller, J. Hillis. *Poets of Reality: Six Twentieth-Century Writers.* Cambridge: Harvard University Press, 1974.

Nevinson, C. R. W. *Paint and Prejudice.* New York: Harcourt, Brace, 1938.

Nietzsche, Friedrich W. *The Birth of Tragedy* [1872] and *The Genealogy of Morals* [1887]. Translated by Francis Geoffing. Garden City, NY: Doubleday, 1956.

Ortega y Gasset, José. *The Dehumanization of Art and Other Essays on Art, Culture and Literature.* 2nd ed. Translated by Helene Weyl. Princeton: Princeton University Press, 1968.

———. *Man and Crisis.* Translated by Mildred Adams. New York: W. W. Norton, 1958.

Paxton, Norman. *The Development of Mallarmé's Prose Style.* Genève: Librarie Droz, 1968.

Perl, Jeffrey. *Skepticism and Modern Enmity: Before and After Eliot.* Baltimore: Johns Hopkins University Press, 1989.

———. *The Tradition of Return: The Implicit History of Modern Literature.* Princeton: Princeton University Press, 1984.

Plato. *The Republic.* Translated by Benjamin Jowett. Oxford: Clarendon Press, 1953.

Pound, Ezra. *Personae: The Collected Shorter Poems of Ezra Pound.* New York: New Directions, 1949.

———. *Selected Cantos of Ezra Pound.* New York: New Directions, 1934.

———. *Selected Letters of Ezra Pound 1907–1941.* Edited by D. D. Paige. New York: New Directions, 1950.

———. "This Hulme Business." *Townsman* 2 (5 January 1939): 15–16.

Richards, I. A. *Principles of Literary Criticism.* New York: Harcourt Brace, 1925.

Roberts, Michael. *T. E. Hulme.* London: Faber and Faber, 1938.

Schuchard, Ronald. "Eliot and Hulme in 1916: Toward A Revaluation of Eliot's Critical and Spiritual Development." *PMLA* 88 (October 1973): 1083–94.

Schwartz, Sanford. *The Matrix of Modernism: Pound, Eliot, and Early 20th-Century Thought.* Princeton: Princeton University Press, 1985.

Scott, Nathan. *The Broken Centre: Studies in the Theological Horizon of Modern Literature.* New Haven: Yale University Press, 1966.

Shusterman, Richard. *T. S. Eliot and the Philosophy of Criticism.* New York: Columbia University Press, 1988.

Smith, Grover. *T. S. Eliot's Poetry and Plays.* Chicago: University of Chicago Press, 1974.

———, ed. *Josiah Royce's Seminar, 1913–1914: As Recorded in the Notebooks of Harry T. Costello.* New Brunswick: Rutgers University Press, 1963.

Sophocles. *The Oedipus Cycle: Oedipus Rex, Oedipus at Colonus, Antigone.* Translated by Dudley Fitts and Robert Fitzgerald. New York: Harcourt Brace Jovanovich, 1977.

Squire, J. C. *The Honeysuckle and the Bee.* London: Heinemann, 1937.

Stead, William Force. "Mr. Stead Presents an Old Friend." *Alumnae Magazine of Trinity College* 38, no. 2 (Winter 1965): 66.

Stock, Noel. *The Life of Ezra Pound.* New York: Random House, 1970.

Valéry, Paul. "Letters from France: The Spiritual Crisis." *Athenaeum* (11 April 1919): 182–84.

Woolley, Grange, trans. *Stéphane Mallarmé 1842–1898: A Commemorative Presentation Including Translations from His Prose and Verse with Commentaries.* Madison, NJ: Drew University, 1942.

Worringer, Wilhelm. *Abstraction and Empathy: A Contribution to the Psychology of Style.* 1908. Translated by Michael Bullock. New York: International Universities Press, 1953.

Yeats, W. B. *The Poems of W. B. Yeats.* Edited by Richard J. Finneran. New York: Macmillan, 1983.

259

Index